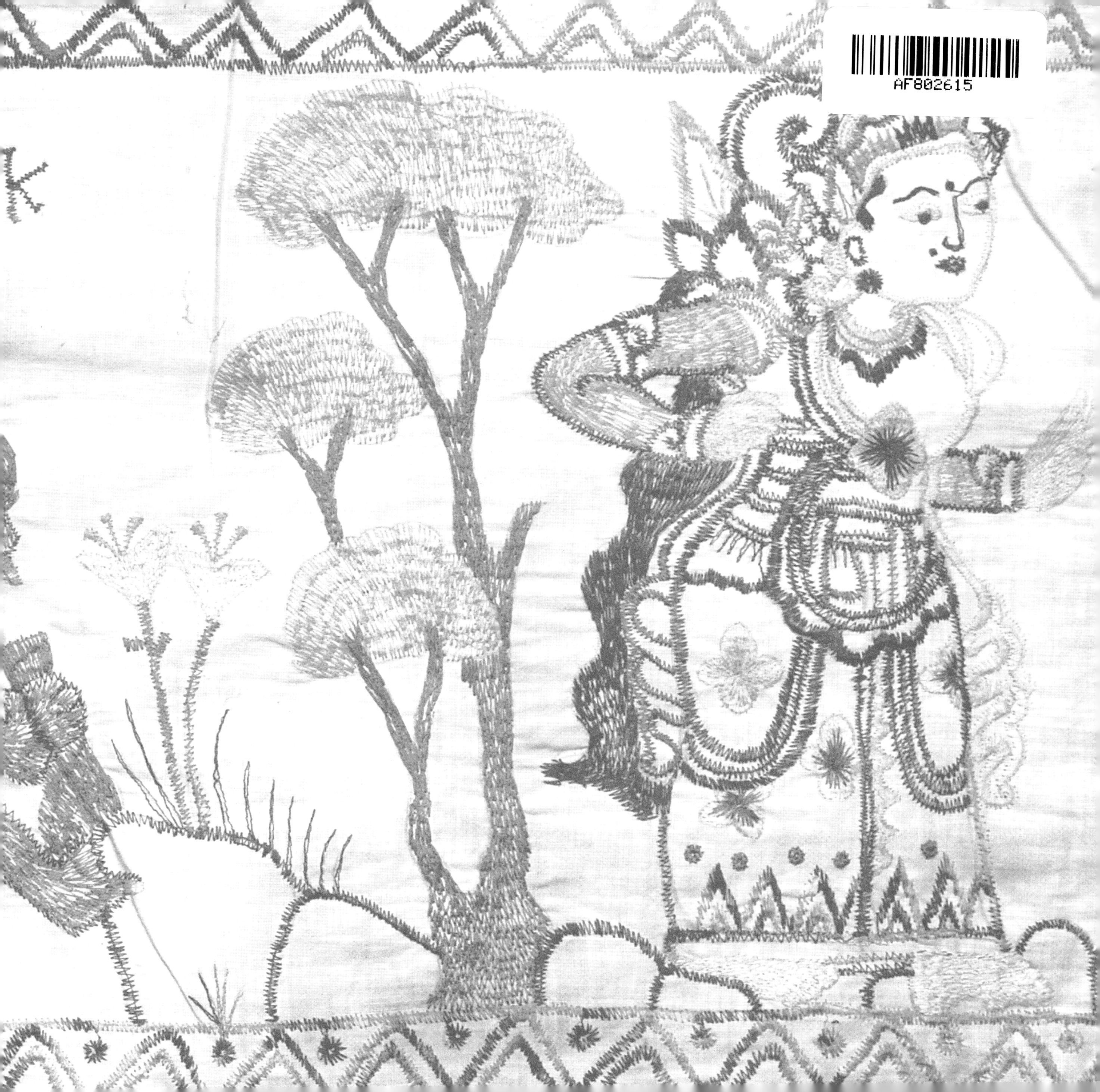

STORY CLOTHS OF

BALI

STORY CLOTHS OF BALI

JOSEPH FISCHER

TEN SPEED PRESS
Berkeley | Toronto

Ten Speed Press
P.O. Box 7123
Berkeley, California
94707

Distributed in Australia by Simon and Schuster Australia,
in Canada by Ten Speed Press Canada,
in New Zealand by Southern Publishers Group,
in South Africa by Real Books,
and in the United Kingdom and Europe by Airlift Book Company.

Cover and Interior Design by Stefanie Hermsdorf

Author's Note: All measurements are in centimeters and denote the overall size of the embroidery. Dates for most cloths are not given because they could not be ascertained.
All threads and base cloths utilize cotton unless otherwise noted.
All embroideries shown are, with few exceptions, from the collection of Clare and Joseph Fischer and were acquired between 1994 and 2003.

Library of Congress Cataloging-in-Publication Data

Fischer, Joseph, 1926-
Story cloths of Bali / Joseph Fischer.
p. cm.
Includes bibliographical references and index.
1. Textile fabrics--Indonesia--Bali Island--Themes, motives. I. Title.
NK8980.A3B354 2004
746.44'09598'6--dc22
2004009712

First printing, 2004

Printed in China
1 2 3 4 5 6 7 8 9 10 — 07 06 05 04

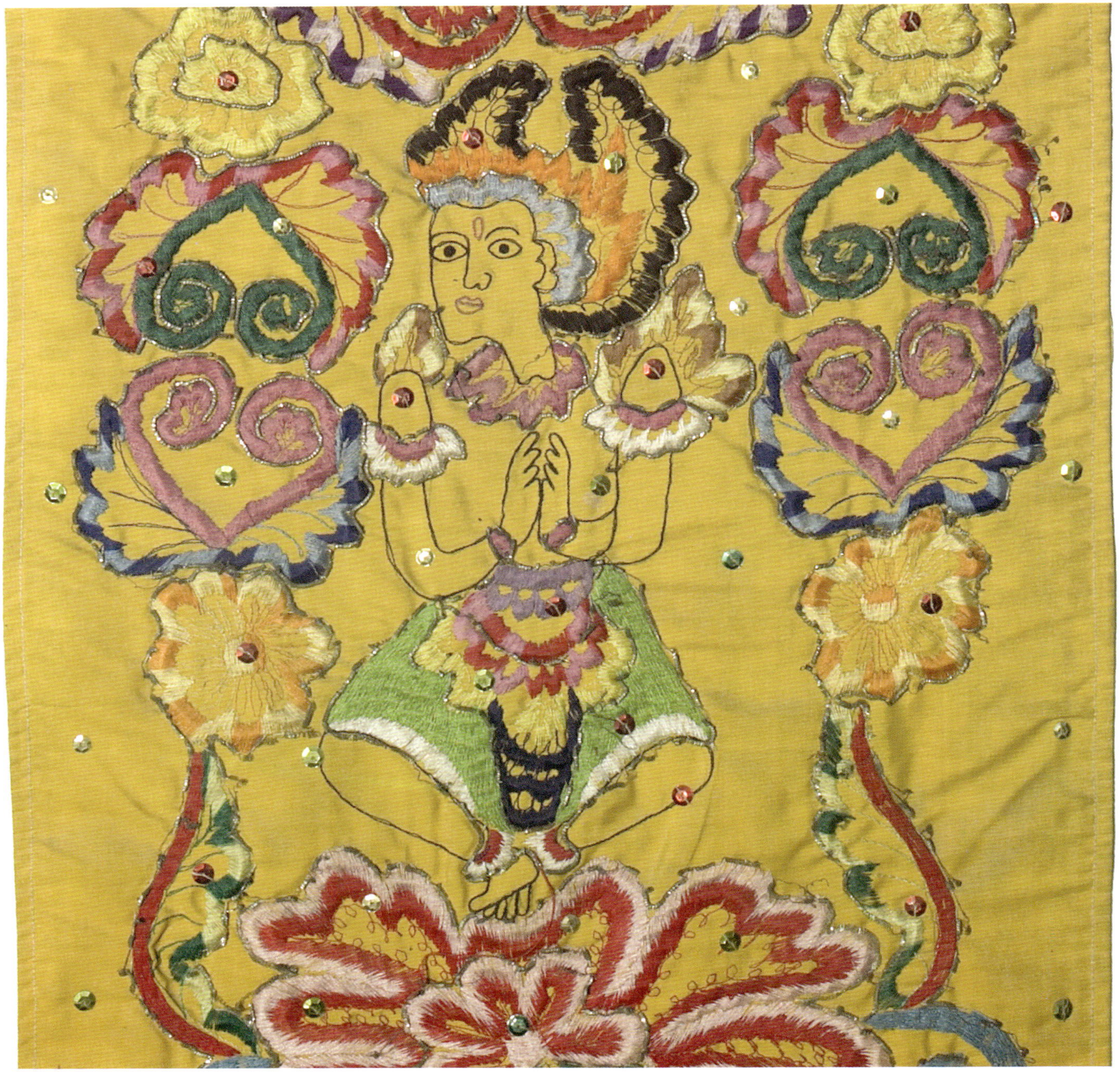

PLATE 1 **Buleleng.** *Lamak,* detail, 31 x 82, *Mahabharata.* Silk threads, gimp, and sequins. Arjuna meditates prior to leading his Pandawa family to victory.

Dedication

To Clare B. Fischer, critic, guide, supporter, and companion for thirty years.
To my daughter, Justine, and my grandchildren, Leonie and Ian,
all of whom have enlivened my life with love and laughter.

To the memory of Molly Kant Achilles, friend, scholar,
and my wonderful next-door neighbor in Indonesia many years ago.

To the many unknown and creative women of Bali
who have embroidered beautiful cloths and helped keep ancient traditions alive.

Acknowledgments

Listed in alphabetical order, these are all the people to whom I am grateful for their contributions to and support of my work in and out of Bali.

Stanley Abercrombie and staff of the Sonoma Valley Museum of Art, for hosting an exhibition of Balinese embroideries in 2002.

Agung Rai and the Arma Museum, for his support of art in Bali.

Agung Tirta, who provided his vehicle and his considerable knowledge of where to go and what to see in Bali.

Agus Indra Udayana, for helping me correct some of my mistakes.

I Made Bandem, who shared his artistry as a dancer and his seminal knowledge and promotion of Balinese traditional performance.

University of California at Riverside and ***Professors Michael Feener, June O'Connor,*** and ***Ivan Strenski,*** for hosting my presentation on the story cloths of Bali.

Thomas C. Cooper, friend and colleague, whose knowledge of Balinese language and culture have been indispensable, especially at times when I sorely needed an answer to questions, and for the loan of seven embroideries.

Nyoman Gunarsa and ***Indrawati***, for their friendship and dedication to local culture in creating the Museum of Balinese Classical Art in Klungkung.

Lucy Harmon, of CFT Tours and Travel (Berkeley), for her excellence in making arrangements.

Kristi Hein, for her superb copyediting.

Stefanie Hermsdorf, for her excellent design.

Dotty Hollinger, for transcibing my unwieldy handwritten manuscript.

I Made Jani and ***Ni Made Tulus*** of Ubud, friends and promoters of traditional and modern textiles.

Koman (Pande Nyoman Wahyu Suteja) and ***Mansri (Ni Nyoman Trisniawati)***, gallery and hotel owners in Ubud, who provided hospitality and introductions over many years.

Professor Kaja McGowan and ***I Ketut Raka***, for their help in explaining some Balinese folk tales.

Thomas Murray, for the use of one cloth, photographed by ***Robert Bengston***.

Carol Nathan, for tips on embroidery techniques.

I Pande Wayan Suteja Neka and ***Ni Gusti Made Suteja Neka***, owners of the Neka Museum and the Neka Gallery, Ubud, who first introduced me to contemporary Balinese culture and art.

Annie Nelson, my astute and helpful editor.

Noni (Luh Estiti Andarawati), like a daughter, always willing to help, especially in translating and recounting her memory of Balinese stories.

Mary Northmore, friend and founder of the Seniwati Gallery of Art by Women in Ubud and ardent supporter of Balinese women's creativity.

Oxford University Press in Asia (formerly in Kuala Lumpur), for publishing my first study of Balinese embroideries.

Pandji Tisna, cultural broker and concerned ecologist.

Ida Bagus Paramartha and his staff, for their hospitality at the Laghawa Hotel in Sanur.

Peneeda View Beach Hotel in Sanur, for its fine service.

Chris Roche and ***Shanenon Starrett,*** for their excellent photography and their geniality.

Nyoman Rudana and ***Ni Wayan Olastini***, proprietors of the Rudana Museum and Gallery in Peliatan, for hosting traditional performances, providing great Balinese food, promoting the arts of Bali, and, most of all, providing wonderful friendship.

Margo Schevill, for her encouragement and support of my textile endeavors.

I Wayan Sinti and ***Ibu Nilawati***, for their commitment to supporting and extending the Balinese musical tradition.

Soedarso SP, my mentor and friend who published my first article on Balinese embroideries.

Blake Summers and his staff at the San Francisco International Airport, who hosted and helped prepare a year-long (2002) exhibition of Balinese embroideries at the airport.

Consul General Susanto Prio Utomo and his staff, for their support and graciousness.

Paulus Edmund Talo and his staff at Floressa Tours in Sanur, for their excellent service.

Laura Tibbals of Moe's Books, for suggesting Ten Speed Press as a possible publisher.

Toko Indra (Klungkung) and ***Oka Sunadi***, for help in identifying and procuring embroideries.

Ubud Inn in Ubud, to ***I Wayan Suparsa*** and his staff, for all their help.

David Weitzman, author, friend, and fellow admirer of Balinese and Javanese traditional culture.

I Made Wianta and ***Intan***, wonderful symbols of generosity, artistry, ecological concern, and political commitment.

Phil Wood and ***Kathy Hashimoto,*** of Ten Speed Press, for their support.

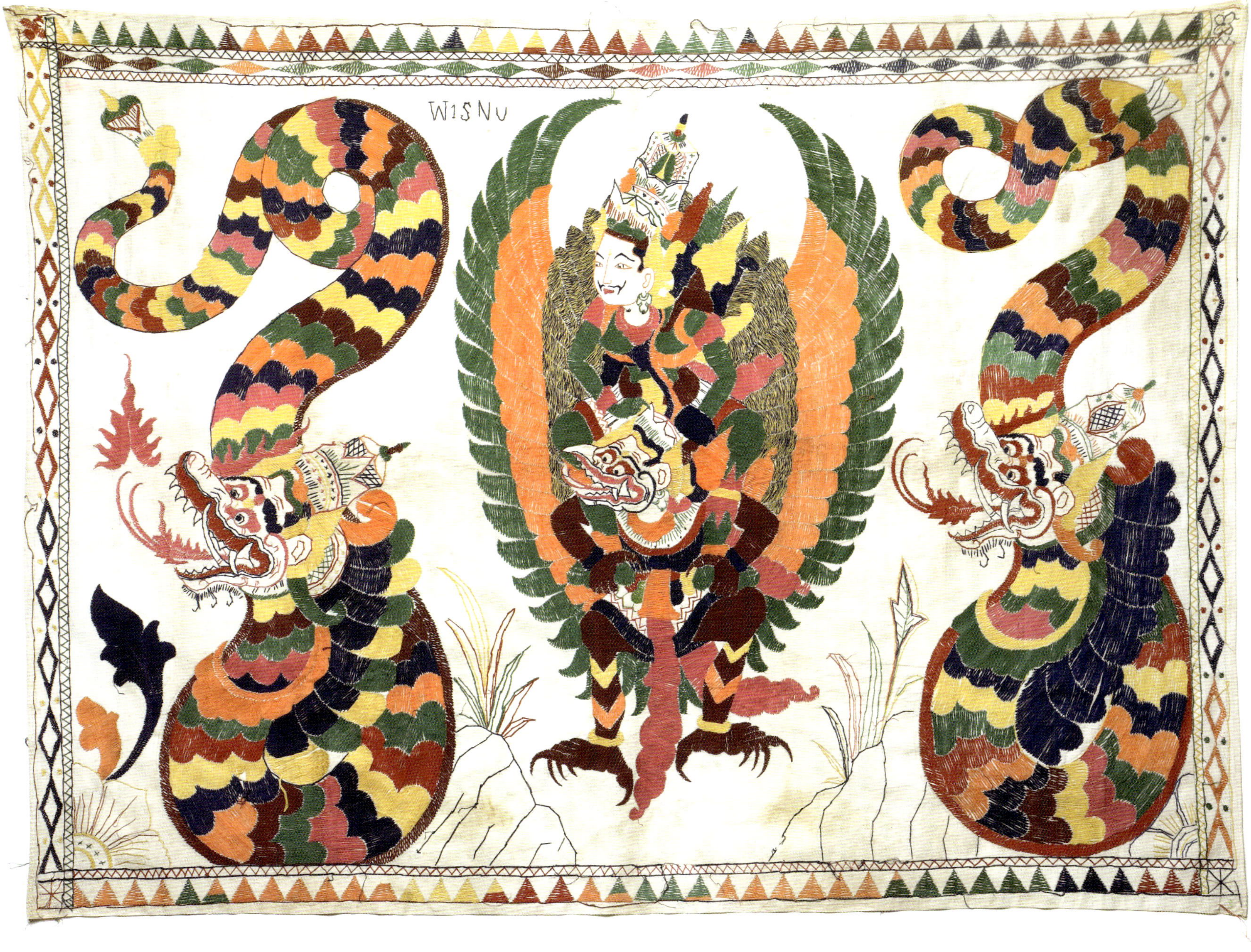

PLATE 2 Negara. *Tabing*, 94 x 120. The god Wisnu astride his vehicle, Garuda, with two multi-colored *nagas*, both unusually facing the same direction.

Contents

Prologue

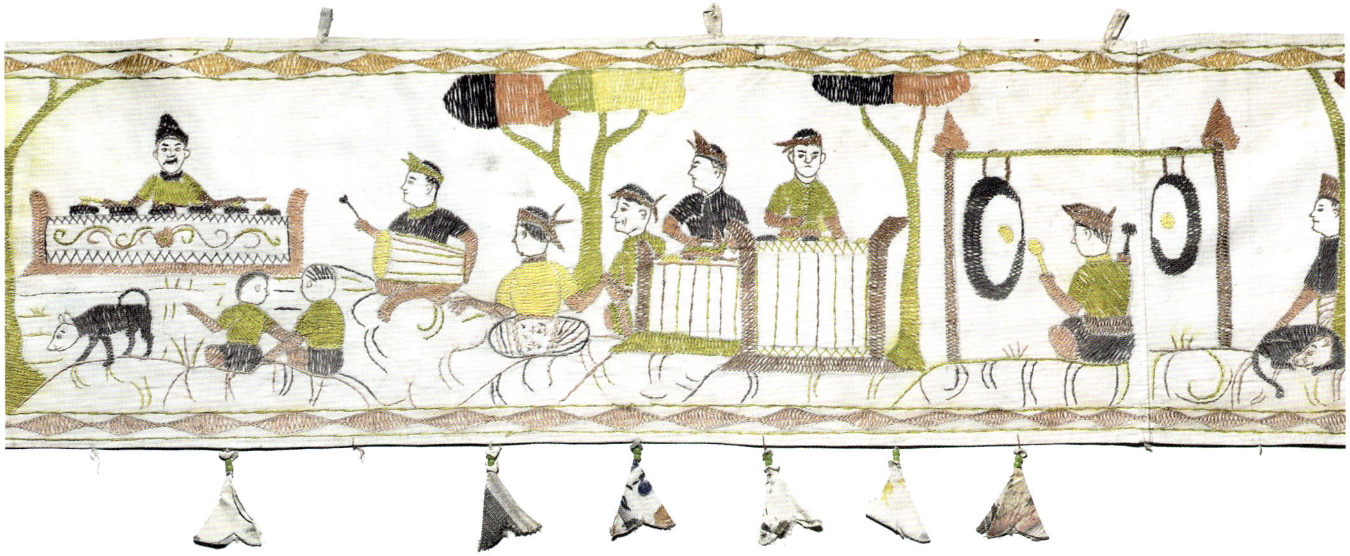

PLATE 3 Negara. *Ider-ider*, detail, 24 x 390. People listen to a Balinese *gamelan* (orchestra) with two large suspended metal gongs, two *gangsa* (xylophones), a *kedang* (drum), and six small gongs mounted on a *trombong* (wooden stool).

In June 1956 I drove a green 1953 Chevrolet sedan from Miami to New York City. I took it to a cargo pier in the harbor, where it was unceremoniously hoisted aboard a Maersk Line ship bound for far-off Indonesia. This car was the best I had owned and I wondered if I would ever see it again.

I arrived in Indonesia first; two months later, the car arrived and was offloaded at Tanjung Priok, the port for Jakarta. The car's battery was dead and the windshield wipers were missing, but everything else was in order. Several dock workers helped push the car to get the motor running. It started quickly, and I immediately drove for eight hours to Yogyakarta in Central Java. It was here that I began to teach in three faculties at Gajah Mada University. I spent two wonderful years there. By the time I left, I had driven my Chevrolet over 200,000 miles without any major repairs. I sold this car to my Indonesian neighbor and for all I know it may still be running. I had enjoyed hospitality, kindness, and friendship from many Javanese. My gratitude to them shall always remain with me.

In contrast to my long stay in central Java, during my ten visits to Bali I never spent more than two months at any one time, yet there, too, I always felt welcome. Many Balinese helped and guided me and provided information about their remarkable traditional culture. Because of them, the complexities of Balinese social and religious life and the high quality of their art, crafts, and performances have enabled me to better understand and appreciate this extraordinary island of creativity and devotion.

I made my first trip to Bali in June 1957. I drove my reliable Chevrolet from Yogyakarta to the city of Banjuwangi at the eastern end of Java. There my car was loaded onto a rusting World War II LCT and transported to the port of

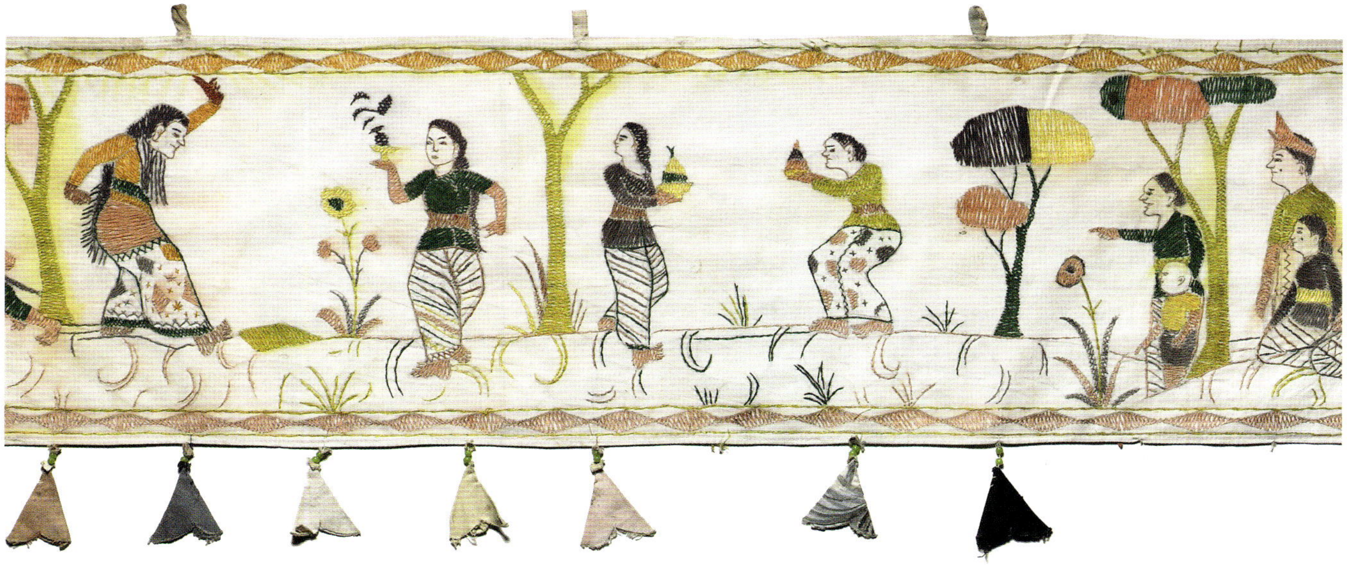

PLATE 4 Negara. *Ider-ider*, detail, 24 x 390. Onlookers observe four Balinese women performing a sacred dance *(mendet)*.

Gilimanuk in westernmost Bali. I drove from that city to Ubud, normally a trip of four hours, but it took me ten. The entire road had been torn up and was later to be repaired in preparation for the first visit to Bali of Nikita Khrushchev, then first secretary of the Communist Party of the Soviet Union, and Soviet premier Nikolai Bulganin. Upon my arrival I had to buy four new tires. My Balinese adventure had commenced.

There were hardly any real hotels in Ubud at that time, so in Ubud I stayed for four weeks in the compound of Prince Tjokorde Gde Agung Sukawati, who provided me with a room, food, and genial hospitality. My gratitude for persons and things Balinese had begun.

It is hard to imagine now, but my expenses in Bali averaged two dollars a day. The rate of exchange was twelve rupiah to one U.S. dollar (in 2004 it was nine thousand to one). Gasoline cost fifteen cents a gallon and an ample restaurant meal averaged about fifty cents. Never before or since have I lived so inexpensively and comfortably. In addition, I had never experienced a place with so many temples, with so many bicycles and hardly any cars—all enveloped in greenery and sweet, clear air. Memories of that first Balinese sojourn still remain happily with me. My nostalgia for that time has never diminished and has helped me over the years to continue to learn about and admire Bali.

PREFACE

Discovery and Demise

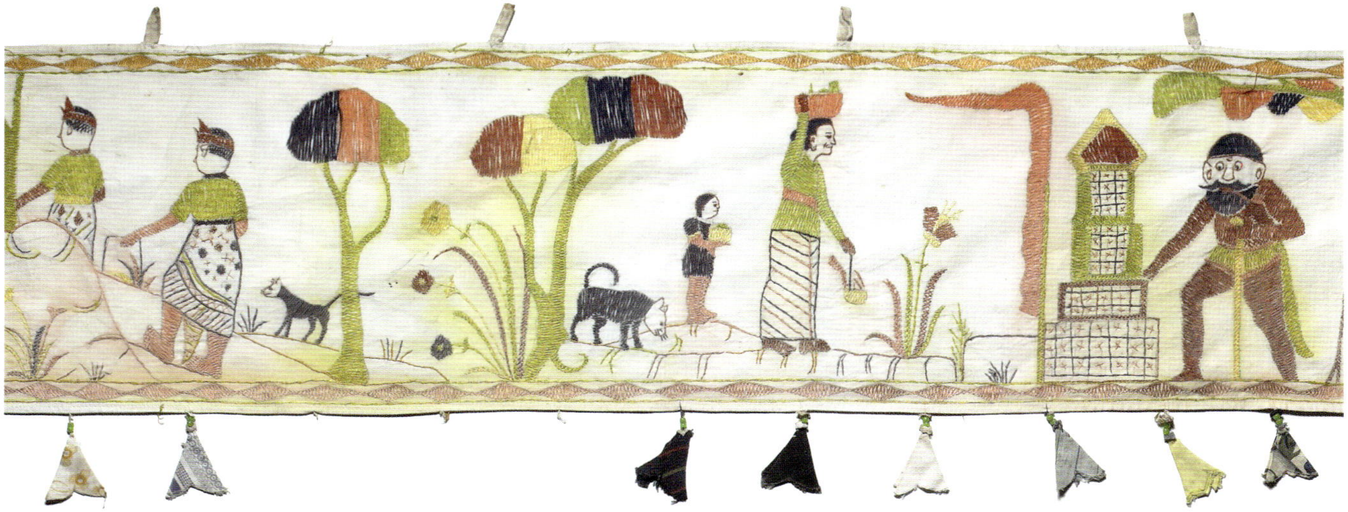

PLATE 5 **Negara.** *Ider-ider*, detail, 24 x 390. A woman and child carry offerings of food to a grandfather during a religious ceremony.

Imagine yourself, with a passion for traditional textiles, walking into an antique shop in Sanur, Bali, in the summer of 1994 and finding a five-foot-high stack of wonderfully embroidered Balinese cloths that you had never known existed. I had already visited Bali more than a dozen times over a period of forty years and yet these embroideries were unknown to me. I unfolded cloth after cloth in amazement, feeling like an explorer who has come upon some great undisclosed treasure. I felt that as an outsider I had "discovered" them, although I later learned they had been around for more than eight decades.

Viewing each embroidery, one after the other, gave me an almost ecstatic feeling. Here in vibrant colors were depicted the gods, goddesses, kings, demons, warriors, and sages of the two great Indian epics—the ***Mahabharata*** and the ***Ramayana***—previously known to me only through books, paintings, and dance/dramas. Here they were, representations of characters both elegant and crude, in intricate stitching, threads of every color imaginable, and decorations of sequins, beads, mirror glass, and gold threads. These embroideries seemed to represent an entire cosmos of the seen and imagined universe—a captivating, mythological world brought forth on cotton cloth.

I succumbed on the spot and bought five of the embroideries. I took them back to my hotel, the Laghawa in Sanur, and showed them to the clerks and the owner. They were unfamiliar with them. My Balinese and foreign friends in Denpasar, Sanur, and Ubud were also unfamiliar with the cloths—which is strange in an island as small and as well-studied as Bali. The antique dealer in Sanur could only tell me that they came from the city of Negara in the district of Jembrana in western Bali.

The next day I returned to the same shop and bought more; the following day I did the same thing. It might have gone on and on in this way, but my travel schedule and my dwindling finances intervened. I determined that I would go to Negara. This was the beginning of my textile journey to find out who had made the embroideries and where they came from. In 1995, in a village eight kilometers from

Negara, a local city official and the village headman arranged for me to meet with a group of forty Balinese women who were part of this unusual embroidery tradition. All of them were over sixty years of age; all knew or were related to each other. I asked them whether these embroideries were still being made and whether they were still used in traditional ceremonies. Of the forty women, about twenty indicated they were still embroidering, but only occasionally. Only one was doing it on a regular basis and only on commission, however, she was using thick yarns instead of thin threads, which made them less attractive (see PLATE 159, page 123). Embroideries were still used as offerings and decorations several times a year to celebrate the Balinese New Year, the birthday of a Hindu temple, weddings, cremations, and the Indonesian national independence day.

No one, local or foreign, had ever before seriously inquired about these cloths, so they were somewhat puzzled by my interest. I particularly wanted to know whether they could identify the inked or penciled proper names and initials on some of the cloths. I had brought with me a list of twenty-five names or initials; the women quickly identified all of them. In fact, several of the artisans were in the audience, but most of the others were deceased. I told them of my research interests and that I hoped to start a project to revive and support their embroidery tradition. I emphasized the value of preserving some embroideries as ***pusaka*** (heirlooms), but it was clear from their responses that the women present were not very interested in them anymore. In fact, one woman ran to her house and came back with a large embroidered cloth that she insisted I buy—so much for my "preservation of antiquities" message!

For the women who embroidered, their work was only a minor source of income, part of which had to be shared with a local agent. Very few of the women had local patrons and until recently collectors and antique dealers had not been interested. There was no local feeling that there might be a potential outside market for their embroideries. Some Negara women, many of whom had Brahman social status, knew that they were doing something quite different from other artisans in Bali, but this did not translate into a commercial or popular enterprise. In addition, western Bali was not and had not been a tourist area, and there were few great artisan traditions associated with the royal courts in Jembrana, as there were in other regions of Bali.

I was unable to secure funds for a local embroidery project, and I did not return to Negara until 1999. I found that of the twenty women who had been embroidering on my first visit, only one was still working at it and she indicated she would soon stop and begin weaving, which was easier to sell. The other nineteen women had become laborers for a living, mainly carrying bricks on their heads for local construction projects. Sadly, the craft was disappearing, and with it an unusual and rich tradition.

The demise of this craft is indeed unfortunate. These women were not merely decorating cloths; they were embodying a profound religion (Hinduism) that contains useful beliefs, ethical principles, models of virtuous behavior, and the requirements for a harmonious and good life—a several-thousand-year-old tradition still popular and meaningful in present-day Bali. It has been written that "the design, workmanship, and coloration of a good piece of embroidery usually embody the wisdom, work, and feelings of generations of women." [1] Their craft and the uses to which these cloths were put had given a few women a semblance of cultural influence and religious status that had always been the province of men. Now, although their lives and their rituals still continue, their embroideries are moribund. The rice still grows in their ***padi*** fields and is duly harvested with hard work and rituals that are still enhanced with old embroideries. I was privileged to know these pious and creative women and sad to witness the demise of their craft. With this book, I seek to at least honor them and their artistry.

I have used secondary sources and information from Balinese informants for the texts of all stories and epics. I have used the terms *story* and *tale* interchangeably. The term *epic* refers only to the ***Mahabharata*** and ***Ramayana.*** Some of the interpretations, descriptions, or identifications may be subject to question or, perhaps, mistaken. The relevant epics and myths are so complex and varied, and different versions so prevalent, that misinterpretations are unavoidable. I welcome any corrections and suggestions.

FOOTNOTE

1. Yarong Wang, *Chinese Embroidery*, 1.

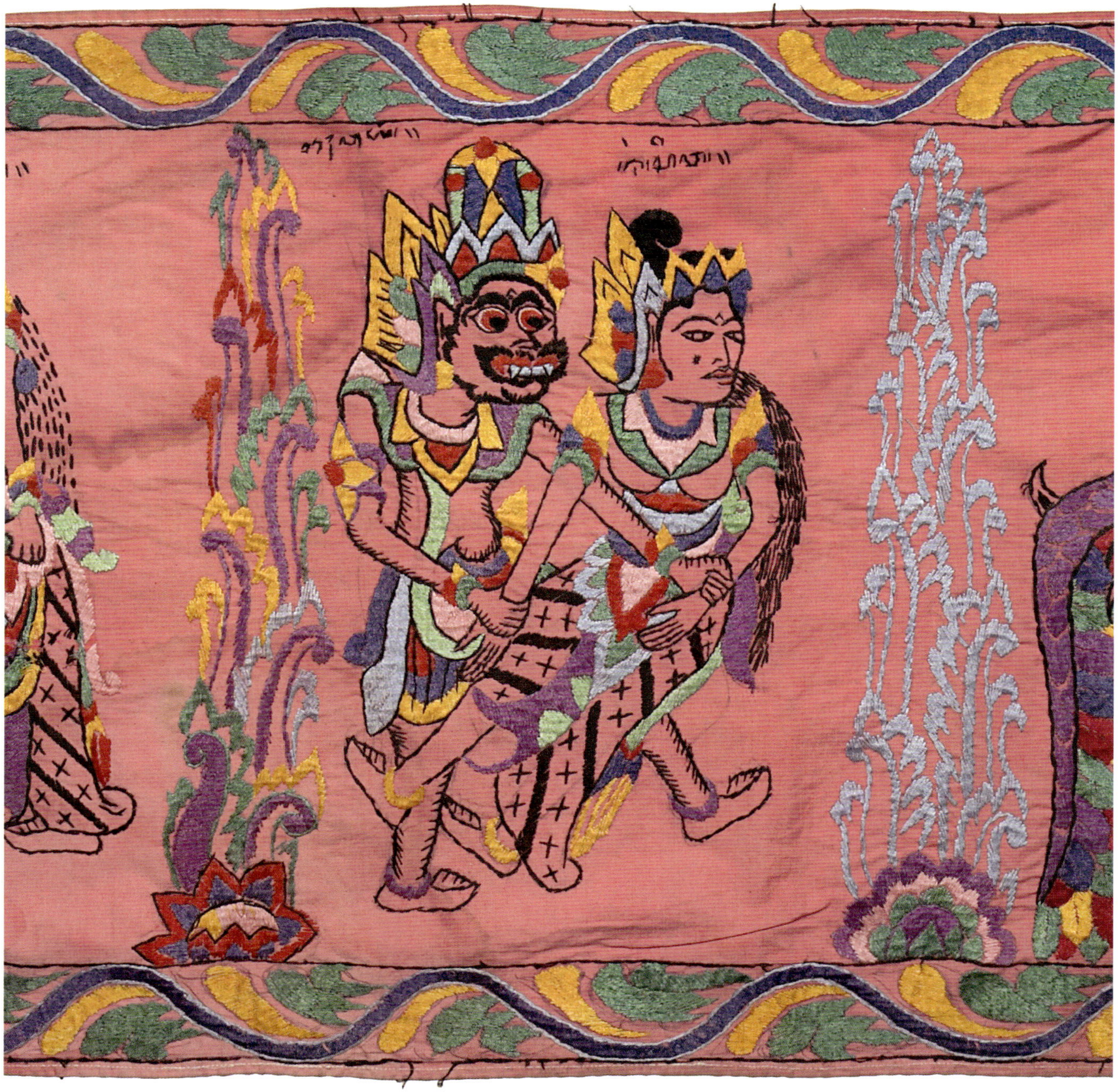

PLATE 6 **Buleleng.** *Ider-ider*, detail, 40 x 227. *Ramayana.* Diverse and intricate stitches on an unusual red satin base cloth show Sita resisting the clutches of Rawana who has kidnapped her. The Balinese script identifies the two characters beneath it.

CHAPTER 1

Balinese Embroideries: Character, Context & Craft

The Indonesian Archipelago of thirteen thousand inhabited islands stretches for three thousand miles across the Indian Ocean, the South China Sea, and the Pacific Ocean. Malay sailors, Dutch sea captains, Indian traders, Bugis pirates, Chinese travelers, and European adventurers traversed these waters, visited many of the islands, and established outposts and settlements there. The seas and oceans that surround what is today the Republic of Indonesia have always been easy to cross. Merchants, missionaries, foreign armies and navies, and immigrants have sought its spices and other natural resources and valued its strategic location across the vital sea lanes of South and Southeast Asia. Four great religions—Hinduism, Buddhism, Islam, and Christianity—came from foreign countries and were established there. With all this movement of peoples and religions came many new languages and customs, diverse literature, and a variety of myths. The ***Mahabharata*** and ***Ramayana*** epics came from India; many stories and immigrants came from China. Bali received myths and tales from Java. Craft and art techniques came from Holland and other European countries. Indonesia's history has been described as eclectic, and the term also applies to the country's arts, crafts, rituals, and beliefs, and, in turn, the embroidered story cloths that are the subject of this book.

A key to understanding the complex cultures of Indonesia, particularly those of Bali, lies in its varied mythology. Myths contain much more than intriguing and colorful plots and characters. They often embody beliefs, customs, and personal traits that reflect traditional practice in everyday life. They can be a veritable cosmos of everything in the universe, seen and unseen. Myths are passed on from generation to generation in Bali and often define the very nature of traditions and what is required for a contemporary harmonious life.

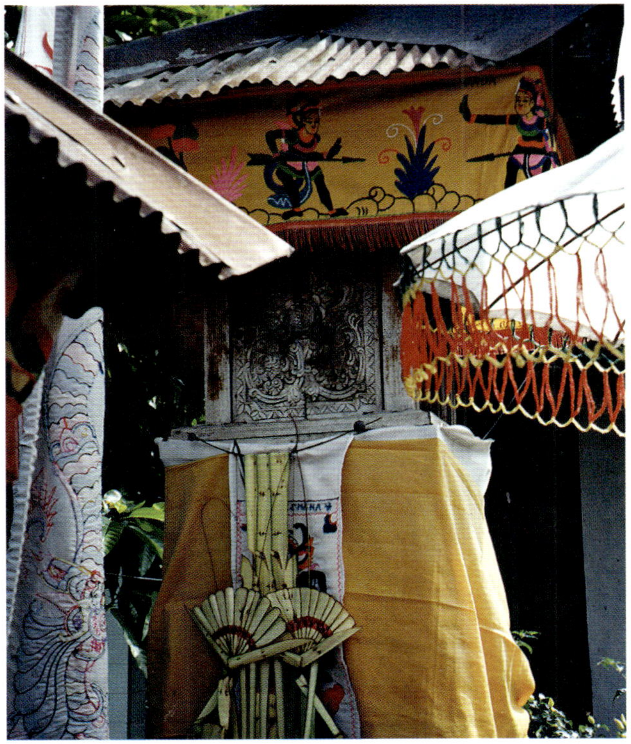

PLATE 7 **Village near Negara,** *c.1995.* A religious celebration is acknowledged with an outdoor *pelangkiran* (family altar), an *ider-ider* hanging from the eaves of a roof, a small embroidered *lamak* hanging in the front above two palm-leaf *cili* (fertility figures), and a *umbul-umbul* (pennant) with an embroidered *naga* (dragon) on the left. Photograph courtesy of Thomas Cooper.

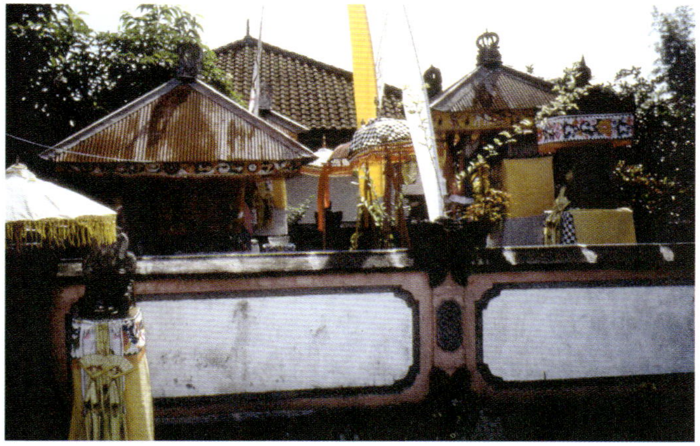

PLATE 8 Village near Negara, *c.1995.* A religious celebration is shown with white and yellow pennants attached to bamboo poles and various *ider-ider* embroideries hanging from the eaves of buildings and around a stone altar. Photograph courtesy of Thomas Cooper.

In Bali, embroideries are used as offerings in rituals and celebrations connected to Hindu religious beliefs and practices. They depict, in striking form, the epics and myths that are an essential part of Balinese culture. Their images mirror ancient history, remind people of their mythological past, and may underscore their relevance to the present. Such embroideries serve the same function as their paintings; their sacred ***lontar*** books, made from narrow strips of cured palm leaf tied together, on which were scratched the text; their temple sculptures; and their dance/drama performances: the preservation and transmission of culture.

Balinese embroideries come from two districts of the island: Jembrana in the west and Buleleng in the north. The greatest number by far come from Jembrana, in and around its central city, Negara. These are embroidered offerings and ceremonial cloths called ***sulaman***. The base cloth for all embroideries is white cotton; the stitchery is done in colored cotton threads. Some finer embroideries, such as those from north Bali, use silk threads and are often decorated with sequins and gold or silver gimp (see PLATE 99, page 64). Other decorative elements, such as mirror glass and mica, may be applied. The cloths were made in six different sizes appropriate to the space in which they were to be used as well as to the particular ritual requirements; these will be discussed in detail. The Balinese names for these different size cloths are the same that have been used for traditional paintings, as follows:

1. ***ider-ider:*** long, narrow cloths hung horizontally from the eaves of temples and other village buildings, averaging 11 centimeters in height and 100 in width (I have seen one that is 1,100 centimeters long)
2. ***tabing:*** rectangular or square hangings in Hindu temples and village buildings, averaging 30 centimeters wide and 60 long
3. ***lalubur:*** a square ceiling canopy used in houses and special ritual structures, averaging 113 centimeters wide and 120 long
4. ***lamak:*** a small vertical hanging for homes and outdoor family shrines, averaging 20 centimeters wide and 75 long
5. ***langse:*** a curtain of varying sizes, used mostly as a room divider
6. ***umbul-umbul:*** a triangular cloth pennant hung atop very tall, bending bamboo poles, marking the entrance to village or temple celebrations

The most common size cloth is the ***ider-ider,*** shown in PLATE 7 in actual use on the eaves of three village buildings near Negara. These clearly are marking an important cultural event, with a shrine draped with embroidered cloths on the left, three long bamboo poles with ***umbul-umbul*** pennants, and parasols sheltering sacred spaces.

Seen from a distance, many of the ***ider-ider*** embroideries appear to have a painterly quality, highlighted with strong and colorful motifs. Fringes are often sewn on the bottom edge; they are made of small triangular cloth scraps, often with beads attached.

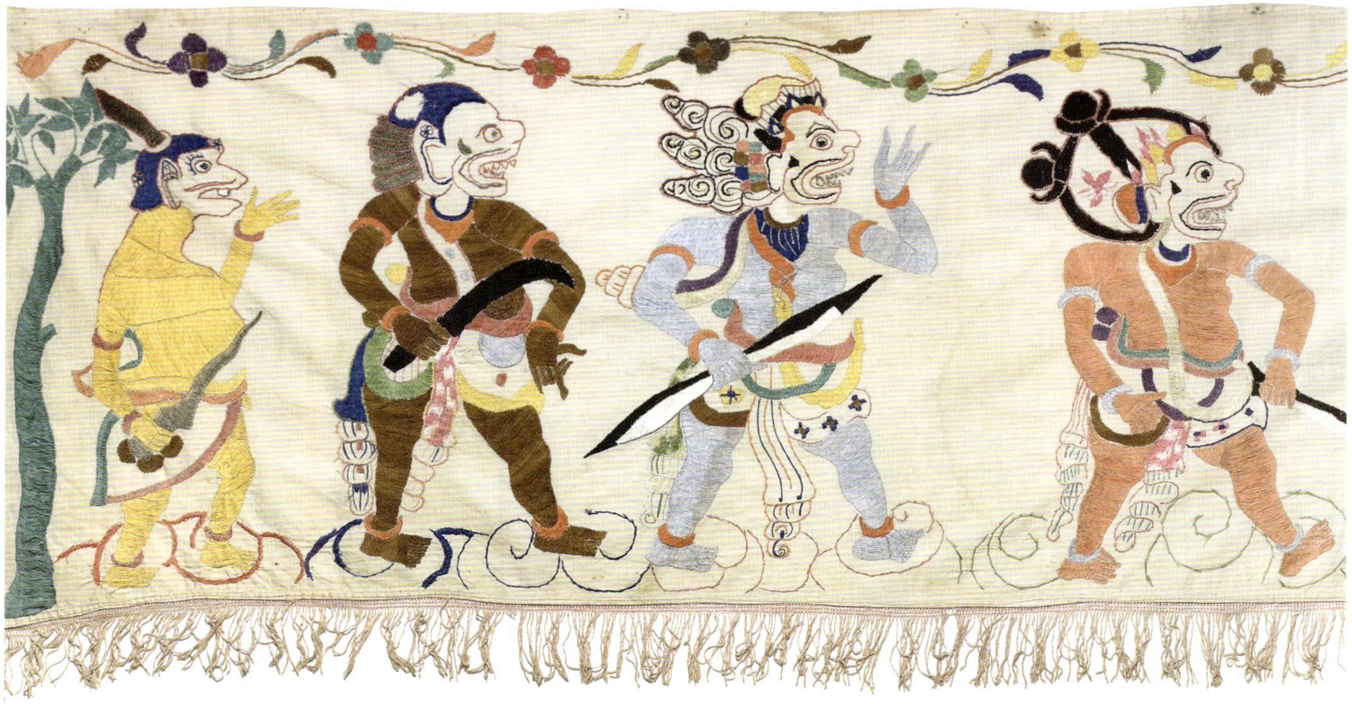

PLATE 9 **Buleleng.** *Ider-ider*, detail, 32 x 200. Various finely stitched characters from the *Ramayana,* including (from left to right) *Sangut* (a clown), a warrior, a soldier, and an officer.

STITCHING TECHNIQUES

An extraordinary variety of stitching techniques are used in these embroideries.[1] For example, in the cloth shown in PLATE 9, stem stitches are used for tree branches and straight stitches for everything in blue, and outlining satin stitches are employed for flowers, faces, bodies, and clothing. The figures are completely filled in; in contrast, the figures in PLATE 11 (page 4) are sparsely outlined with some traces of golden gimp and most of the white cloth is left as a plain background.

An example of superb overall stitching is seen in PLATE 13 (see page 6), an ***ider-ider*** with silk threads. The eyebrows of all the characters are chain-stitched and the entire embroidered surface is done in satin stitch. The ***Ramayana*** story in PLATE 10 uses diverse stitches on an unusual red base cloth. All the figures are entirely filled in with intricate, multicolored threads. The black crosses and the blue upright ones are cross-stitched; the hair on the legs is chain-stitched. The blue border is in stem stitch, as are the character names in Balinese script. Straight satin stitches that go back and forth through the cloth predominate. All of this results in a very unusual and strikingly dramatic depiction. Another highly skilled and elegant embroidery technique is called shading in which threads are closely intermingled so as to create an extraordinary multi-color effect. PLATE 12 shows two monkeys (***kerak***) rendered using this technique. PLATE 112 (see page 78) demonstrates another way of embroidering images with a minimal use of threads against a plain cloth background.

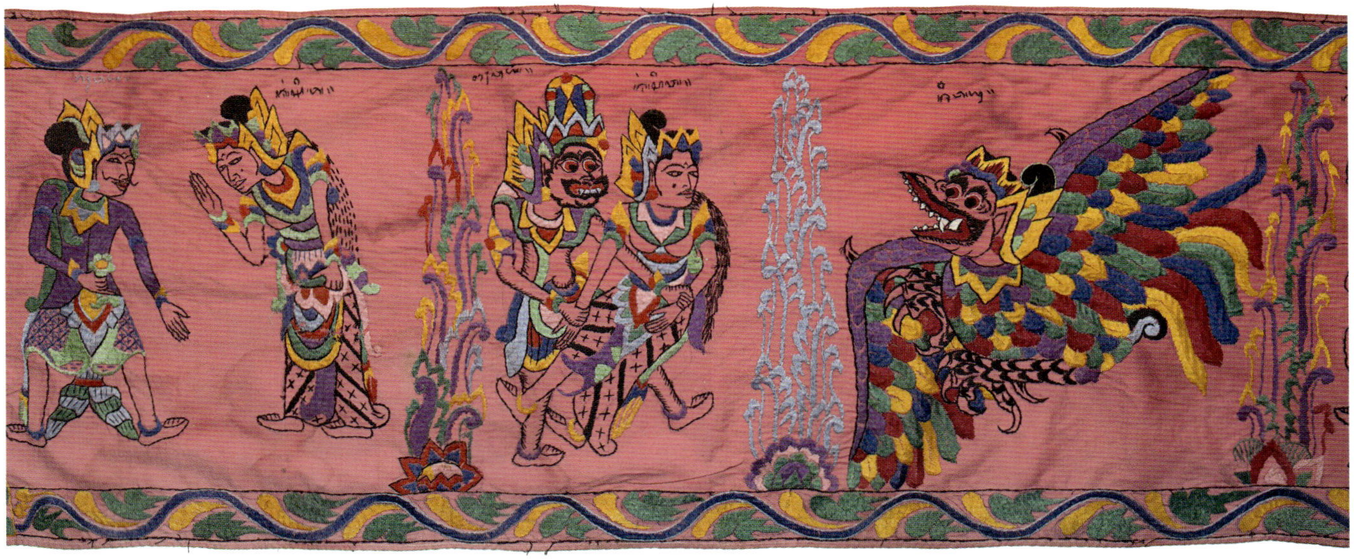

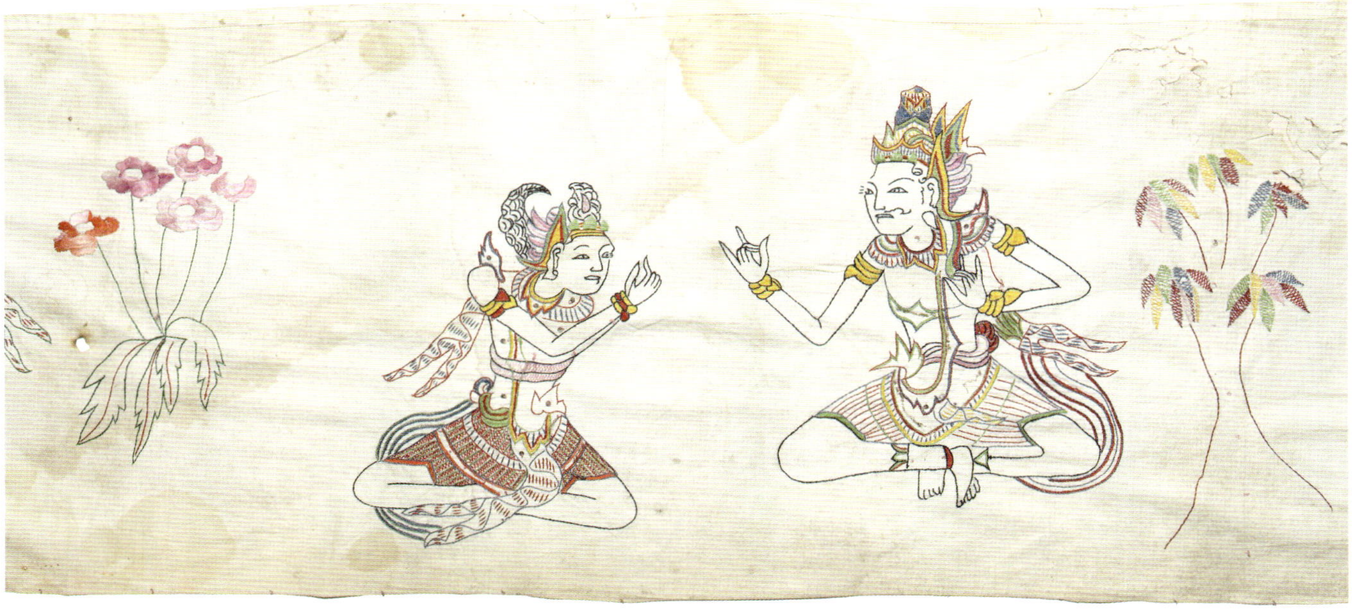

PLATE 10 Buleleng. *Ider-ider*, detail, 40 x 227. Balinese script. Diverse and intricate stitches on an unusual red base cotton cloth show *Ramayana* figures (right to left): Rawana disguised as a priest to lure Sita; the real Rawana kidnapping Sita while the mythical bird Jatayu tries in vain to protect her.

PLATE 11 Tabanan or Buleleng. *Ider-ider*, detail, 37 x 275. Outline stitching of *Mahabharata* characters including Brahma (right) and Arjuna (left).

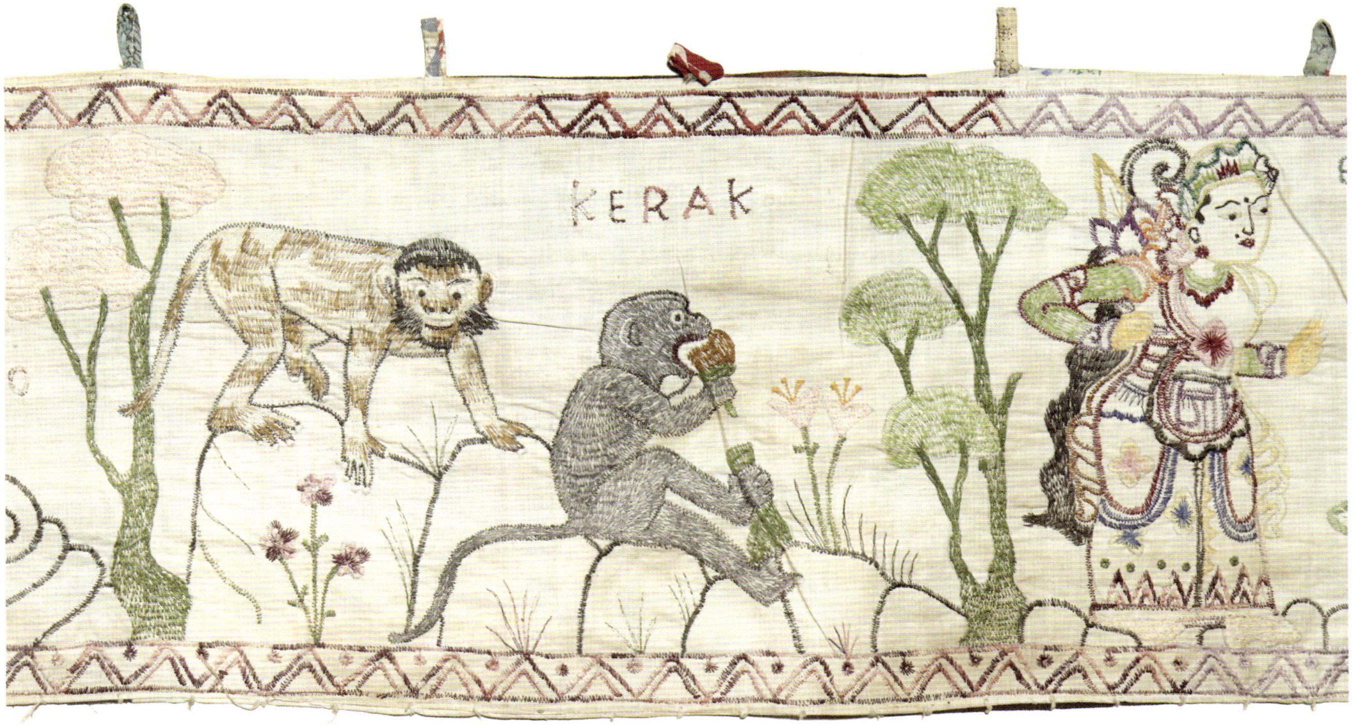

PLATE 12 **Negara.** *Ider-ider*, detail, 26 x 252. Two monkeys *(kerak)* humorously rendered in a shading technique on a cloth depicting many *Mahabharata* characters.

TABINGS

The most aesthetically satisfying and perhaps the most spectacular of Balinese embroideries are the ***tabings***. The stitching techniques and materials used are similar to those described above; however, each ***tabing***, no matter the quality and extent of the stitching, is a complete composition in itself within a discrete square or rectangle. This sharply contrasts with the seemingly never-ending sequences in scene after scene in the ***ider-ider*** cloths. A typical ***tabing*** example is shown in PLATE 16 (page 7); it is a made-up scene from the ***Mahabharata***. All the characters appear animated, which heightens the visual effect of the cloth and makes it akin to an actual live dramatic performance. This ***tabing***, like many other embroidered cloths, shows a faithful rendering of traditional characters, but their appearance is not part of a specific event in the story. They are there to make the embroidery more attractive and meaningful to viewers and thus add to their connection to Balinese culture. It may also be that the artist simply put into her embroidery the characters and scenes that she liked the best. One Negara woman told me this was her customary practice. Similarly, the ***tabing*** in PLATE 15 (page 7) is a composition of various characters from the ***Ramayana*** who may or may not have been together in any actual scene from the epic.

A somewhat different but still highly decorative ***tabing*** (PLATE 14, page 6) features a typical Balinese/Hindu pagoda-shaped structure. Embroidered are letters spelling ***Pure*** (*pura*; temple) and ***Agung***, which is its specific name. This is another arranged scene using ***Mahabharata*** characters with common Balinese motifs all chosen by the artisan.

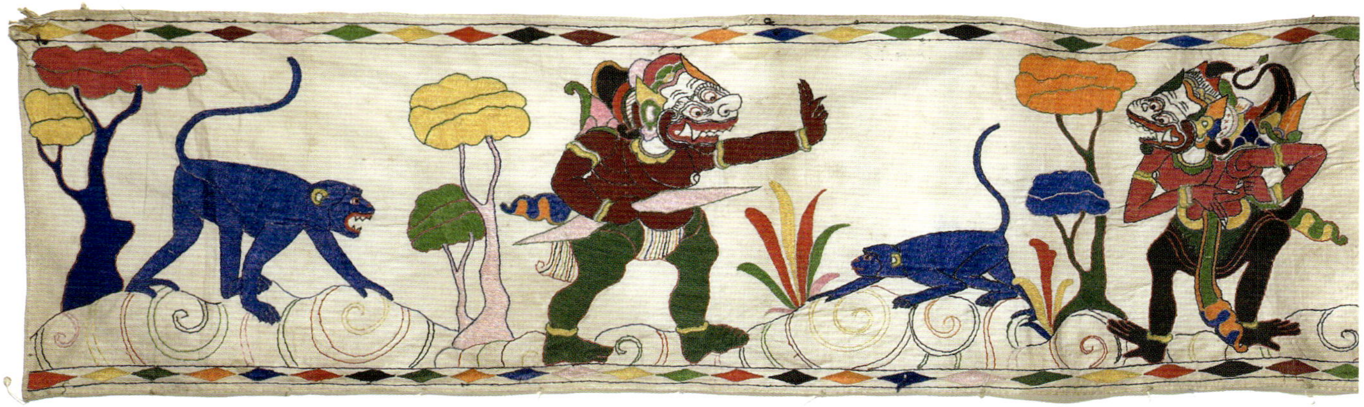

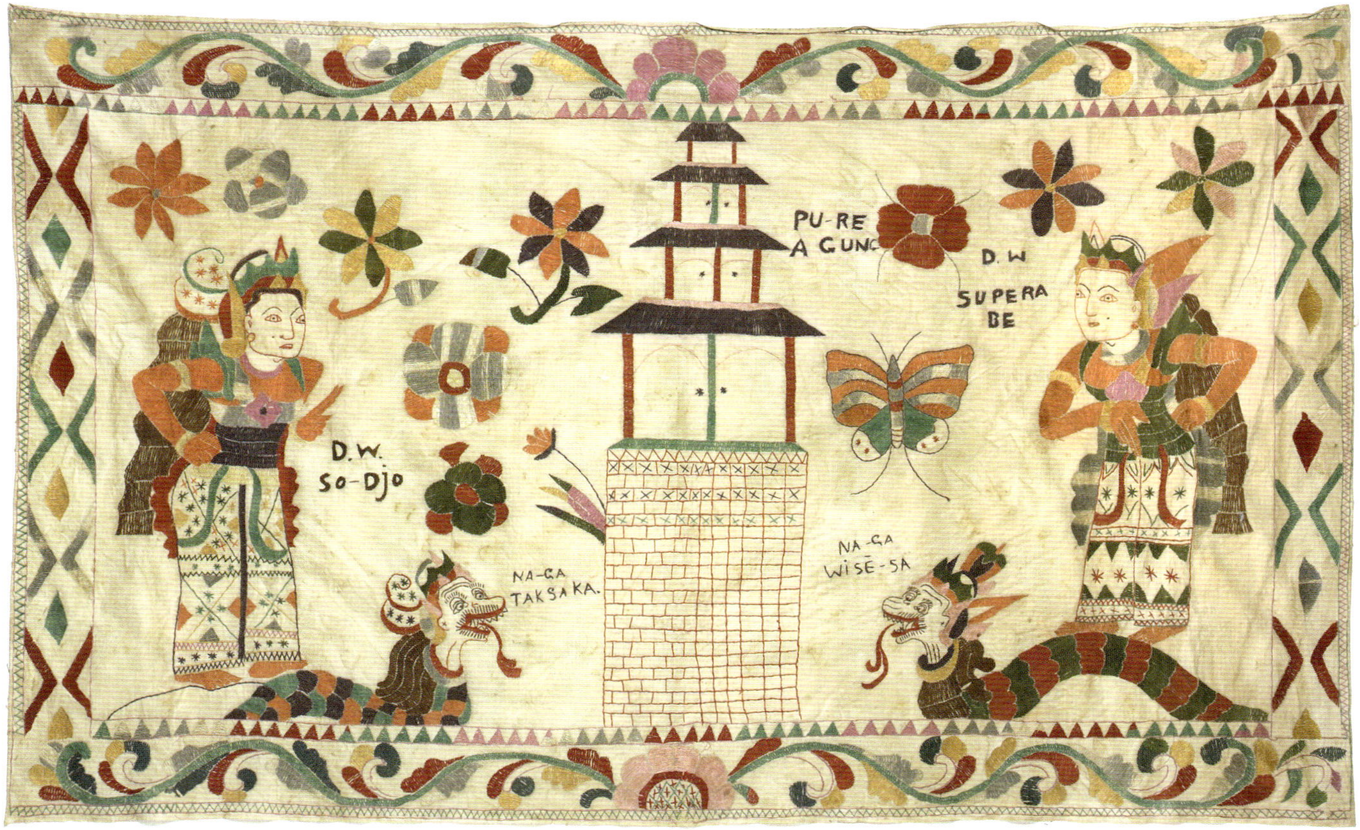

above: PLATE 13 **Negara.** *Ider-ider*, detail, 25 x 250. Silk threads. A variety of stitching techniques depicting *Ramayana* characters, including Hanuman (right), a warrior, and two engaging blue monkeys.

below: PLATE 14 **Negara.** *Tabing*, 86 x 150. *Mahabharata.* A made-up scene of a Balinese temple structure, Pure Agung (its name), D. W. So-djo, and D. W. Supera Be, who are perhaps the wives or consorts of the two regal *nagas*, Taksaka and Wise-sa.

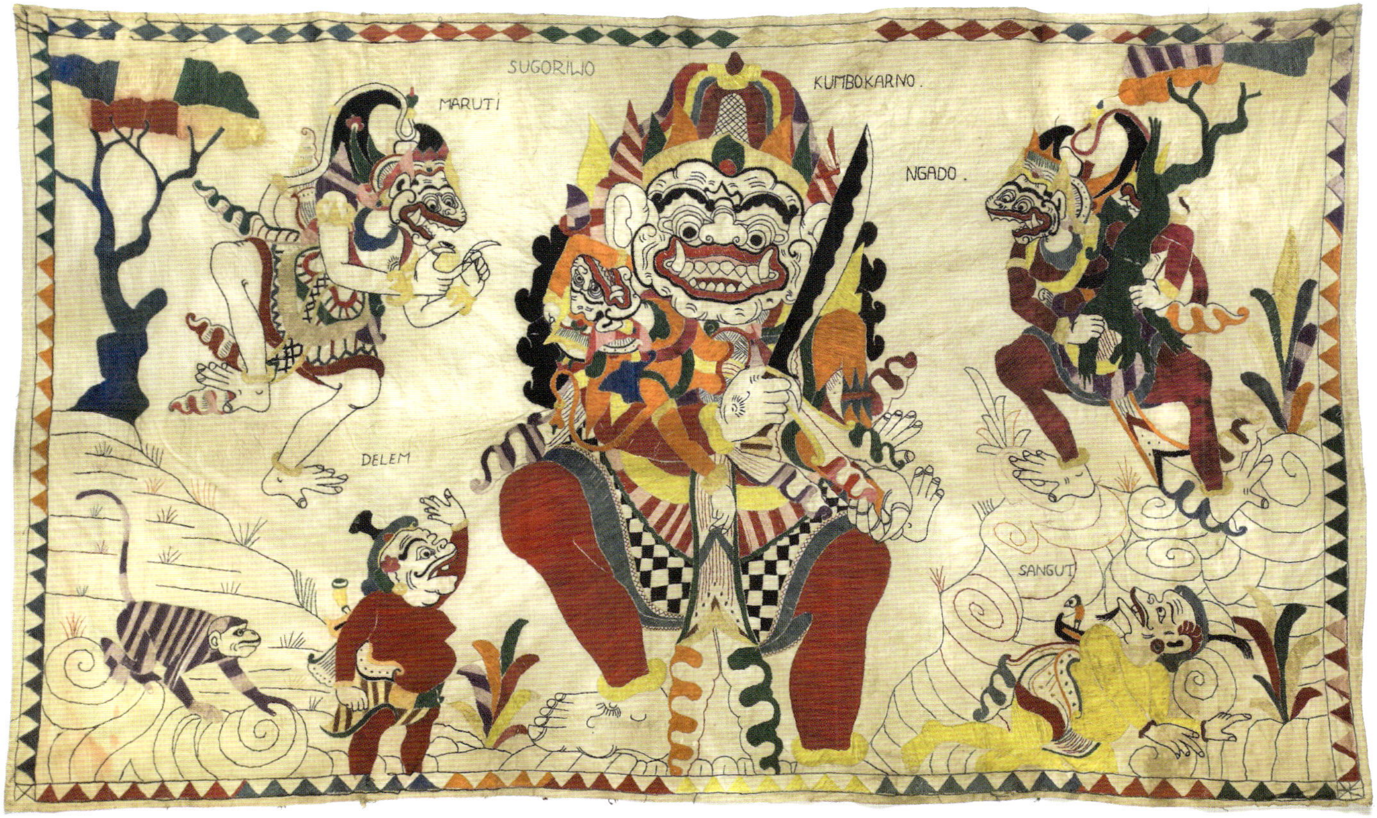

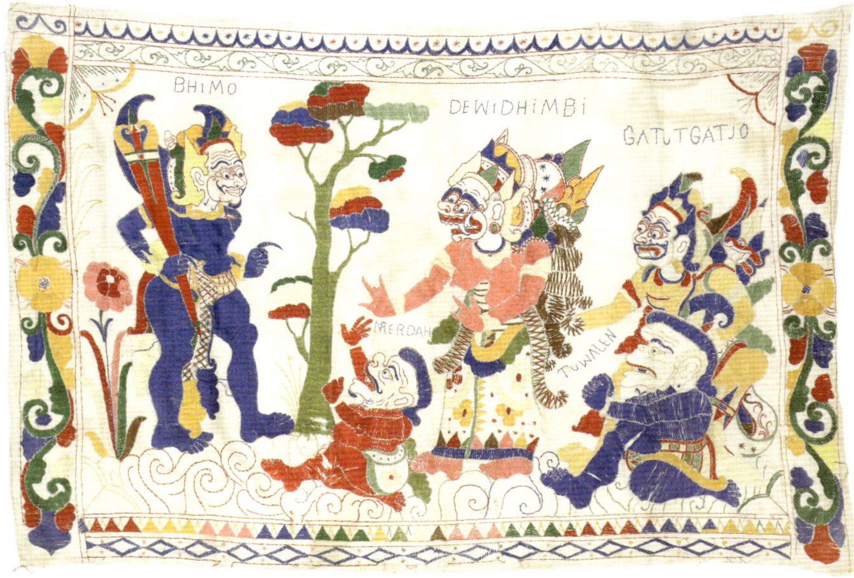

above: PLATE 15 **Negara.** *Tabing*, 87 x 136. *Ramayana*. Kumbakarno (Kumbakarna), the giant brother of King Rawana, with the protagonist monkey general Sugoriwo (Sugriwa) in his grasp and being menaced by the monkey-warriors, Maruti (Hanuman) and Ngado (Anggada) with the clowns, Delem and Sangut engaging in their inexplicable antics.

left: PLATE 16 **Negara.** *Tabing*, 82 x 128. A fine stitching technique of the following *Mahabharata* characters: Bhimo (Bima), strongest of the five Pandawa brothers; Dewi Dhimbi (Arimbi), his *raksasa* wife; Gatugatjo (Gatokaça), their son; and the clowns Twalen and Merdah.

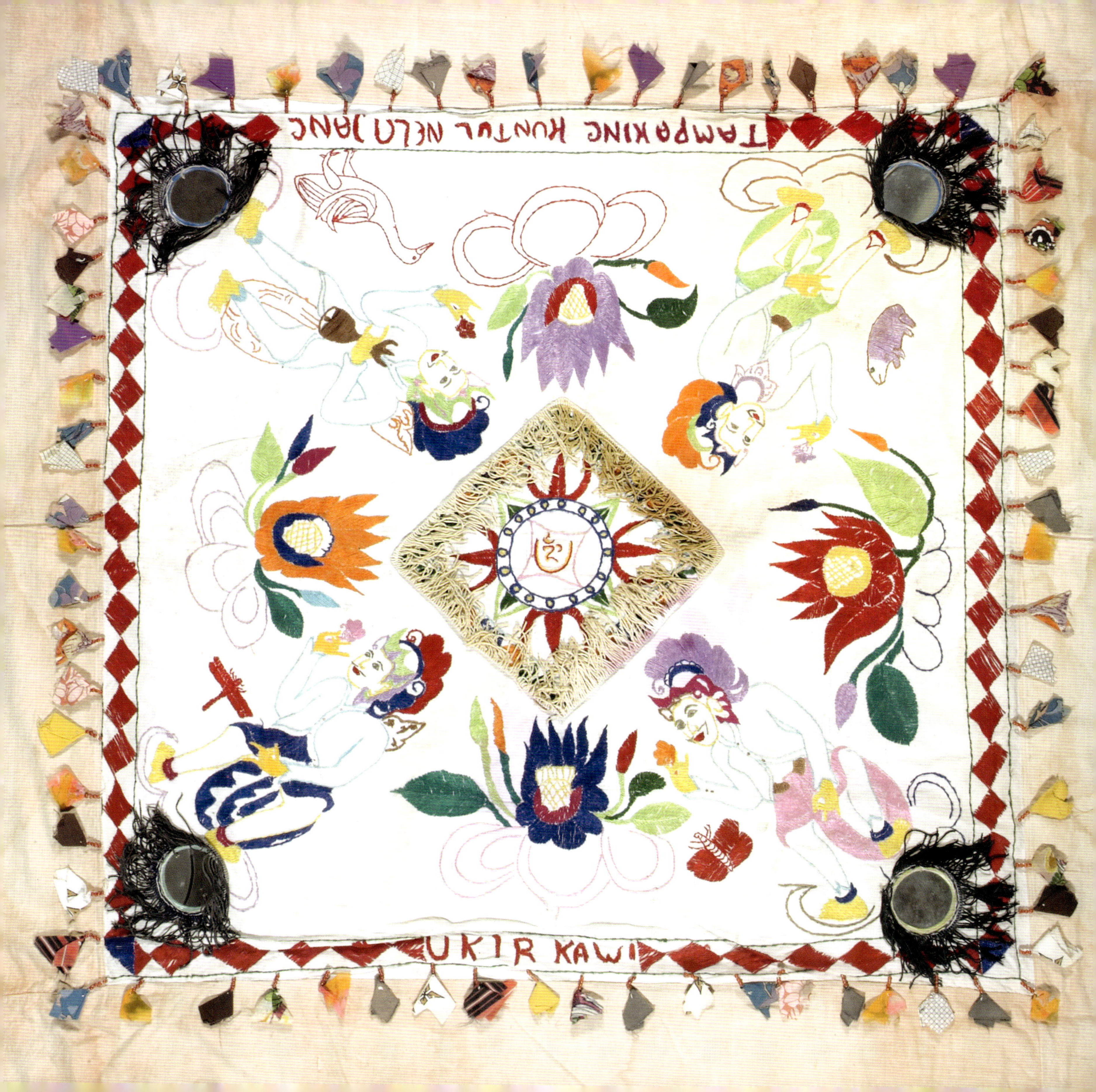
TAMPAKING KUNTUL NGLAYANG
UKIR KAWI

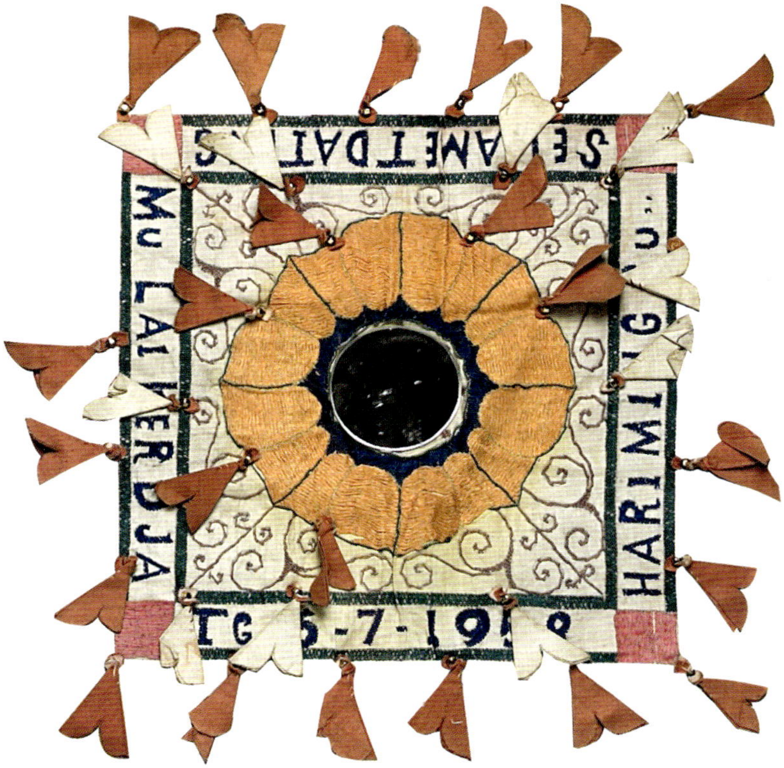

CEILING CLOTHS

A third and less common type of embroidered cloth is the ***leluwuor***, used solely as a ceiling canopy in celebrations and rituals. **PLATE 18** shows one that is dated July 6, 1958.[2] The Indonesian words *mulai kerdja* indicate the cloth was completed on that date. *Slamet datang* means welcome and *Hari Minggu* means Sunday. Such a cloth may have been used in special events such as a tooth-filing ceremony or a traditional wedding. ***leluwuor*** mainly have floral and geometric motifs; they rarely depict persons. An unusual exception is the cloth shown in **PLATE 17**, which shows Balinese ascetics, or holy men, in various praying poses. These cloths are almost always dated and usually, as noted above, contain some Indonesian words. Not all the work in ***leluwuor*** is embroidery; in some, many of the decorations are precut cloth designs such as leaves and flowers, which are attached by couching.

opposite: PLATE 17 **Negara.** *Leluwuor,* 110 x 124. Silk threads on cotton, mirror glass, scrap cloth triangles, and nylon fringes. Ceiling canopy used in ceremonies and rituals. Balinese script in the center is composed of sacred letters, here denoting the god Siwa. The four persons are Balinese ascetics or holy men with their traditional jackets and elaborate headdresses. Each is holding a petal and one holds a *bajra* (sacred bell); which are used in meditations and prayers. Depictions of persons on these embroidered ceiling canopies are rare, as most have sewn floral and geometric motifs with little embroidery. There are four large lotus motifs. The dragonfly, goose, and pig are apparently just decorations. The six words are transliterations from the Balinese language but their precise meaning and significance is unclear: *Ukir* (carved or engraved), *kawi* (ancient form of Javanese), *nelayang* (fisher), and *tampaking kuntul* (a heron who catches fish).

this page: PLATE 18 **Negara.** *Leluwuor*, 135 x 140. Embroidery, dated July 6, 1958. A ceiling canopy used in rituals and celebrations. The Indonesian words *mulai kerdja* mean the work was completed on the above date; *Hari Minggu* denotes Sunday; and *slamet datang* means welcome.

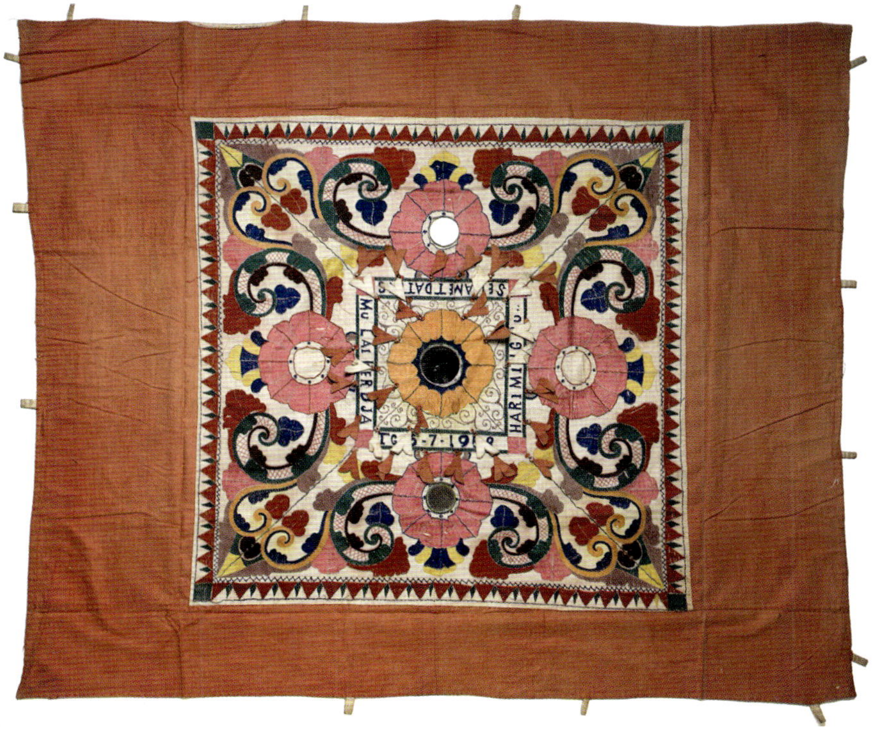

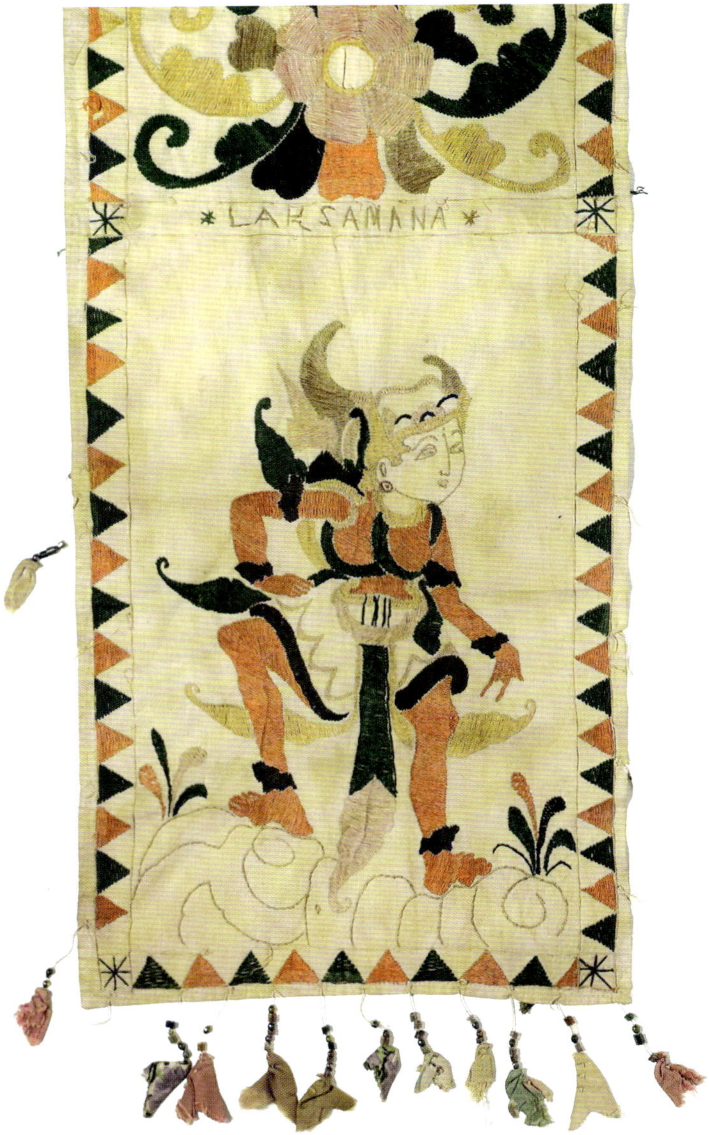

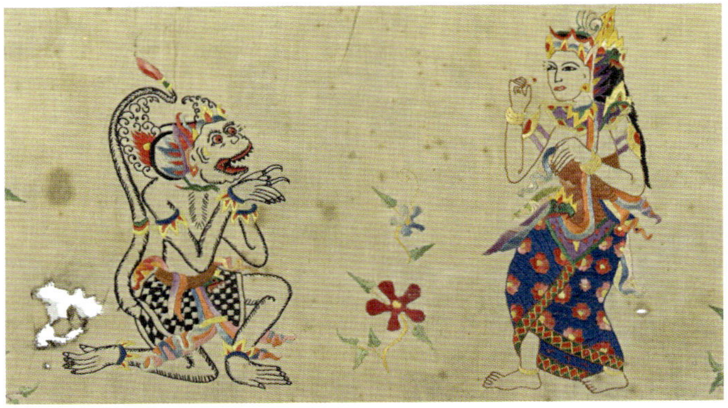

above left: **PLATE 19 Negara.** *Lamak*, detail, 29 x 87. A small offering cloth used on shrines and altars. Depicted is Laksamana (Laksmana), Rama's faithful brother in the *Ramayana*.

above right: **PLATE 20 Buleleng.** *Langse*, detail, 88 x 180. A curtain or a room divider with small finely embroidered images of *Ramayana* characters spaced on a wide expanse of undecorated cloth. This cloth has an unusual feature in that there is no wrong side. The holes are from exposure and long usage. Shown are Hanuman and Sita in captivity identifying Rama's ring.

LAMAKS

A fourth type of embroidered cloth, the small ***lamak,*** is hung vertically to adorn household altars and outdoor shrines during daily or special religious observances. Used as offerings, they usually contain one figure drawn from the many characters in the traditional stories. The designs and embroidery are simple. Typical examples of ***lamak*** with ***Ramayana*** characters are in **PLATES 19** and **21**. Two characters from the ***Mahabharata*** are shown in **PLATES 87** and **90** (see pages 56 and 58). A few ***lamaks*** are quite long; for example, that depicting Widur Budi, a fearsome ***raksasa*** (demon/warrior) measures 43 centimeters in width by 226 centimeters in length (**PLATE 22**). An even longer ***lamak*** (39 by 240 centimeters), shown in **PLATES 38** and **39** (page 23), includes three gods, one goddess, and two ***nagas*** (dragons) with names. This cloth is discussed in chapter 2.

ROOM DIVIDERS

All of the previously described embroidery sizes come from the Negara area. The fifth type, the ***langse*** or curtain, apparently was made only in northern Bali around Singaraja. It was used primarily as a room divider, hung from ropes or wires to separate rooms in modest village homes that have few interior walls. ***Langse*** were only embroidered with a few figures positioned on a large expanse of otherwise undecorated cotton cloth. The stitching technique was highly skillful, using silk threads in attractive pastel colors. **PLATE 20** shows two characters from the ***Ramayana.*** This ***langse*** measures 38 centimeters high and 180 centimeters long.

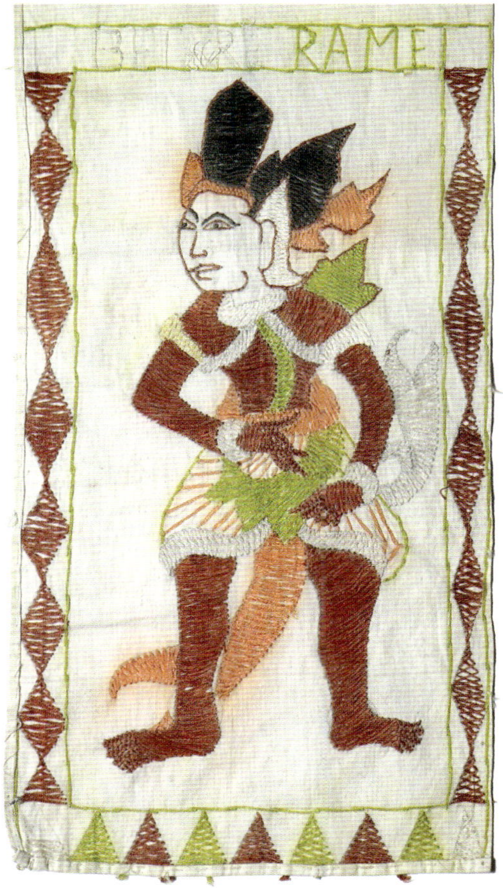

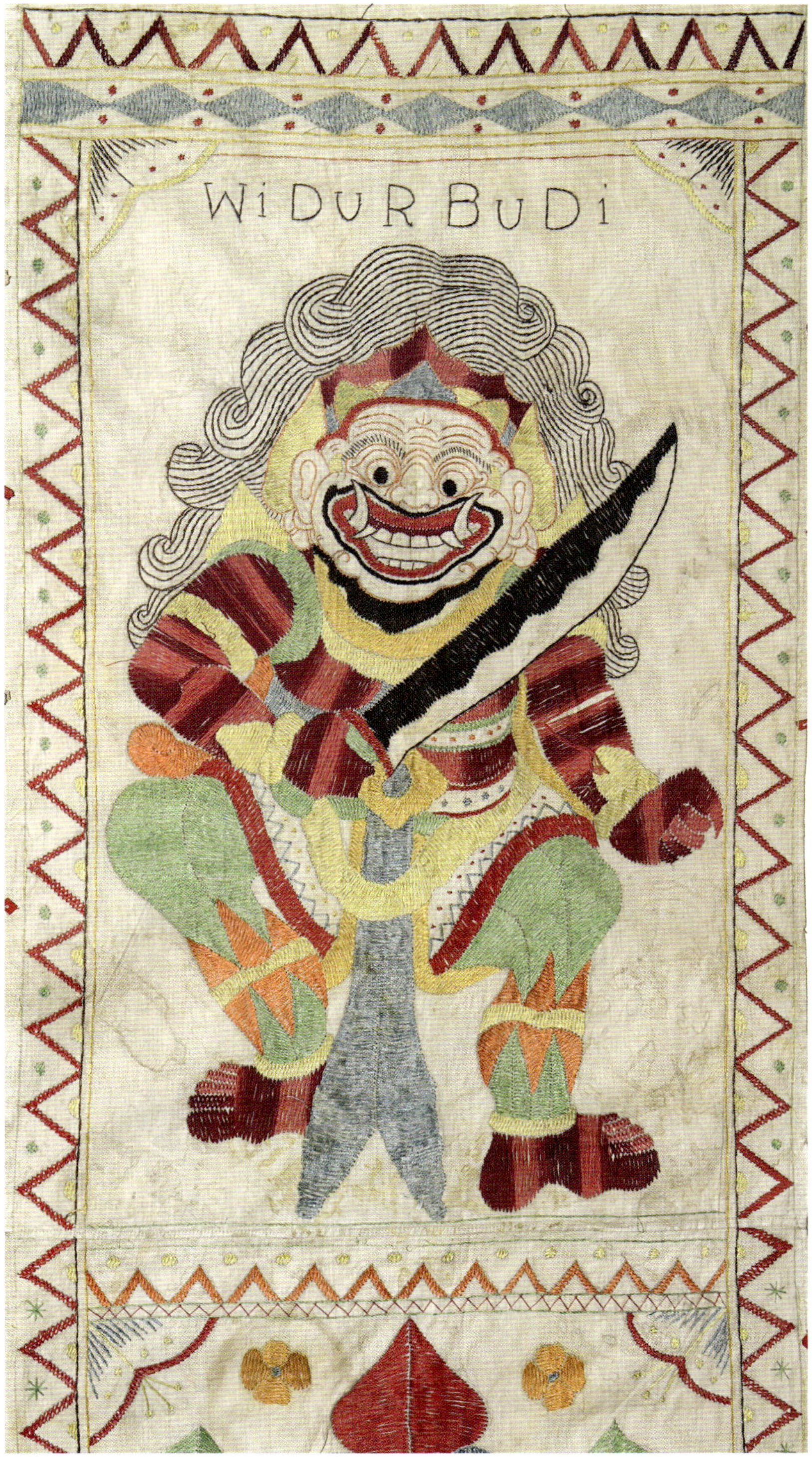

above left: PLATE 21 **Negara.** *Lamak*, 20 x 73. Betare Ramei (Rama) hero of the *Ramayana.*

above right: PLATE 22 **Buleleng.** *Lamak*, detail, 43 x 226. An unusually long vertical offering cloth with a demon warrior (Widur Budi) who may be a character from the Panji cycle of stories emanating from East Java.

PENNANTS

The sixth and last size cloth is the ***umbul-umbul,*** a pennant usually attached to the top of a very long, thin, curving bamboo pole. These are used to mark the entrances to villages and temples when special ceremonies are taking place. Examples can be seen in the elaborate temple ceremonies in **PLATE 25**, with pagoda towers, nine bamboo poles, a ***keris*** (knife) dancer, seven ***gamelan*** (orchestra) players, and four women with offerings. This is just one half of the cloth; the other shows Arjuna and two of his wives (see page 60). You can see such village scenes with poles everywhere on festive occasions throughout Bali. Usually the ***umbul-umbul*** are either plain white or yellow; however, some special ones contain exquisitely embroidered ***nagas*** that seem to fly when the wind blows. Such pennants ordinarily contain only one figure, almost always a ***naga.*** A typical one is shown in **PLATE 23**; it measures 33 centimeters at its widest and 112 centimeters long, and the ***naga*** seems to slither down its length. Another example, in **PLATE 24**, has a tinsel-like thread at the end of its tail and the name of the maker on the cloth. (The significance of the ***naga*** is discussed in chapter 4, which features the depiction of animals in the story cloths.)

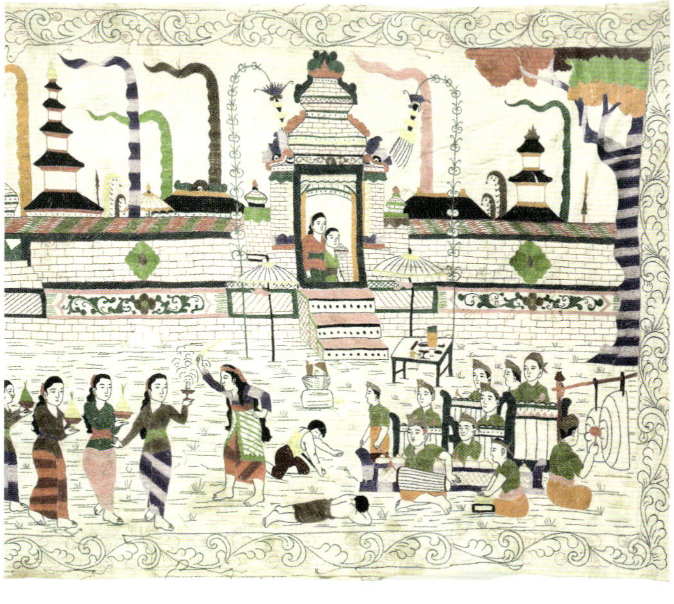

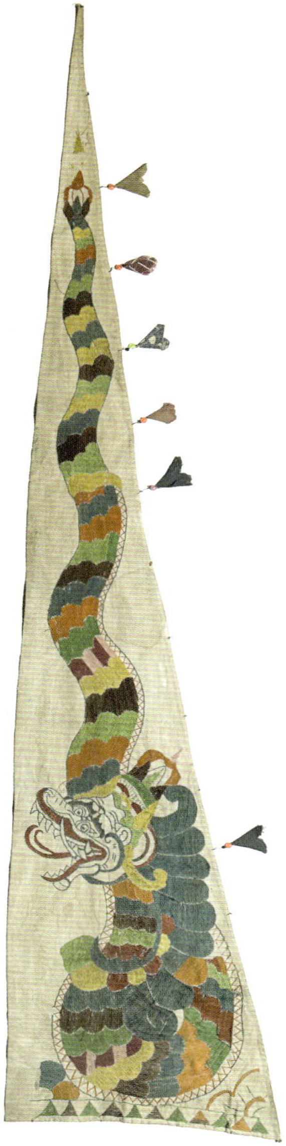

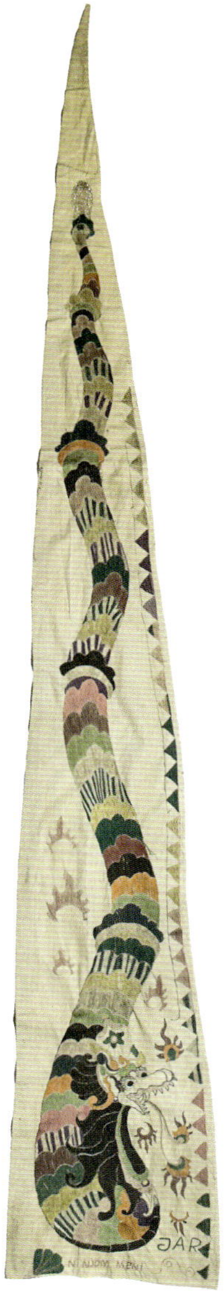

above left: **PLATE 23 Negara.** *Umbul-umbul,* 33 x 112. A pennant attached to a bamboo pole marking a religious event or celebration in a village, a temple, or a house. The *naga* (dragon) decoration is typical for such pennants.

above right: **PLATE 24 Negara.** *Umbul-umbul,* 30 x 206. Ni Njonm Meni probably is the name of the maker. The word that looks like JAR refers to the *naga* (dragon).

left: **PLATE 25 Negara.** *Tabing,* detail, 88 x 192. A temple celebration marked by long flowing pennants *(umbul-umbul)* on bamboo poles with religious pagoda-like structures. Depicted are women dancing, one man ritually stabbing himself, another in a trance, and an *gamelan* orchestra playing.

ARTISANS

These Balinese embroideries are referred to as ***sulaman*** and the technique of embroidering as ***bordir***. Within Indonesia, embroidery is not common in traditional textiles; ***ikat*** or resist methods of dyeing and loom weaving predominate. Embroidery is a very simple craft, requiring only needles, threads, and cloth, most of which are cheap and readily available in local markets. What makes these Balinese embroideries unusual is that they can be viewed not only as attractive decorative cloths but as informative narrative texts. The characters and scenes depicted in colored threads come from the great storytelling traditions that have been and still are popular in Bali—namely, the ***Mahabharata***, the ***Ramayana***, the ***Calonarang***, and many other tales.

It is always women who embroider these story cloths. However, in order to do this properly, they must have some knowledge of the traditional characters depicted. One such woman is I Ketut Wandi (**PLATE 26**) who lives in a village near the city of Negara. Her background is typical of the several women I interviewed who did embroidery. She was born in 1956, had three brothers, six sisters, and three children. She began to embroider in 1980 and was self-taught. Her income from her craft was modest. She seemed to know very little about the history of this Negara tradition of which she was a part. She was relatively familiar with the ***Mahabharata*** and used many of its characters in her embroidery. I asked her who her favorite character was in this epic, and she said, "It is Arjuna, and I like to put him in as many of my embroideries as possible." She was polite and hospitable and answered my many questions with candor. She was an excellent embroiderer, but not skilled enough to make the required drawings of the various characters beforehand.

Usually a local man steeped in Balinese traditions will outline in pencil the characters and motifs to be embroidered by a woman. In the Negara area, such a man is a woodcutter named I Wayang Putra who lives in Sangkaragung village, ***banjar*** (subdivision) Samblong; the female members of his family do the actual embroidering. One of his drawings, before embroidering has been done, is shown in **PLATE 28**. Another such person is a ***dalang*** or puppeteer, I Ketut Sukarela, who lives in Mendoyo in the same area. Thus, these embroideries are the result of a collaborative craft involving a traditional artist such as a male illustrator or puppeteer and a traditional artisan such as a female embroiderer.

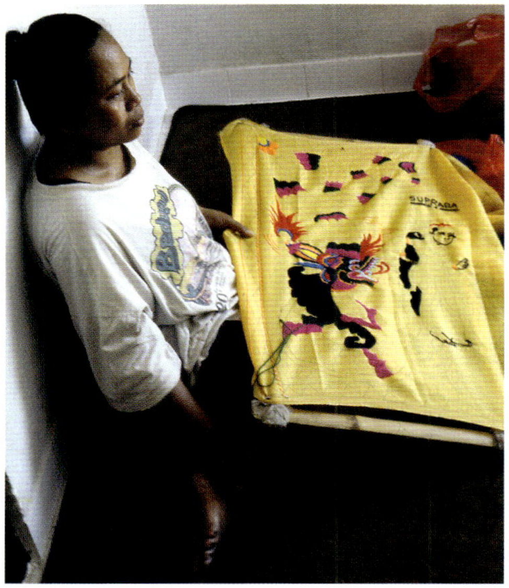

PLATE 26 Griya or Brahman village, near Negara, July 1995. I Ketut Wandi working on an embroidery.

The original drawings are entirely dependent on the artist's knowledge of traditional stories. This is not a simple matter of common knowledge. I have determined that in the embroideries in my collection some three hundred characters are either depicted or referred to; all must be drawn clearly to make understandable the scenes to be embroidered. This means knowing the genealogies and features of the embroidered characters in relation to what is being portrayed. It also means knowing the facial characteristics and the appropriate dress and adornments of each character, as well as all the symbols associated with them.

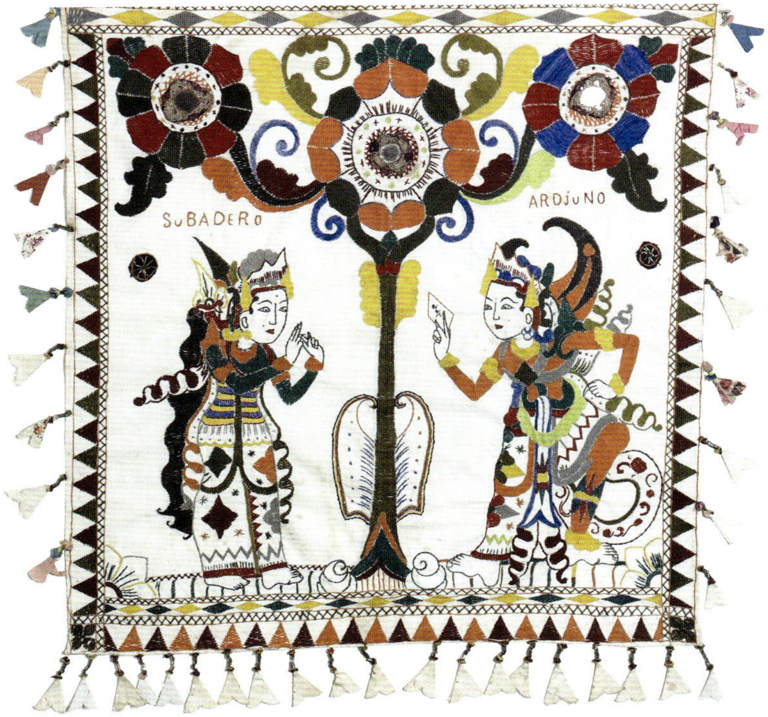

PLATE 27 Negara. *Tabing*, 63 x 130. *Mahabharata*. An elaborate, highly stylized tree-of-life with symmetrical lotus motifs perhaps signifying rootedness and a fruitful life for Ardjuno (Arjuna) and one of his wives, Subadiro (Subadra).

PLATE 28 Jembrana. 89 x 145. Pencil and ink on cotton. *Wisnu Astride Garuda*, by I Wayang Putra of Sangkaragung, March 2003. Also depicted are Dewi Winata, the wife of *naga* Tasaka and Dewi Kadru (Gadru), the wife of *naga* Basuki. The embroiderer will choose her own colored threads for the outline and for the spaces to be filled in.

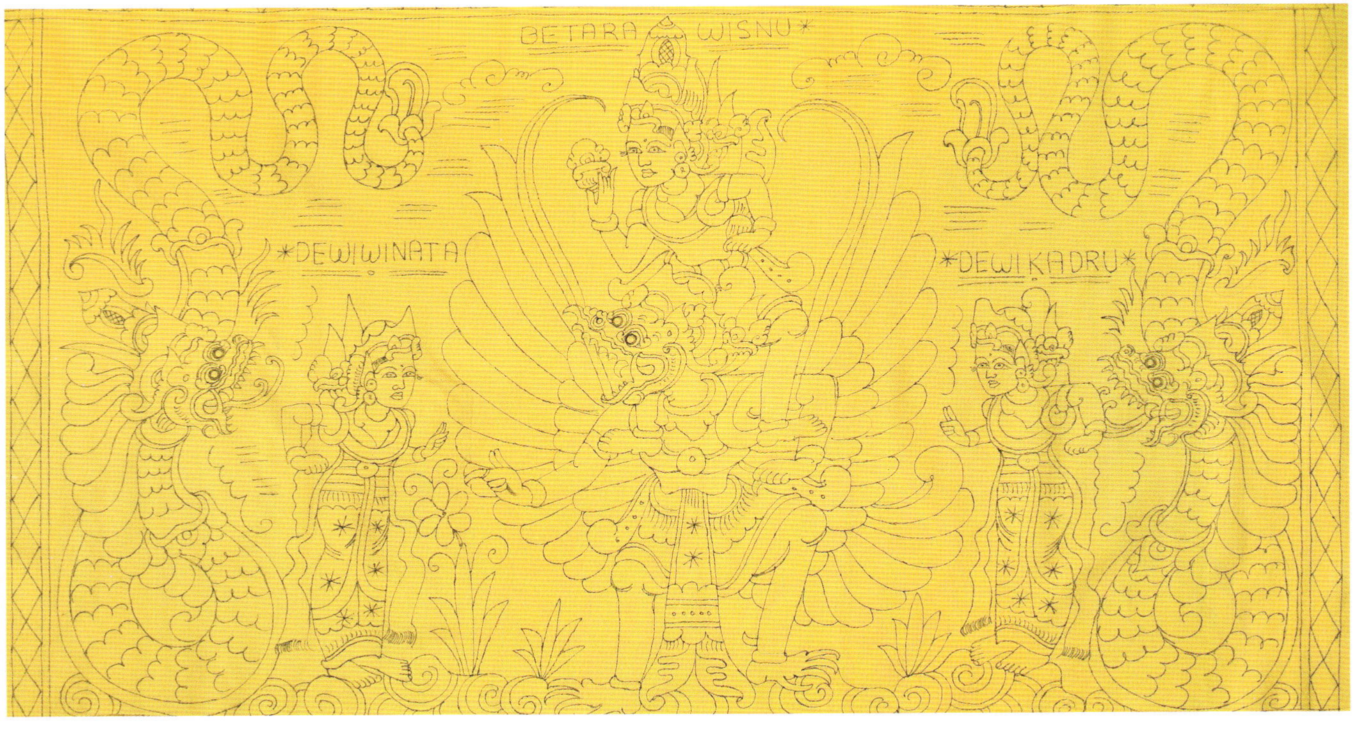

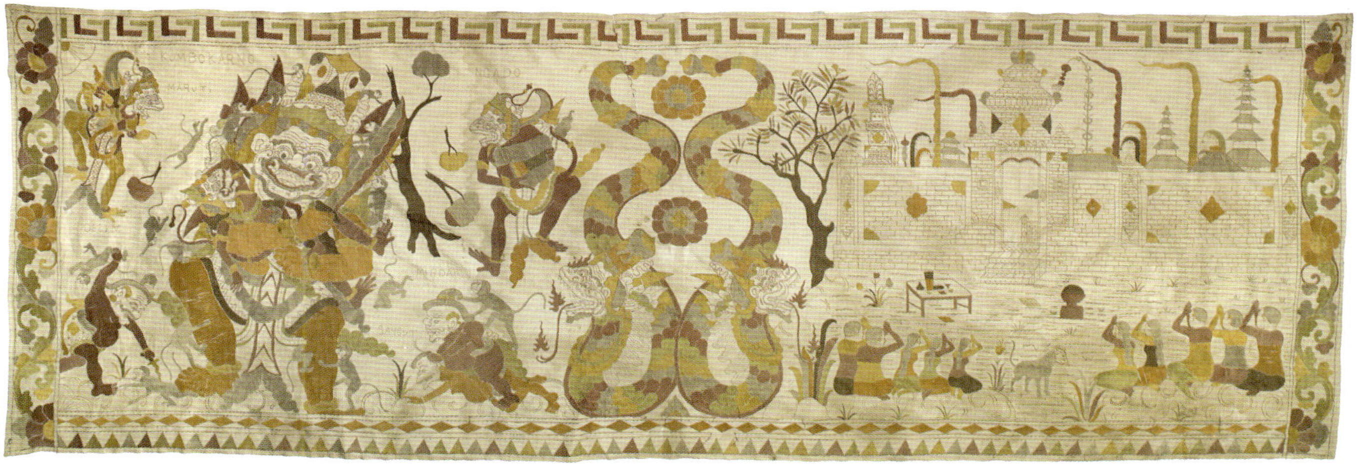

PLATE 29 **Negara.** *Tabing*, 85 x 226. A very large cloth with two separate scenes divided by two spectacular *nagas*. The right half depicts a major Hindu temple ceremony with five men and five women praying before a table with vessels of offerings and a large ritual bowl. The left half depicts Kumbakarna battling Maruti (Hanuman) and Ngado (Anggada) in the *Ramayana*.

DESIGN & DECORATION

Several elements are common to most of these embroideries. They are rarely backed. Decorations may include sequins, mica, mirror glass, gimp, beads, nylon fringes, and scraps of cloth dangles. All the cloths have continuous borders that may include diamond or triangular shapes, flowers, tendrils, and various wavy lines. Many have symbols such as a tree-of-life (PLATES **52**, page 33 and **27**, opposite). Symmetry is an important feature, exemplified by paired ***nagas*** or ***panasars*** (clowns) and the spacing of other characters and motifs. (See the exquisite examples of orange lotus amidst carefully placed flowers and leaves (PLATE **30**, page 16). The specific characters depicted have generally been modeled after the same characters as shadow puppets with respect to dress, adornment, skin color, body, position and the like. However, some characters in the older embroideries appear to be modeled on traditional dancers rather than puppets. The scenes in long ***ider-iders*** unfold in cartoon-like sequences with clear divisions among them. Some ***ider-iders*** and some ***tabings*** are divided into two parts, each depicting related but different scenes, as in PLATE **29**. Humorous or comic touches are added to many cloths by including clowns in ludicrous positions, animals in funny poses, and odd gesturing by many characters. All of these features can be achieved with embroidery, which is free from the limitations imposed by the loom.

These Balinese embroideries exhibit several particularly distinctive characteristics. For one, the depicted characters almost always have their own names embroidered beside them.[2] Names such as Wisnu, Arjuna, Rama, Sita, and Merdah appear, mostly in Indonesian; some are in Balinese script, but only on older cloths. This is, of course, a direct and graphic way of identifying traditional images so that everyone can easily recognize them. In any case, all characters must conform to the conventions of what they should look like. However, it is not clear why this explicit identification is needed, since most Balinese, young and old, know traditional characters by their image alone. From talking to several Balinese women about this, I have concluded that this "captioning" was most likely a style that developed and endured over time. However, it may be related to notions of identity and social status, which are significant aspects of Balinese traditional culture.

Another unusual element is the names or initials of the maker that sometimes appear in ink or pencil on the back or, less often, on the front of the embroidery. Since almost all the embroidering work was done in a small area around Negara, one could actually identify the maker or her family—and in many cases I was able to do so. This is perhaps a unique characteristic in any folk art, particularly in traditional textiles for which the maker is ordinarily anonymous. It suggests the possibility of productive field research to trace the evolution of such an embroidery tradition and the people that have been closely involved in it. Regrettably, I would need another lifetime to undertake such a task—but the opportunity certainly exists for others.

REGIONAL CONTRASTS

Some embroideries from Negara were made between 1920 and 1929 in Buleleng. Most, however, were done between 1940 and 1995. The earliest dated one in my collection is 1958, but I know by style characteristics and aging that some are much older. The oldest Negara embroideries often have names on them in Balinese script (PLATE 32). In addition, they usually contain muted thread colors, mostly tans and browns. Most of the cloths from this area feature ***Ramayana*** characters and scenes and, to a lesser extent, scenes from the ***Mahabharata***.

In contrast, the Buleleng cloths from north Bali come mainly in the ***ider-ider*** size and generally favor the ***Mahabharata***. The stitchery is finer and silk rather than cotton threads are often used in a range of exceedingly bright colors including purple, orange, pink, and green. Buleleng embroideries are more decorated than their Negara counterparts, with bright sequins and silver and gold threads that are sewn or couched, not embroidered. The effect of all this can be dazzling and the stitching so intricate and so finely meshed that the cloth, even up close, looks like a painting (see PLATE 99, page 64). Such a fine ***ider-ider*** compares favorably with the best embroideries from India and China.[3]

Folk art is often mistakenly described as repetitive in subject, relatively uncreative, and not adherent to the so-called cardinal rules of perspective and design. If you accept a very different basis for creativity and representation, the Balinese embroideries belie such descriptions. They contain many variations of color, form, and spacing that reflect both aesthetic and creative elements. Body colors associated with traditional monkey/soldier characters such

PLATE 30 **Buleleng.** *Lamak*, detail, 43 x 226. The bottom of half of a long cloth showing a fine example of meticulous spacing and beautifully embroidered lotus leaf and tendril motifs.

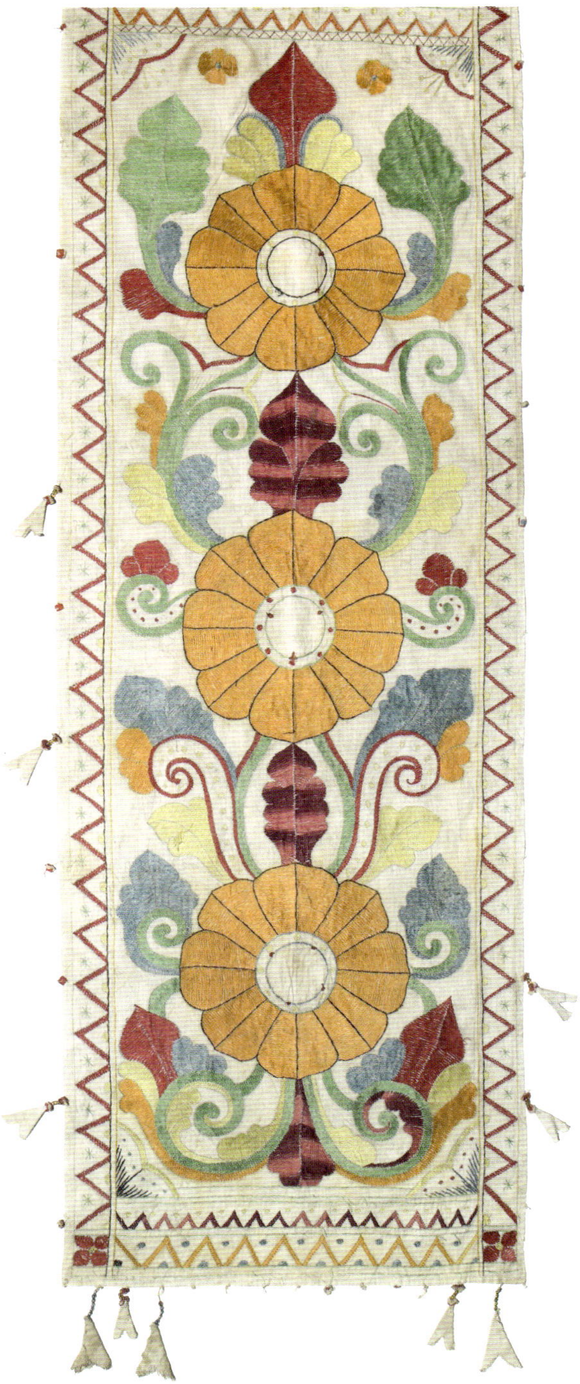

right: PLATE 31 **Negara.** *Tabing*, 87 x 106, dated August 8, 1975. *Mahabharata.* Arjuna sits on a mound of rocks, holding an arrow symbolizing his fame as a great archer and wearing a crown indicating his incarnation as a god. Two of his many wives, Nilotama and Supraba, stand dutifully at his side. Two large multi-colored *nagas* or mythical dragons frame the scene.

below: PLATE 32 **Negara.** *Tabing*, 77 x 128. This is an older (pre-1945) cloth unusual in that it has lettering in both Indonesian and Balinese. The male figure holding the pretzel-like object is Gatokaça (an ardent ally of the Pandawa family) and Swatama (a Korawa supporter). Satijawati is the wife of Salya, a Korawa general. Djenaki is related probably by marriage to the Korawa family.

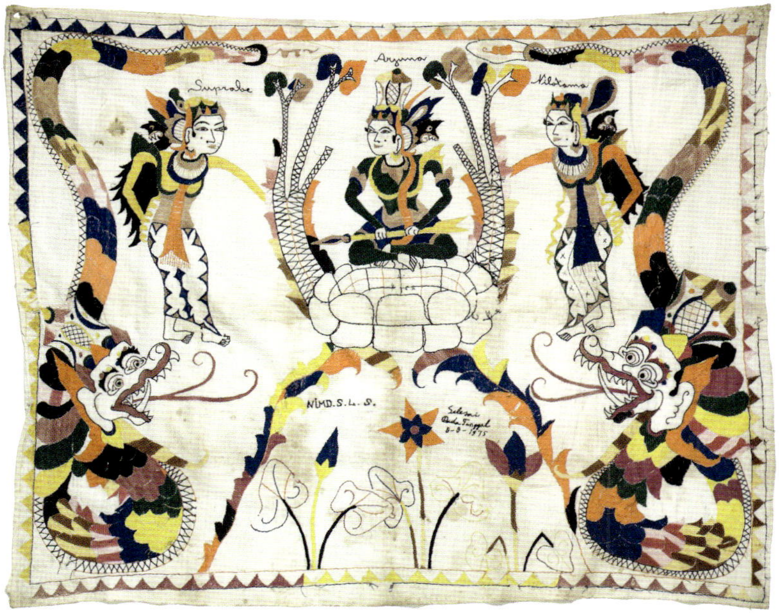

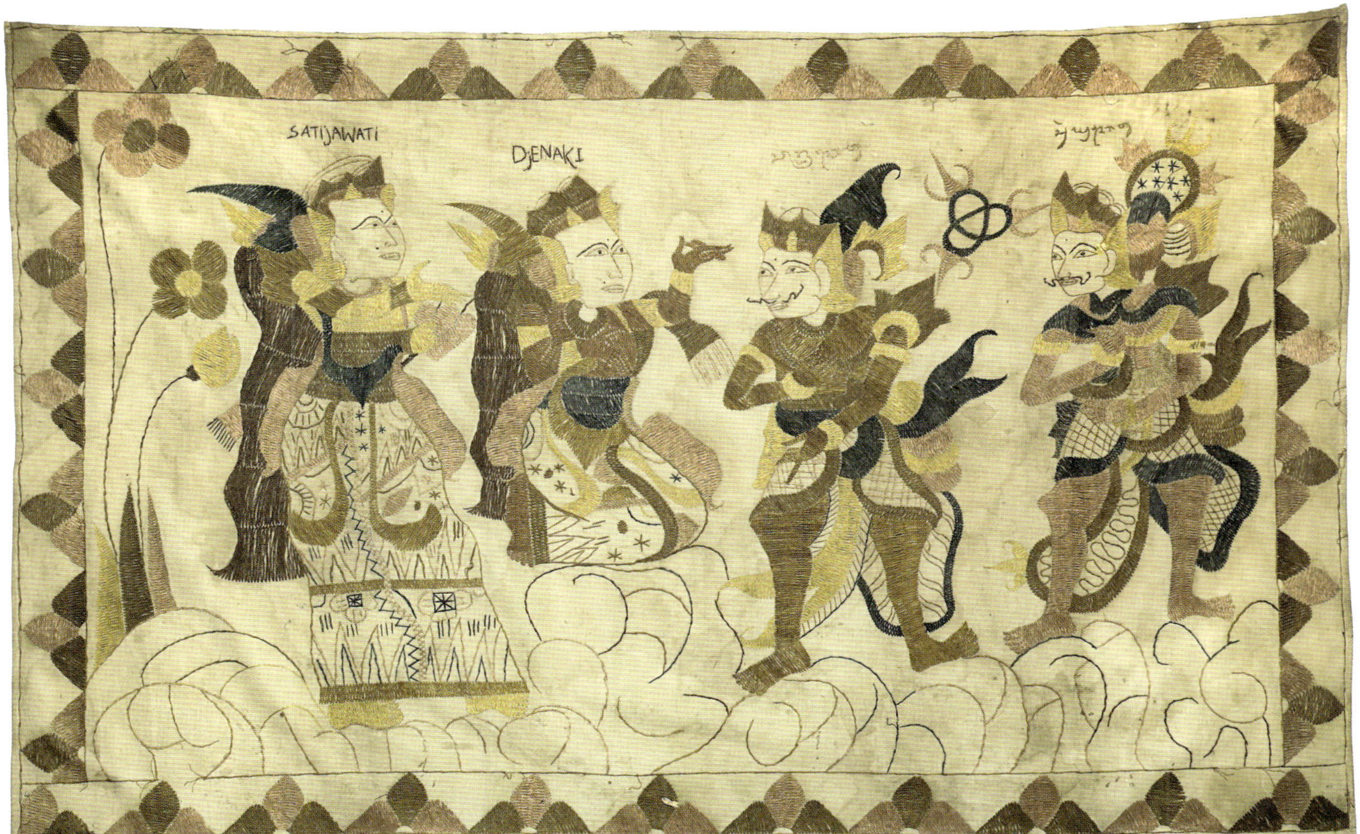

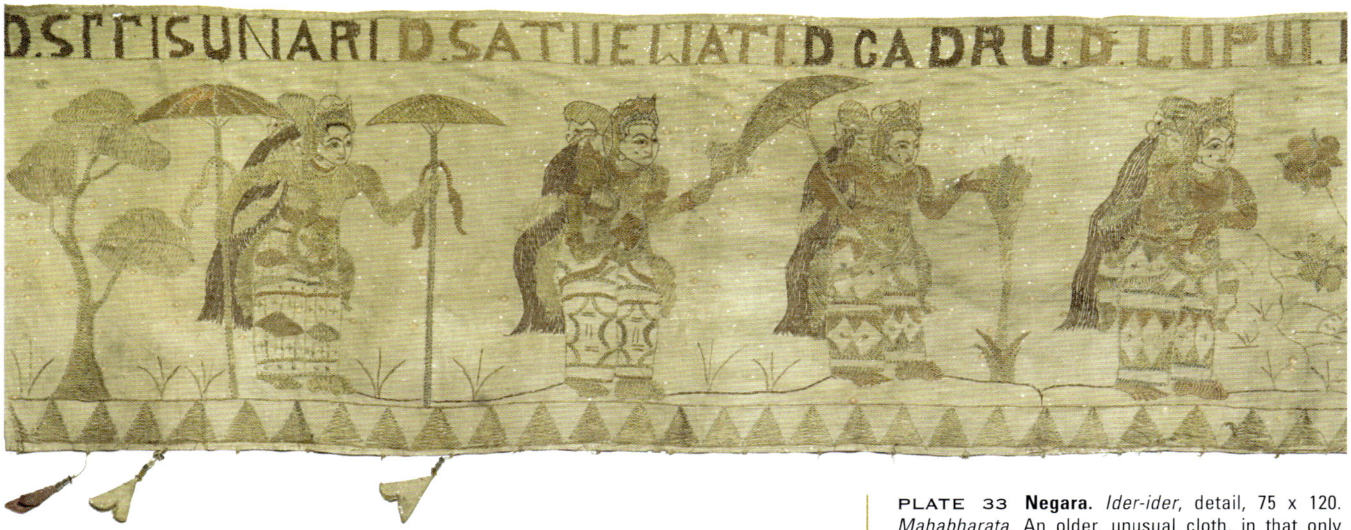

PLATE 33 Negara. *Ider-ider*, detail, 75 x 120. *Mahabharata*. An older, unusual cloth, in that only women are depicted and their names are embroidered in large letters above them. Shown from left to right are: D. Sunari (Kresna's daughter and wife of Abhimanyu); D. Satijawati (the wife of the Korawa general, Salya); D. Gadru (wife of a *naga*), and Lupui (princess daughter of Priest Kanwa).

as Hanuman (white), Anila (red), and Anggada (green) are not constant. The clowns should be depicted with black bodies, but this varies. One might think that the selection and arrangement of characters on cloth would conform to an actual scene from one of the stories. However, as mentioned previously, this is not necessarily so, as the personal taste of the maker and the preference of a client may determine what any scene contains, so long as it is relatively appropriate to the story.

Some common popular Balinese preferences come into play, such as clowns appearing in many, many scenes irrespective of their part in what is really going on in the original story. Some of the women told me they sometimes like to place characters from different stories on the same cloth, apparently as a creative diversion. An apt example is the ***ider-ider*** (PLATE 111, page 77) in which one half depicts a scene from the ***Ramayana***, and the other half is from the ***Mahabharata***.

The choice of border designs and other motifs appears to be mainly subjective, allowing the embroiderer a certain amount of free play. However, when very well-known scenes are to be embroidered, they normally present a conventional and realistic depiction of the characters. These include such favorite scenes as Arjuna meditating, surrounded by seductive nymphs (PLATE 34, opposite and PLATE 97, page 63); Rawana abducting Sita (PLATE 108, page 74); Hanuman showing Rama's ring to Sita and her resisting Rawana (PLATE 115, page 80); and so on. Personal choices of stitching, color, design, and content are all evident to some extent in all the embroideries shown in this book. However, they are always done in a frame of reference that is more or less conventional and that easily fits Balinese notions of story, character, and style. The embroideries, nevertheless, can certainly be appreciated for their aesthetic as well as their technical qualities.

For me and, I strongly believe, for the Balinese, what makes this folk art embroidery so attractive and popular is its narrative content, which reflects some of the most important and ancient elements of Balinese traditional culture. In some sense they are unusual world-class textiles. It is sad that this Balinese embroidery tradition is now moribund. What we have left, fortunately, is the marvelous stories they still show us. And now to the stories.

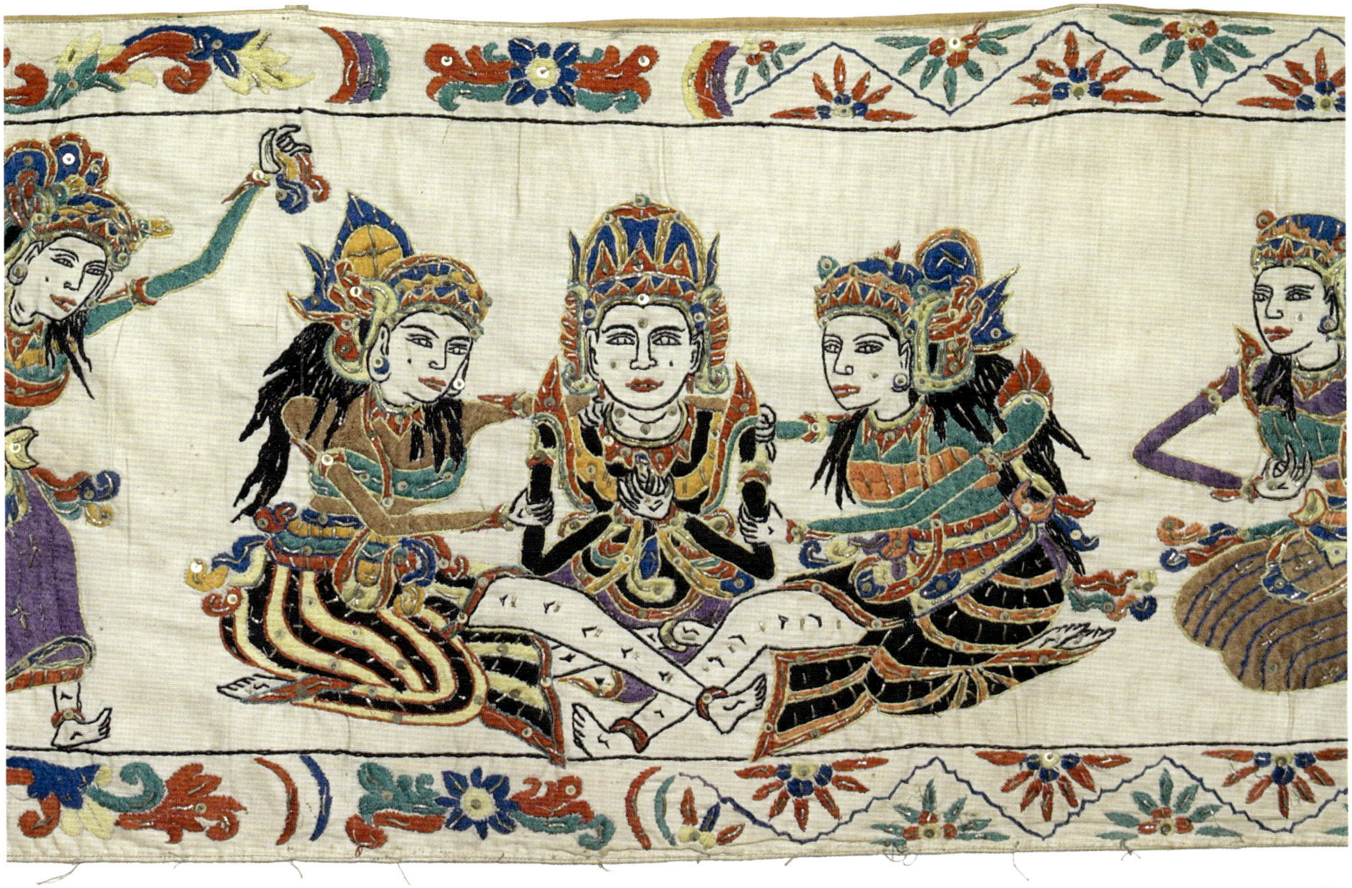

PLATE 34 **Buleleng.** *Ider-ider*, detail, 37 x 164. Silk threads, gimp, and sequins. *Mahabharata*. A finely stitched depiction of Arjuna meditating and resisting the seductive distractions of maidens. This is one half of the cloth, the other is a different scene. (See PLATE 106, page 72.)

FOOTNOTES

1. The major sources on stitching techniques that are relevant to those used in Bali are Rosemary Crill, ***Indian Embroidery***, particularly pp. 140–143, and Anne Morrell, ***The Techniques of Indian Embroidery***, particularly pp. 137–140.
2. Please note that the spelling of the names of characters may vary from cloth to cloth. This is mainly due to a narrative tradition that encompasses three different languages: Indonesian, Balinese, and Javanese. It is also a characteristic of folk art that correct spelling is not critical as long as the character is readily identifiable. In addition, Indonesian names for the Hindu gods, for example, differ from those used in India–Siwa for Shiva, Wisnu for Vishnu, and so on. Another complication is that the same character may have more than one name; for example, Hanuman is also known as Maruti, and Siwa also goes by Batara Guru. I have tried in most cases, where necessary, to identify all the names and their alternatives. Note, also, that almost all of the embroidered names on the cloths are pre-1972 Indonesian spellings, which are slightly different from those used today.
3. For examples to compare from these countries, see Subashini Aryan, ***Himachal Embroidery***; Rosemary Crill, ***Indian Embroidery***; and Beverly Jackson and David Hugus, ***Ladder to the Clouds: Intrigue and Tradition in Chinese Rank***.

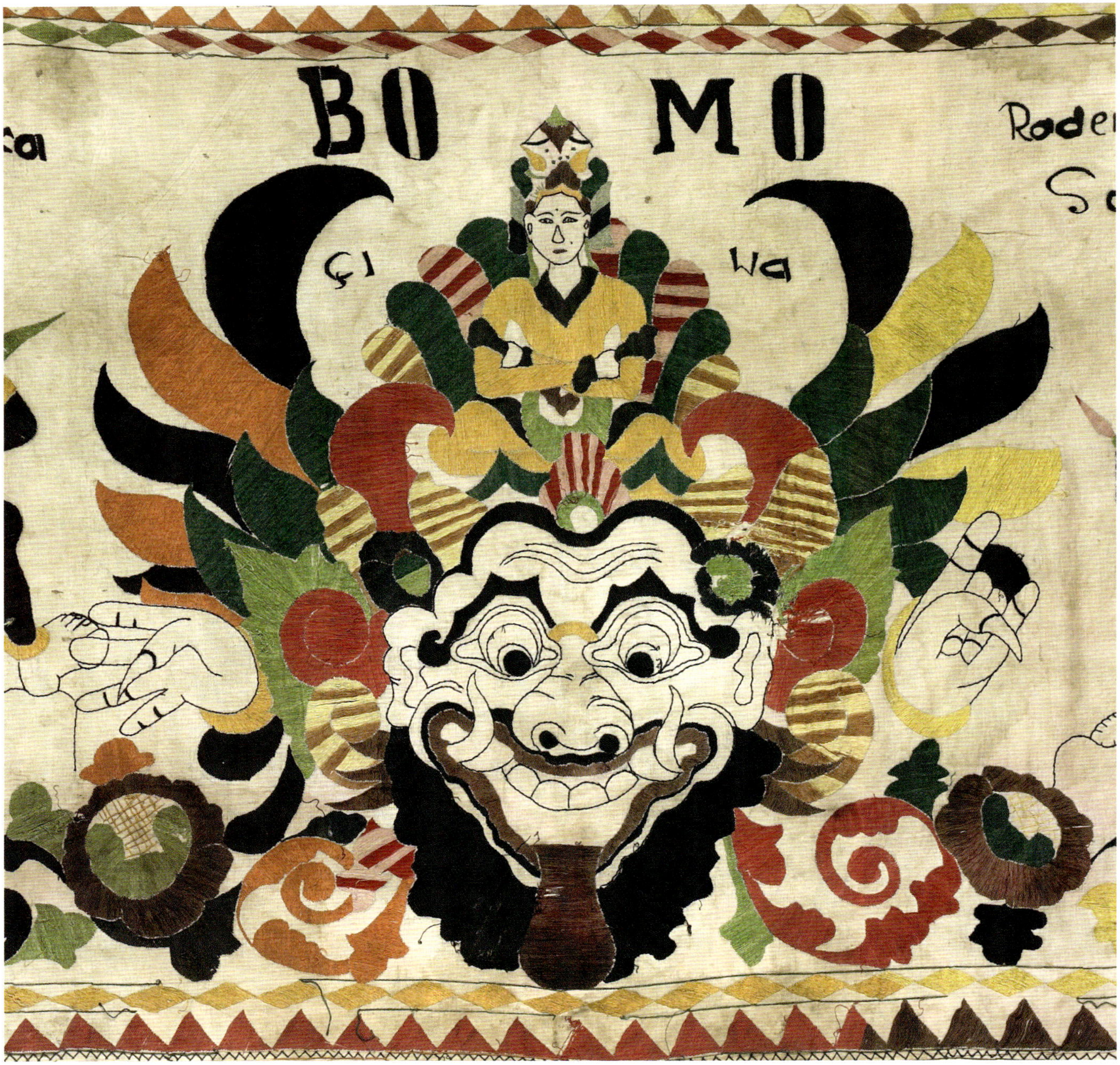

PLATE 35 Negara. *Tabing*, detail, 58 x 100. *Mahabharata*. A splendid depiction of the all-powerful god Siwa sitting atop his protector Bomo. On both sides of Siwa are Balinese letters, which name him.

Chapter 2

Gods, Goddesses & Great Demons

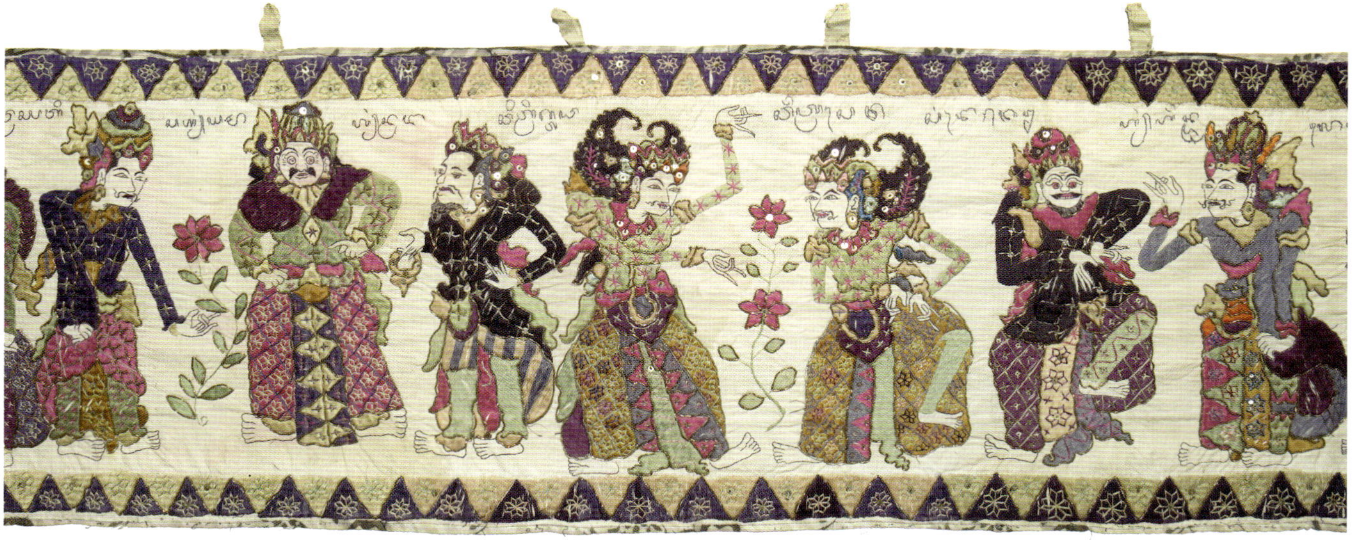

Of all the major religions in the world, Hinduism probably has the largest body of sacred texts, the greatest number of gods, and the most extensive mythology. As an outsider, I find its vast literature and extraordinary deity relationships difficult to understand and, at times, truly baffling. Fortunately for me, a detailed analysis of the Hindu tradition is beyond the purpose of this book; in any case, it is well-described elsewhere in hundreds of volumes. However, within this literature from India are two great epics that are known all over the world and particularly popular in Bali.

The ***Mahabharata*** and the ***Ramayana*** contain an amazing array of diverse personalities and complicated human and superhuman relationships. Within these great epics, you enter a world of gods and goddesses, kings and royal families, priests and sages, warriors, clowns, witches and ghosts, and animals both mythical and real. Some characters are transformed into others; some are incarnated and reincarnated; some are merely disguised. Many have more than one name. It is a complex and sometimes confusing populated universe subject to interpretation

PLATE 36 **Buleleng.** *Ider-ider*, detail, 40 x 360. Silk threads, gimp, and sequins. *Mahabharata*. A rare embroidery with names in Balinese script depicting among others the god Indra (far right); and the God of Death, Yama (second from left); Drona, center (magician and half-brother to the Pandawas, killed by Bima); Duryodhana, leader of the Korawas (second from right); and Citrasena, one of the one hundred sons of Dhrtarasta (third from right).

and reinterpretation. Fortunately, the stories themselves have been worked out and their ancient texts fully edited and translated. Almost all the various characters have extensive genealogies and their own personal names, so they can be easily identified through physical characteristics and dress. In this cosmos, the gods and goddesses of Hinduism who appear in the ***Mahabharata*** and the ***Ramayana*** are appealing and powerful from both a religious and an aesthetic perspective. Their dominant positions as figures of worship, as supernatural actors in human affairs, and as icons in art, craft, and performances present us with an intriguing panorama for storytelling, for both enjoyment and cultural understanding.

"The number of Hindu gods is … the same as that of the possible aspects of manifestation, created or potential."[1] In other words, the number of gods is seemingly inexhaustible. Along with their wives and consorts, the gods inhabit the entire universe: sitting on clouds, flying on air currents, meditating on mountain tops, and inhabiting trees, lakes, rivers, and oceans. They are everywhere and everything. There are thirty-three recognized main gods that compose the Hindu pantheon[2] and roam the episodes of the ***Mahabharata***. The number three is significant in that the supreme gods are three in number: Brahma (ruler of the heavens), Wisnu (the preserver; in India, Vishnu), and Siwa (the creator and destroyer; in India, Shiva).[3] They constitute what is called in Bali the *Trimurti* (the godly triumvirate). They are represented in paintings, as masks, embroideries, and as shadow puppets.

Siwa, the Lord of Sleep, has one body with many arms and three faces; he is the centrifugal force of inertia, resulting in annihilation, dispersion, and disintegration. He is the embodiment of a dreamless sleep in which all reality is transparent and the science of the mind is all that exists. He has one thousand and eight names. He is the death of death—that is, of eternal life. Siwa's two main aspects are opposite: the immediate one is fearful, the transcendent one is desirable. He is usually depicted with four arms, symbolizing power and the four directions in space. In **PLATE 37**, he is depicted in the center of the embroidery with Brahma to his left, Wisnu to his right, Bomo above, and Garuda below. His position in the center symbolizes his preeminence in the world of Hindu gods. The Balinese respect and fear Siwa as the creator and destroyer of life.[4] His appearance can be regal and striking, as in the embroidery shown in **PLATE 35** (see page 20), on which he sits as if on a throne with his name in Balinese script and with the protector Bomo beneath him. Again, this does not represent any particular scene from the ***Mahabharata*** as is the case so often in these embroideries.

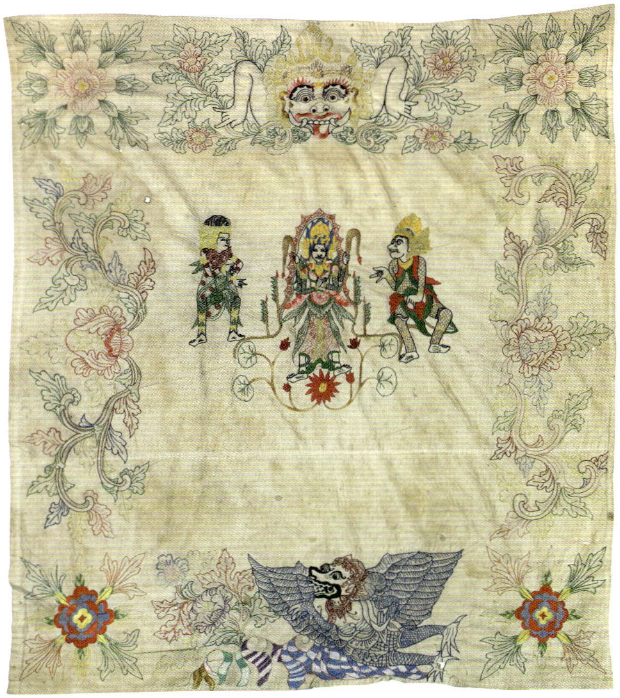

PLATE 37 **Buleleng.** *Tabing*, detail, 109 x 132. The four-armed great god Siwa, attended by a wife and a supporter. Above him is the face of Bomo, his protector, and below him is the powerful mythical bird, Garuda.

PLATE 38 shows a ***lamak*** or vertical offering cloth on which Batara Guru or Siwa is portrayed with his conventional four arms, one holding a discus (his weapon) and another a trident (his unifying symbol). On the same cloth is Sangjang Surya (the Sun God), Sangjang Ulan (the Moon Goddess). The full, rather than partial, depiction of Siwa perhaps

Chapter 3

Send In the Clowns

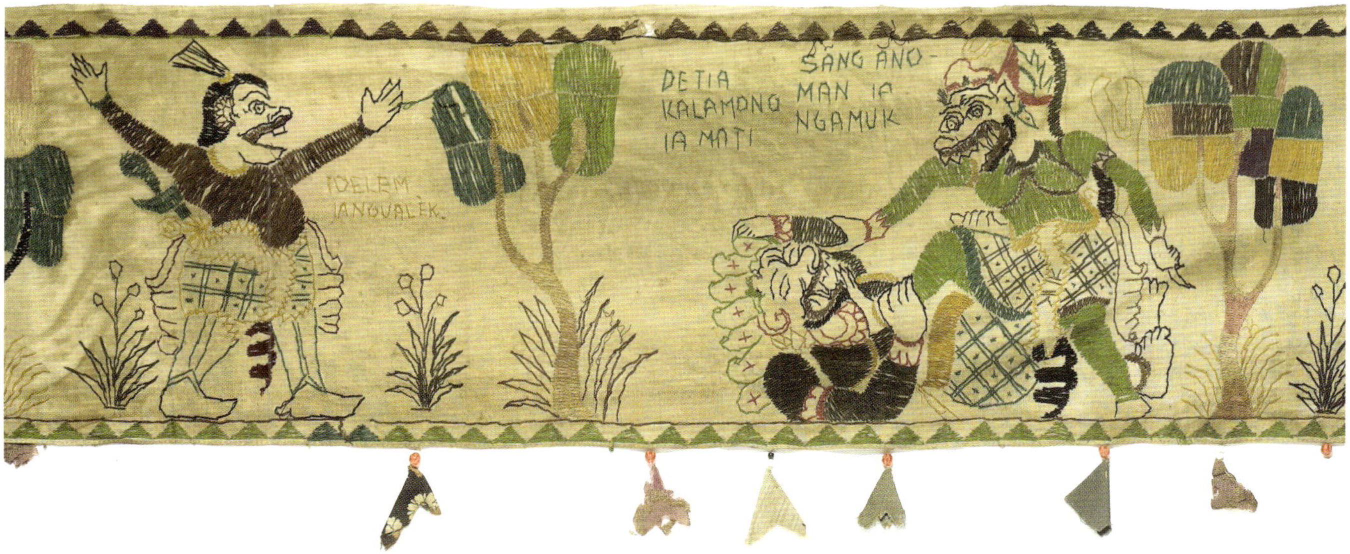

The original ***Mahabharata*** and ***Ramayana*** epics are full of adventures, romances, and battles, but there is not much humor to offset all the plots, intrigues, and frightening supernatural events. There is little or no relief from all the beheading, animal sacrifices, violent contests, and bloody battles. How it came about is unclear, but Bali and Java added four clown characters to both of these Indian epics. In Bali they are called ***panasars***. They appear in scenes throughout the ***Mahabharata*** and ***Ramayana*** as played, painted, and embroidered in Bali, although they may have little to do with the real outcome of any of the episodes. They may be seen in many embroideries gesturing, pointing, biting, wrestling, fighting, and just generally horsing around. They are always naked from the waist up and usually barefoot; they never wear a hat, but wear their hair in a knot. Each of the four ***panasars*** has his own well-known name[1] and his own distinctive appearance and behavior.

Twalen, the oldest, is purported to be the smartest; he is somewhat bumbling and fat, with a distinctive hair knot, and is often full of hubris.[2] He is usually depicted with his brother Merdah, who is shorter, with a curled hairpiece, and very outspoken; he loves to ask generally unanswerable questions and is a perfect foil for his older brother. The other two ***panasars*** are considered less intelligent than their two brothers. The diminutive Delem (sometimes spelled Melem) has a knobbed-shape hair knot, carries a kris tucked into his waistband, and is often shown scolding his brother Sangut, with whom he is usually paired. Sangut seems to be the stupidest of the four ***panasars***, with a thin upper body, a fat belly, and a ponytail topknot; he carries a ***keris*** and is often depicted gesturing frantically for some unknown reason.

PLATE 58 **Negara.** *Ider-ider*, detail, 28 x 183. *Ramayana.* The clown Sangut rejoices after Hanuman kills an enemy.

The ***panasars*** of the Balinese narrative tradition serve at least four important dramatic functions:

1. They provide simple entertainment for all ages.
2. They can engage in impolite, insulting, and salacious speech and behavior—part of their attraction for many Balinese, whose traditions prohibit such things in daily life.
3. They act as messengers and mediators among the many characters and provide a gossipy link to the unfolding episodes.
4. Their highly animated behaviors provide comic relief, an entertaining counterbalance to all the constant intrigues and struggles.

Almost half of the two hundred Balinese embroideries that I have seen depict one or more ***panasars***. On some long ***ider-ider*** cloths, they may appear many times doing different things in cartoon-like sequences. They may have aimless or trivial conversations with each other, particularly when one ***panasar*** gets bored and wants to proclaim his importance. There is, however, some ambiguity in the way they are regarded by the Balinese. On the one hand, their behavior may not be taken seriously; on the other, they may be linked to wise men and the gods. They appear in one embroidery or another among all of the principal characters of the ***Mahabharata*** (for example, Arjuna, Bima, and Kresna) and the ***Ramayana*** (for example, Rama, Sita, Hanuman, and Rawana). The presence of Twalen and Merdah is significant in the embroidery in **PLATE 40** (see page 24), as they are associated with the national logo of Indonesia. The ***panasars*** can say what they want and do what they want, while most of the other characters must conform to the traditional rules governing their status,

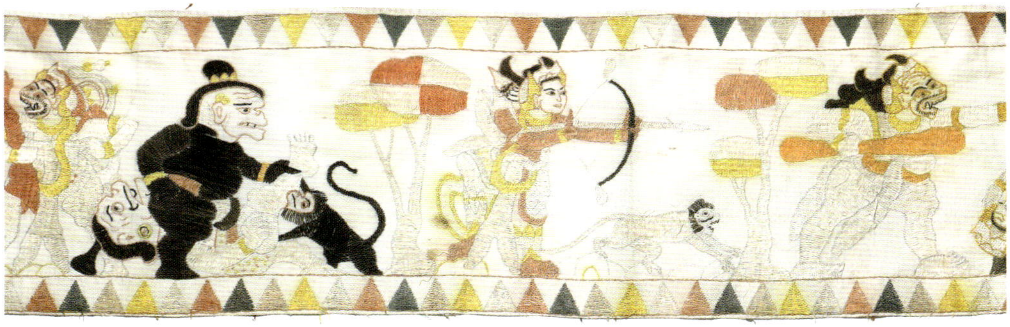

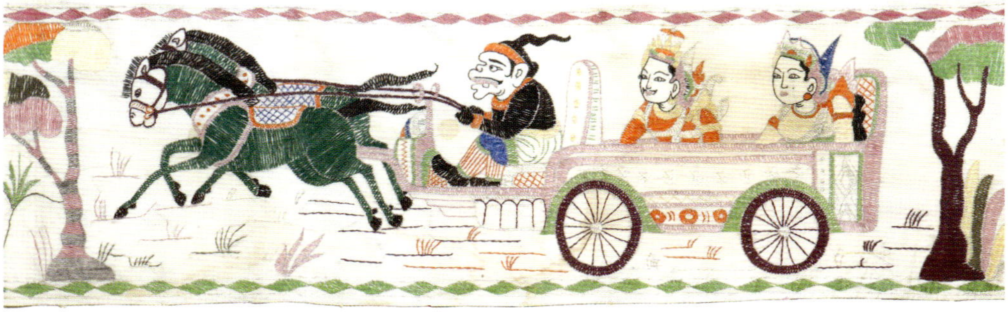

top: **PLATE 59** *Ider-ider*, detail, 26 x 120. *Ramayana* battle scene in which Twalen sits on Merdah, who is attacked by a monkey. The clowns are at it again.

bottom: **PLATE 60** **Negara.** *Ider-ider*, detail, 26 x 183. A made-up scene in which the clown Twalen is driving a carraige with Rama and Sita, something which is not in the written or performed *Ramayana.*

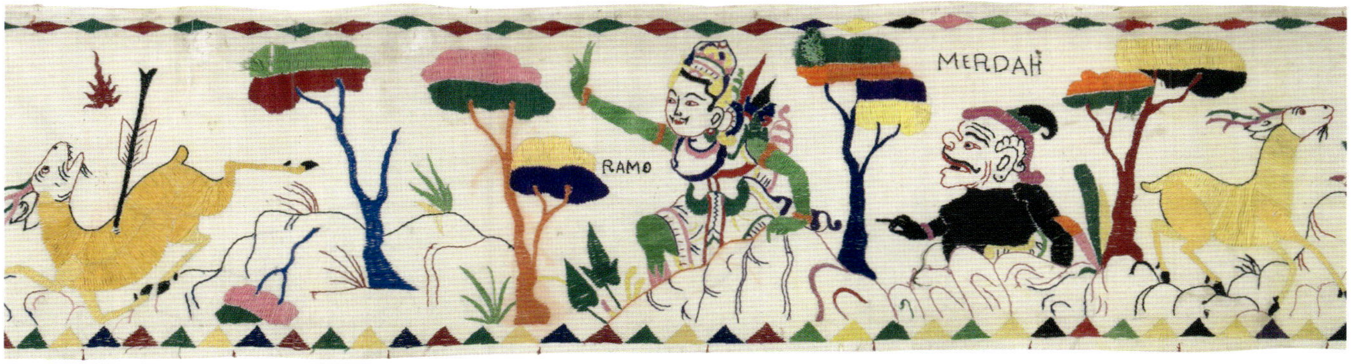

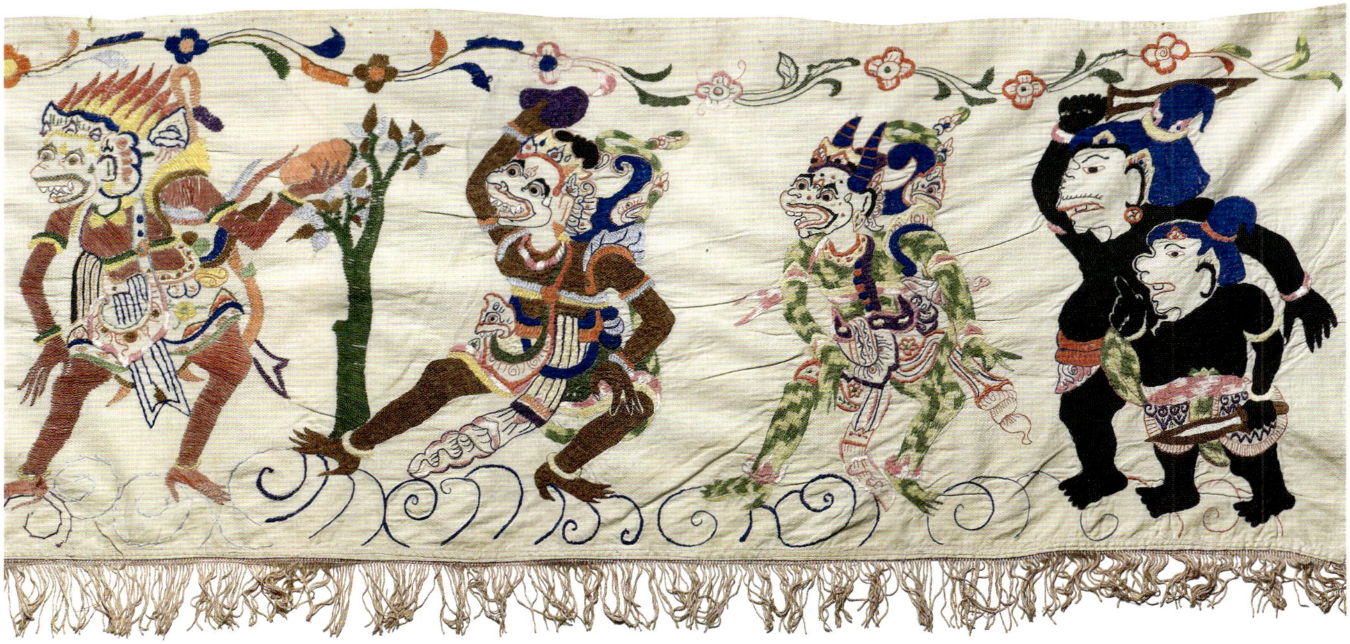

top: PLATE 61 **Negara.** *Ider-ider*, detail, 26 x 355. The clown Merdah witnesses Rama's killing of the ogre, Marica, who is disguised as a golden deer in order to lure Rama away from Sita resulting in her kidnapping by Rawana.

bottom: PLATE 62 **Buleleng.** *Ider-ider*, detail, 32 x 200. Silk threads. *Ramayana.* A battle scene showing two clowns in black, Twalen (with raised sword) and Merdah, along with three monkey officers in Rama's army, from right to left: Predjangga, Anggada, and Anila.

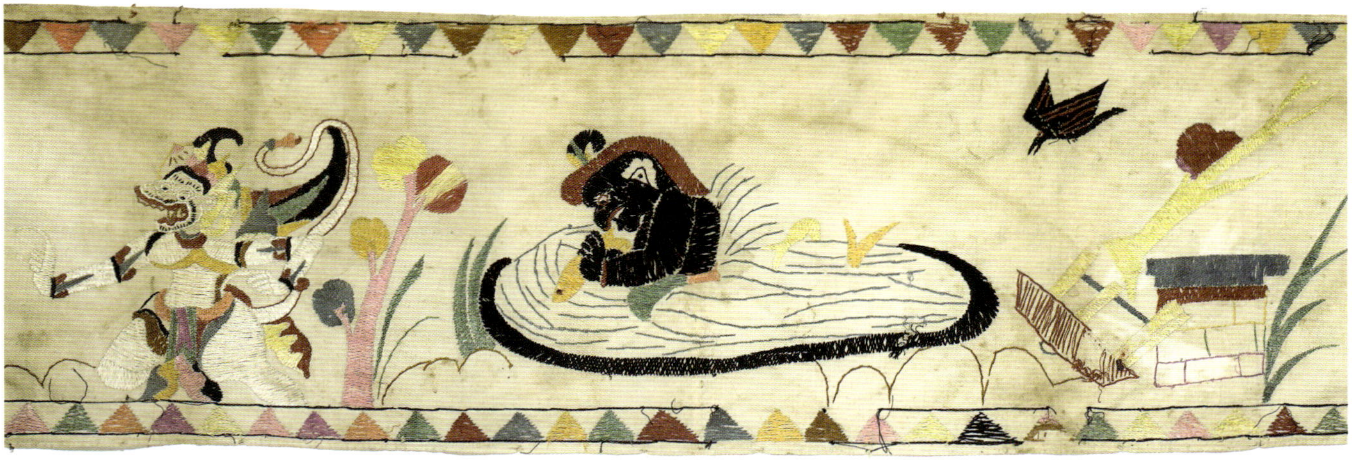

PLATE 63 Negara. *Ider-ider*, detail, 27 x 328. In the midst of a *Ramayana* scene with Hanuman, the White Monkey, engaged in battle, the clown Twalen sits in a pool biting a fish.

roles, age, and gender. Their behavior, as both dramatic actors and single entertainers, gives them a freedom not available to their audiences or to other actors. Of course, this is part of their attraction and popularity among the Balinese. Anyone can empathize, fantasize, and hear their own aspirations through the actions and words of their beloved clowns and still be entertained.

When I attended a drama performance in Ubud, Bali, some years ago, I noted that the ***panasars*** asked many questions, argued about all sorts of matters, and paid an excessive amount of attention to themselves. I recall my Balinese friend who accompanied me saying, "Yes, it is true, but we still enjoy them and even learn from them." It occurs to me now that too much analysis may impede the simple enjoyment of these captivating clowns, their roles, and their clowning. I particularly enjoy the depictions of ***panasars*** in the following Balinese embroideries.

PLATE 62 (page 39) is a finely embroidered ***ider-ider*** showing two clowns: Twalen and Merdah in black. This made-up battle scene is crammed with an assortment of ***Ramayana*** characters. All of the clowns have weapons but, as is usually the case, they rarely hurt anybody or get hurt themselves. The depiction in **PLATE 59** (see page 38) is typical of their buffoonery and, I am sure, this cloth was intentionally embroidered as such. Twalen is sitting on Merdah, apparently holding up his foot so that it can be bitten by a monkey. **PLATE 57** (see page 36) is a kind of funny snapshot of Twalen and Merdah wrestling for no apparent reason—or are they embracing? **PLATE 61** (page 39) merely shows Merdah observing the killing of the golden deer by Rama. Is he a witness or just a decoration? I don't know. In **PLATE 60** (see page 38), Twalen is driving a carriage with what appears to be Rama and Sita as passengers. Could this be an imitation of the famous ***Mahabharata*** scene in which Kresna is driving a chariot to take Arjuna to a battle? Again, I don't know.

Humor is evident in many of these embroideries. In **PLATE 65**, Twalen sits nonchalantly under a parasol while his companion Merdah is being menaced by a tiger. In **PLATE 63**, Twalen placidly sits in a pool eating a live fish while Hanuman looks on. Finally, in **PLATE 64**, Twalen lies on the ground with a rock in his mouth and at the same time seems to try to uproot two trees. Is Twalen trying to imitate Hanuman? Who knows? Two other clowns— Sangut, with his mouth open, and Merdah, wielding a club—are not telling us anything. I have included many depictions of the four clowns apparently doing nothing—or a variety of puzzling and/or ludicrous things. Think of what these serious tales, the ***Mahabharata*** and the ***Ramayana***, would be without them. The Balinese and the Javanese have provided us with marvelous comic additions to these great epics.

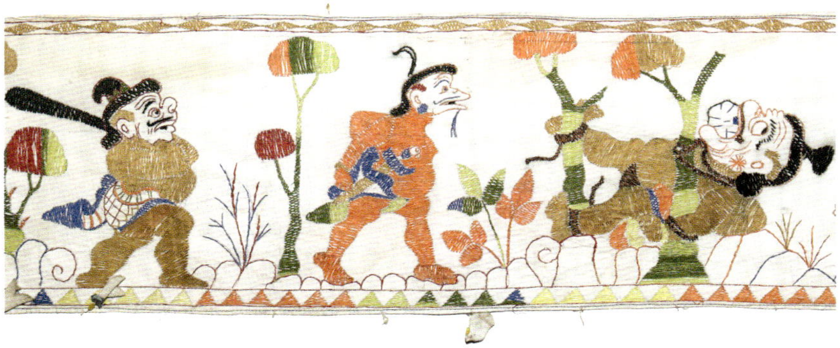

left: PLATE 64 **Negara.** *Ider-ider*, detail, 20 x 330. Part of another *Ramayana* cloth showing the clown Twalen (with a rock in his mouth trying to uproot two trees) while the clowns Sangut and Merdah (carrying a club), look on.

below: PLATE 65 **Negara.** *Ider-ider*, detail, 36 x 360. The clown Twalen (in black) nonchalantly sits under a parasol while his fellow clown Merdah is attacked by a tiger. The rest of the cloth depicts other *Ramayana* characters.

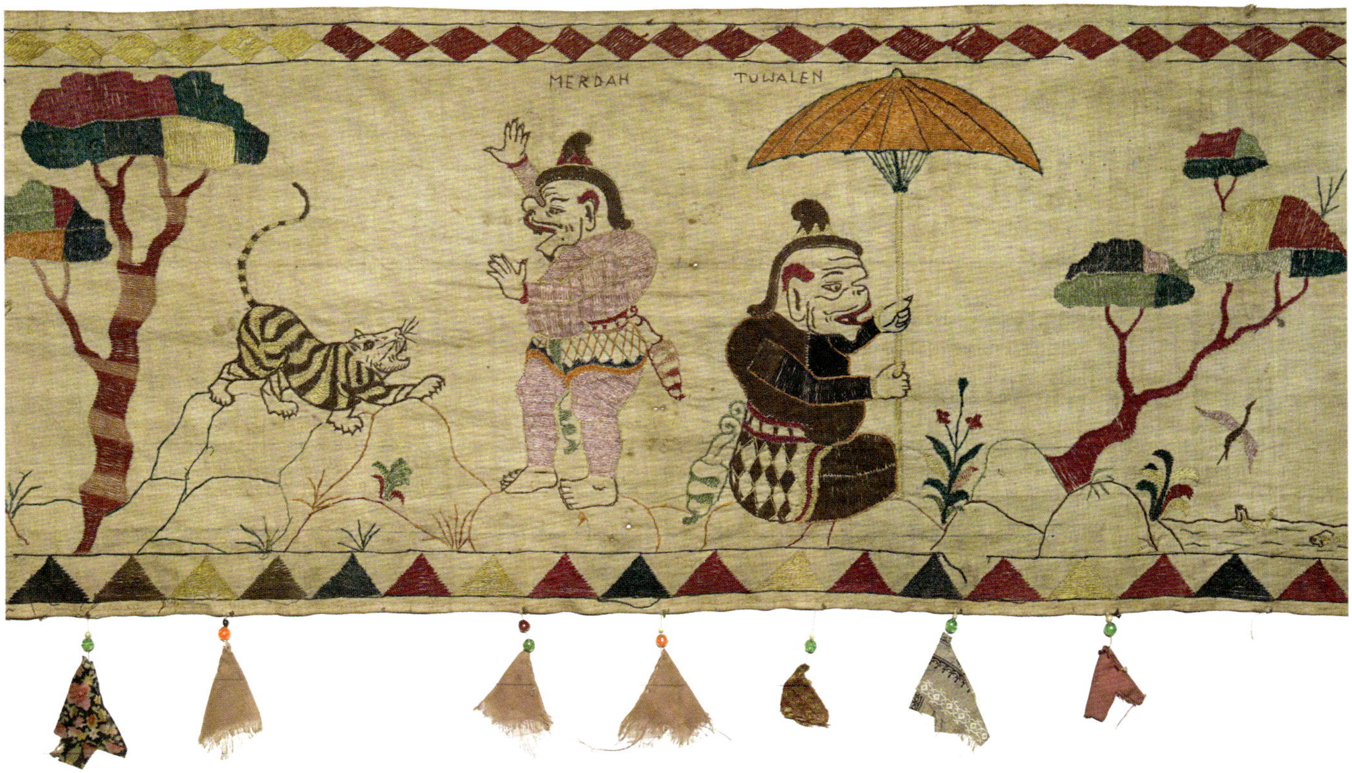

FOOTNOTES

1. In Java the clowns are called ***panakawans*** and there are six: Semar, Petruk, Gareng, Bagong, Togog, and Çepot. There are many other humorous characters, particulary in the ***Mahabharata*** such as gossips, buffoons, servants, and various strange-looking figures. However, none of them compare in popularity or importance as the added Balinese ***panasars*** and their Javanese counterparts.
2. For a contemporary painting of Twalen with an insignia of power, see Klaus D. Höhn, ***The Art of Bali: Reflections of Faith; The History of Painting in Batuan, 1834-1994,*** 169.

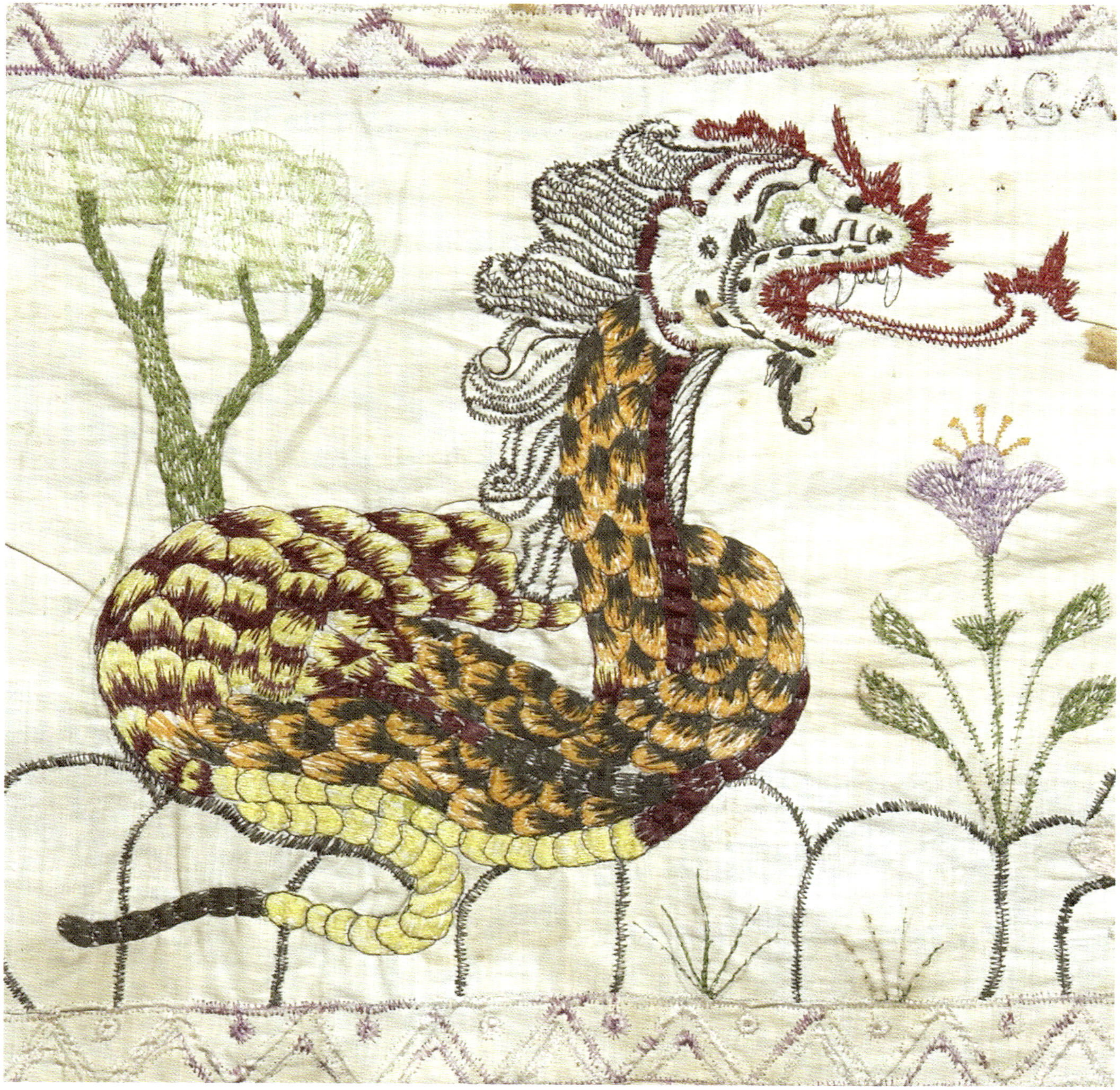

PLATE 66 **Negara.** *Ider-ider*, detail, 26 x 252. An elaborately stitched *naga*.

CHAPTER 4

Animals: Mythical and Real

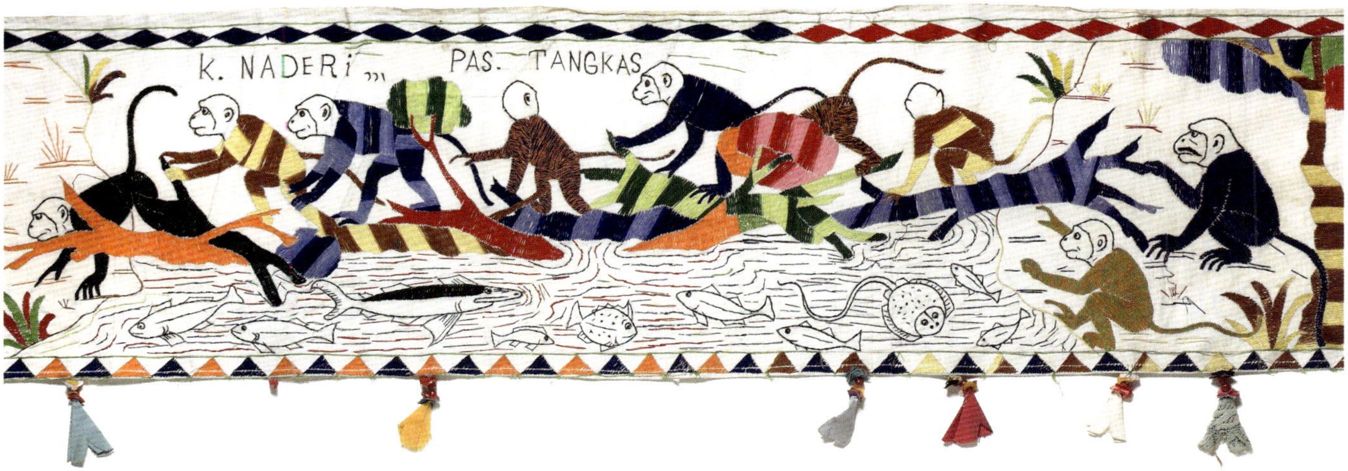

Many years ago, on a dark night in Bali, my wife and I were riding in a taxi when the driver suddenly stopped the car in the middle of the road. He had run over a black cat. He got out of his taxi to look, then quickly returned to his seat and drove on. I assumed he had thrown the dead cat off the road into some bushes. It was pitch black in the taxi and there were no road lights. I noticed nothing unusual until we arrived at our hotel. As the hotel's outdoor lighting illuminated the cab's interior, I saw that there, on the seat between the driver and me, was the dead black cat.

I asked the driver what he was going to do with it. He said, "I killed the cat, and as a Balinese Hindu I must take it home and provide a proper burial."

... all animals may be... the source of a myth that we share with Hindus and Buddhists, the myth of a magic time or place that erases the boundary between man and animals; the ancient time when humans spoke the language of animals; the magic place in the... forest where things have no name.... The time of this animals' paradise... is about a time when gods walked among men... and the individual who possesses the power of animal speech may be likened to... a shaman or a priest.... Who alone is able to traffic with the gods.[1]

There is a veritable zoological world in the ***Mahabharata***, the ***Ramayana***, and other tales to be found in these Balinese embroideries. Mythical animals such as ***nagas*** (dragons) mingle with real ones such as monkeys. Birds, insects,

PLATE 67 **Negara.** *Ider-ider*, detail, 26 x 420. A group of monkeys walk across a fallen tree over water with various fish swimming below.

and sea creatures are scattered throughout the cloths, mostly as decorations or to enhance scenes. Some are symbols, such as an ogre disguised as a golden deer; others are there as additions to battle scenes, such as fighting monkeys. Some may merely reflect a favorite choice of the embroiderers, such as a cat, dog, or elephant. Many animals are often depicted in humorous and colorful poses (see the two monkeys in PLATE 12, page 5). I have counted thirty different real animals in the cloths in my collection and another twelve that are mythical. It is a rich zoo on embroidered cloths, placing nature directly in the scheme of things in these epics and tales.

The mythical animal figures have the most significance because they play real roles in the stories and have symbolic meaning as well. Perhaps the foremost of these is the great mythical bird Garuda. In one episode in the *Mahabharata*, the father of gods, Brihaspati, learns that Garuda is going to steal the *amerta* (the Milk of Immortality). The *amerta* is kept in a dark grotto protected by a hot furnace, a tenacious snake, and a wheel of revolving sharp blades that blocks the entrance. The mighty Garuda sucks in seawater and puts out the fire. He devours the snake, then makes himself so tiny that he can slip through the wheel and steal the *amerta*. He carries it off but, in deference to the gods, he is careful not to drink any of it. As a reward, the god Wisnu makes Garuda his vehicle and they ride around the universe together forever.

PLATE 2 (page x) shows Garuda with Wisnu astride him. It is an image often seen in paintings and as a subject for wood carvings. Many shops and various enterprises are named after Garuda, including Indonesia's national airline. By himself, Garuda is viewed as a symbol of strength and

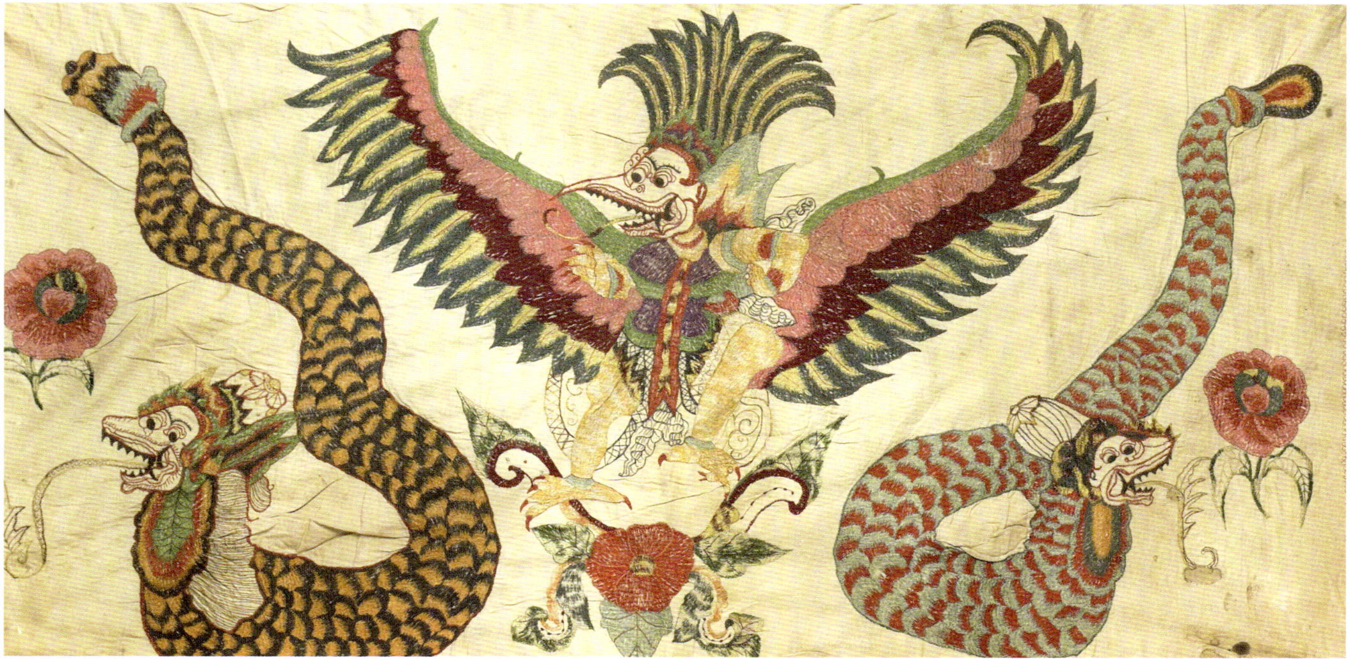

PLATE 68 **Buleleng.** *Tabing*, detail, 86 x 150 Silk threads. A splendid depiction of Jatayu, the protector of Sita, bordered by two *nagas*.

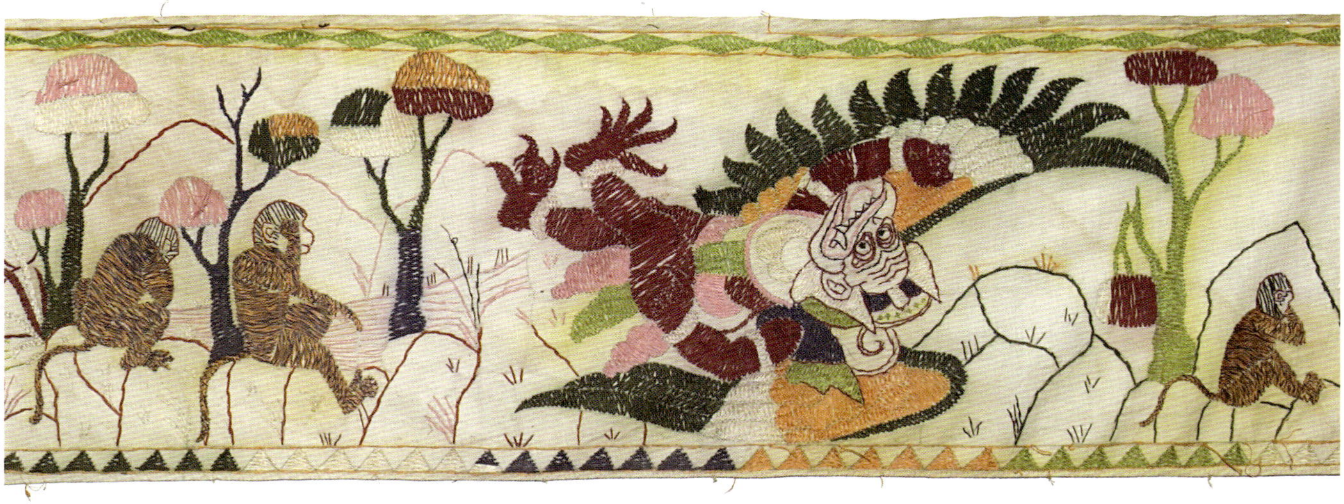

PLATE 69 Negara. *Ider-ider*, detail, 22 x 280. *Ramayana.* Jatayu, the defender of Sita, lies dying while three monkeys cover their ears so they cannot hear his groans.

national identity, as shown in **PLATE 70**, in which he is at the center of the logo of the Republic of Indonesia.

Another great mythical bird is Jatayu, one of the heroes of the ***Ramayana***. Jatayu's loyalty and heroic death have made him legendary in the popular mythos that surrounds the ***Ramayana*** in Bali and throughout South and Southeast Asia. He is the faithful and constant protector of Sita, as shown in **PLATE 109** (page 75) and in **PLATE 111** (page 77), which shows Jatayu battling Rawana, who already has Sita in his grasp. Jatayu is slain and is shown dying on the ground in **PLATE 69**; three monkeys hold their hands over their ears so as not to hear his groans. **PLATE 68** (opposite) is a splendid embroidered example of Jatayu in his almost majestic splendor, surrounded by two colorful ***nagas***. Contrast this with the delicate rendition of Jatayu (**PLATE 20**, page 10)—which appears on a ***langse*** or curtain—and lastly, in **PLATE 71** (page 47), an imposing depiction of Jatayu, finely stitched with muted color threads and decorated with large lotus motifs.

The mythical ***naga*** or dragon is a semi-divine animal portrayed in many embroideries. On his head he wears a royal crown, and he always has a long, protruding, flaming tongue. The ***nagas*** are a race apart that come from the regions below, where they reign supreme. They are the descendants of Kashyapa, a prolific sage who had thirteen wives, and Kadru, whose family was an enemy of Garuda.[2] The ***nagas*** are renowned for their wisdom and their magical powers. They have come to signify protection and authority in the Balinese narrative tradition. With their enormous tails, the ***nagas*** helped dislodge and move a mountain in a churning ocean so that it could find a resting place and start the land mass known as the earth. In these embroideries they are ordinarily depicted in pairs, with striking symmetry. ***Nagas*** often have their own names (which are embroidered on the cloths) and, because of their human attributes, they also have their own wives. **PLATE 72** (page 47) shows the two most important of these ***nagas***, Basuki and Taksaka, with their wives. In the center is a mythical bird, Paksi Winate, who may be Jatayu. (See also the finely depicted ***naga*** in **PLATE 74**, page 48.)

On a long ***lamak*** cloth (**PLATE 49**, page 31, Tahsaka (Taksaka) is associated with Batari Serisutji or Dewi Sri, the Rice Goddess. Two spectacular ***nagas*** are shown in **PLATE 29** (page 15); they serve as scene dividers on this very large Negara embroidery. There is a colorful and very sinuous red ***naga*** in **PLATE 73** (page 48).

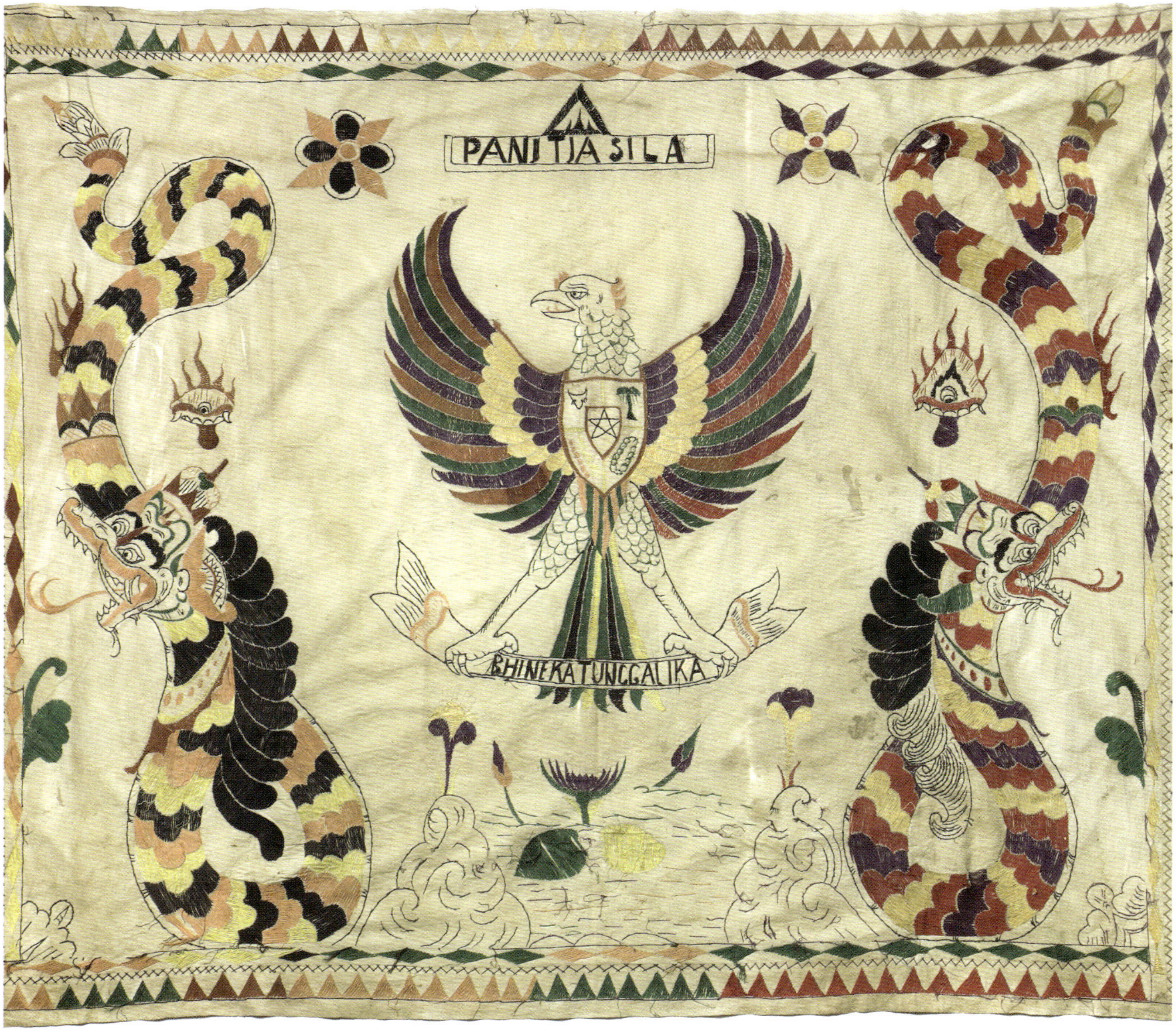

PLATE 70 Negara. *Tabing*, 118 x 113. An excellent example of the use of national symbols and a political motto on a cloth. Shown is the Indonesian national logo consisting of the mythical eagle Garuda. On its chest is a shield containing five symbols: the head of a *banteng* (buffalo), a *beringin* (banyan tree), *padi* (rice plants), a *bintang* (star), and a *rantai* (unbroken linked chain). All of these items symbolize the nation of Indonesia. Its national ideology is called *Panjtja Sila* (Pançila), which embodies five principles: faith in one god, nationalism, humanism, democracy, and social justice. *Bhineka (Bhinneka) Tunggal Ika* means "Unity in Diversity" and is a recognition of the more than one hundred different ethnic groups that live within the country.

On ***umbul-umbul*** or pennants, only a single ***naga*** motif is used. These pennants are hung from very tall bamboo poles to mark and decorate village and temple ceremonies. Some of the best examples of these in design and stitching technique are shown in **PLATE 23** and **PLATE 24** (see page 12).

A great mythical turtle called Bedawang appears in a famous episode in the ***Mahabharata***. This turtle was created by Antaboga, King of the Undersea Snakes. The story is told that the gods and demons had heated up the milky ocean by churning it with their ***naga*** tails to produce the ***amerta***. The ***naga*** Basuki coils his body around a sacred mountain; it comes to rest upon the floating turtle, who carries it to land where the earth can begin. **PLATE 75** (page 49) shows the clown Twalen holding a turtle. It may be just a whim of his, but it also may remind a Balinese viewer of the mythical Bedawang.

A popular Buddhist story that shows the close association of men and animals is that of Prince Sutasoma. It is found in the ***kakawin*** text tradition that came from Java to Bali.[3] However, it is probably derived in part from an earlier collection of Buddhist tales known as the ***Jataka***. These were popular in East Java at the height of the Majapahit kingdom in the mid-fourteenth century and were also to become popular in Bali, as did many other animal tales.

This Buddhist tale of devotion and sacrifice tells of Prince Sutasoma, who is born under auspicious circumstances after his father practiced yoga to enhance his birth. The king's chief Brahman priests had said a son was needed to bring peace to the kingdom. The gods descend to earth to ensure a safe birth and use the occasion to heal all the sick and deformed people. Seven months after his birth, the baby is named Sutasoma. He is handsome, obedient, and much beloved by his father, the king, and his mother, the queen. He matures quickly and possesses many virtues and skills that will prepare him for his future role as a prince and king. He is particularly adept in the performance of religious rituals, guided by the king's chief teacher and sage. In fact, Sutasoma is such a model student that the teacher trains him to be his successor. This was not what the king wants for his son, who is eventually supposed

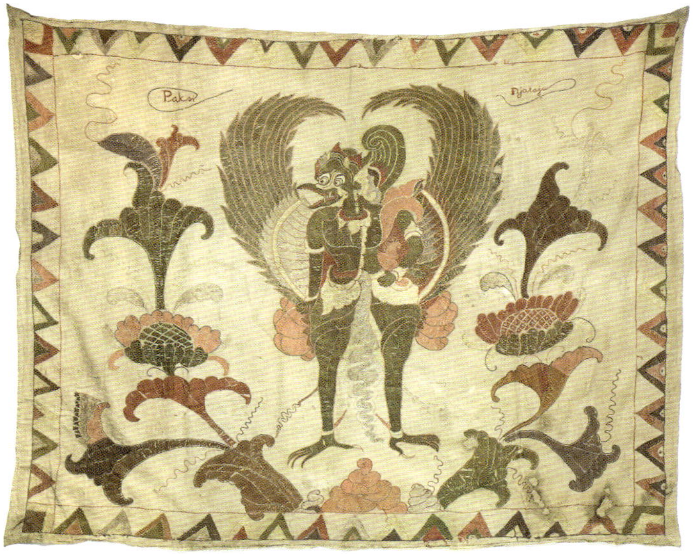

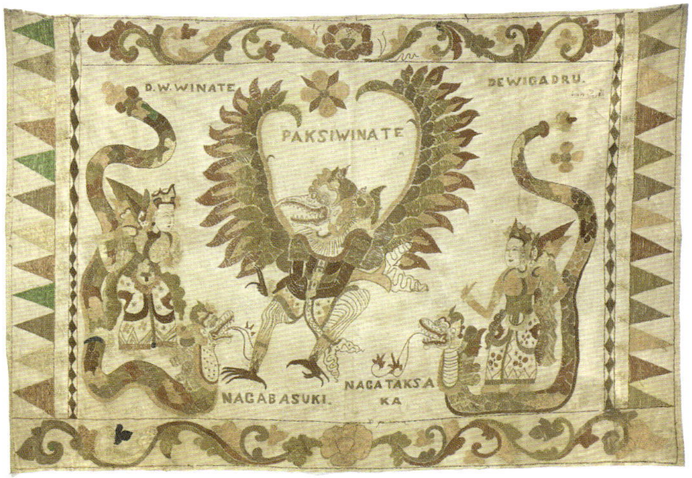

PLATE 71 **Negara.** *Tabing,* 96 x 99. *Paksi* (bird) Djatayu (Jatayu) the heroic protector of Sita in the *Ramayana.*

PLATE 72 **Negara.** *Tabing,* 58 x 130. The most important *nagas* in the *Mahabharata, Naga* Basuki and *Naga* Taksaka, depicted with their wives. Paksi Winate is really Jatayu but probably renamed after the woman who embroidered the cloth, D. W. Winate.

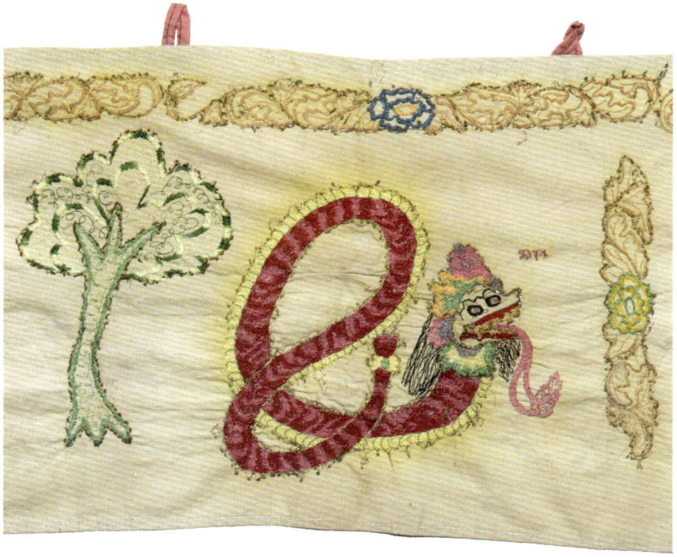

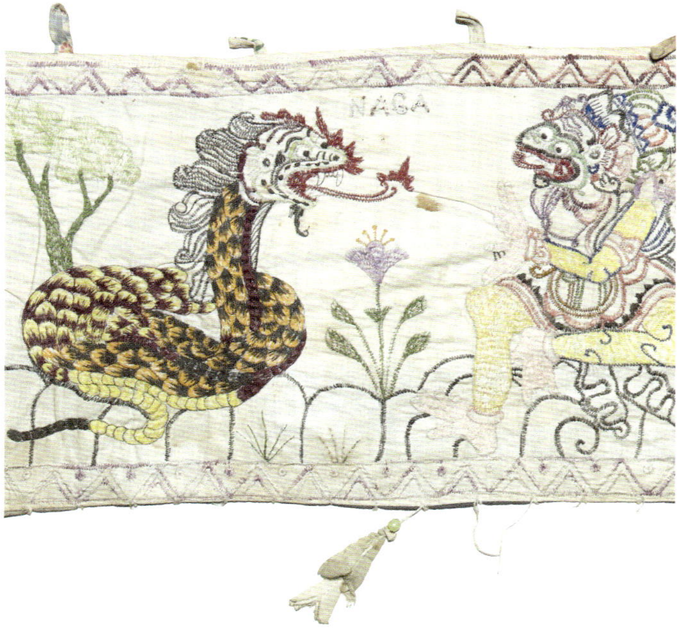

PLATE 73 Buleleng. *Ider-ider*, detail, 22 x 237. Silk threads. A delicately embroidered and colorful *naga*.

PLATE 74 Negara. *Ider-ider*, detail, 26 x 252. A finely stitched *naga*.

to succeed him. Sutasoma is summoned to the court, where the king lectures him on his royal duties and social obligations as a future monarch. He must, states the king, be at one with the Buddha and use his wisdom to lead a moral life and rule the kingdom wisely. Sutasoma, modest and contemplative in manner and thought, is too aware of his own imperfections to undertake the burden of rule. He resolutely decides that he will begin a journey in search of "emptiness" and serenity.

His parents are grieved by their son's decision but they do nothing to prevent his departure. Sutasoma first gives away most of his possessions; then one night he steals away through the palace gates, which mysteriously open by themselves. He journeys as a monk, seeking truth while fully experiencing the bountiful life around him in the forest and on the mountains. He has many adventures, one of which will test his Buddhist principles.

In the forest he meets a desperate tigress who is about to devour her cubs because she is starving and cannot feed them. In PLATE 76 (page 50), a priest and a ***raksasa*** seated on a ***naga*** are looking on. Sutasoma admonishes the tigress for her terrible intention, but he is faced with a dilemma. The tigress is starving, her cubs cannot be fed, and there is no food to be had. Sutasoma quickly offers himself as food for the starving animals.[4] The tigress and the onlookers are amazed by the offer, but she has no alternative—she eats the prince. As Sutasoma's blood flows over the ground, the tigress is filled with guilt. She cries out for other animals or anyone else to kill her, but none will. The tigress is about to kill her cubs and commit suicide when the god Indra intervenes. He descends upon the tragic scene and, through his power of deep meditation, brings Sutasoma back to life.[5] The tigress and her cubs have been given food and everyone rejoices. However, Sutasoma questions Indra's motives in the use of his magical power. It seems that in the pursuit of perfection, someone like Sutasoma cannot be completely satisfied, even with the happiest of outcomes. Indra is not put off; he explains that what he did was to save the tigress from death and "preserve the life of the prince for the good of the world." Sutasoma accepts the explanation and Indra departs. The prince becomes the friend and idol of all

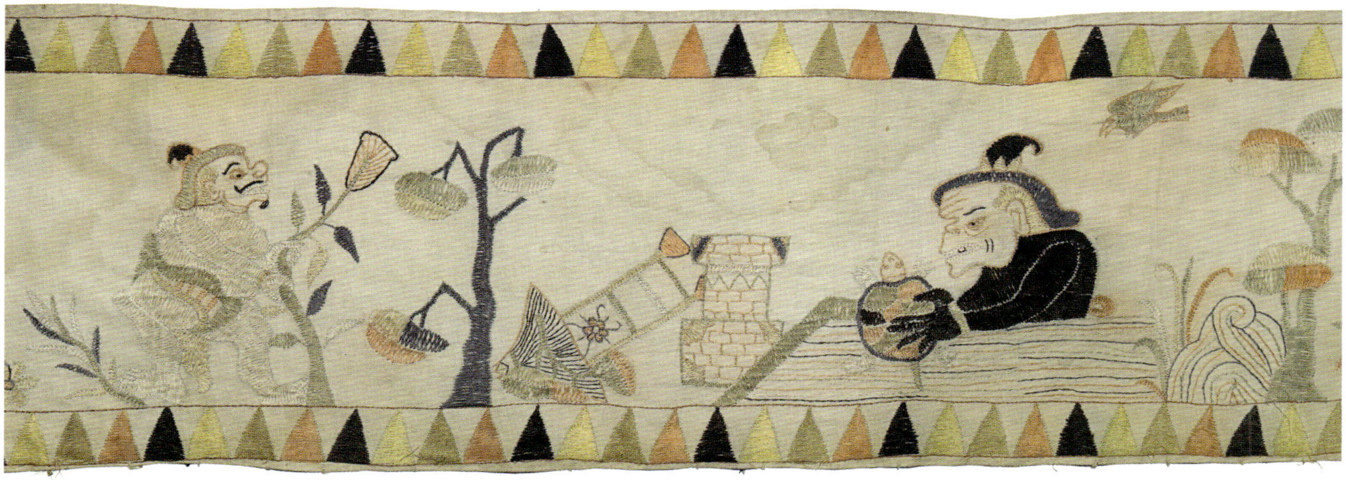

PLATE 75 **Negara.** *Ider-ider*, detail, 25 x 290. The clown Twalen holds a turtle, a *pelangkiran* (altar) has fallen, tree branches break, and the clown Merdah looks on sheepishly. One of many humorous scenes added to the *Ramayana* by the Balinese women who stitched the embroidery.

of the animals forever. It is another traditional tale that illustrates the virtue of personal sacrifice, the value of a moral and spiritual life, and the unalterable connections between humans and animals.

PLATE 77 (page 50) shows Sutasoma's return, upon which he finds his kingdom beset by Durokalo, one of Durga's minions, and Purosado, a demon king also known as Janantaka, the Man-Eater. After many more adventures and battles, the demons are defeated and Sutasoma resumes his life as a Buddhist.

Ordinary animals seem to appear at random throughout the embroideries, simply as decorative expressions of folk art, for example, the multi-colored lion in **PLATE 80** (page 51). One of the women from Negara, who liked tigers, lions, and all cats in general, often put them on her embroidered cloths. **PLATE 79** is a good example depicting a realistic tiger. On the same cloth, two monkeys sit on top of a golden deer and two wild boars are copulating (**PLATE 78,** page 51). There are no lions in Indonesia, although a mythical version of them with wings, called a ***singa***, is common in Balinese woodcarvings and paintings. The golden deer (***kijang mas***) is modeled after the one in the ***Ramayana***. The boars may be a symbolic reenactment of Wisnu in the guise of a boar, ravishing Pertiwi. In some of these assumptions I may be just speculating, but the richness of these narrative stories tempts one to do so.

Monkeys are depicted everywhere in these embroideries, some with natural coats, others with gay stripes. **PLATE 67** (see page 43) is an excellent example of this mix, with eight animated monkeys walking on a tree trunk that has fallen into a pond filled with fish. On some cloths, monkeys appear to be just quietly enjoying life, while other animals race by (**PLATE 83,** page 53); on others they are depicted in struggles and battles (**SEE PLATE 55**, page 34). The embroidery in **PLATE 81** (page 52) contains monkeys, fish, and birds. More importantly, another scene shows four of the five principal mythical monkeys with human attributes that appear in the ***Ramayana***: Anggada, Predjangga, Anila, and Hanuman (**PLATE 81,** page 52). **PLATE 95** (see page 62) shows a gently swimming fish with a prominent blue crab nearby, seemingly just as a charming decoration. In my collection of embroideries, there are also depictions of roosters, rabbits, herons, insects, bulls, reptiles,

PLATE 76 *Tabing*, 83 x 151, Sutasoma tale. Prince Sutasoma and a priest confront a starving tigress and ultimately prevent her from eating her cubs. Looking on is an elephant-like character (perhaps Ganesa) and a snake.

PLATE 77 Negara. *Tabing*, 60 x 120. Sutasoma tale. Shown are Prince Sutosomo (Sutasoma), his enemy Purosado, Durokalo (an ally of Durga), and three clowns, Merdah, Mangut (Sangut), and Twalen.

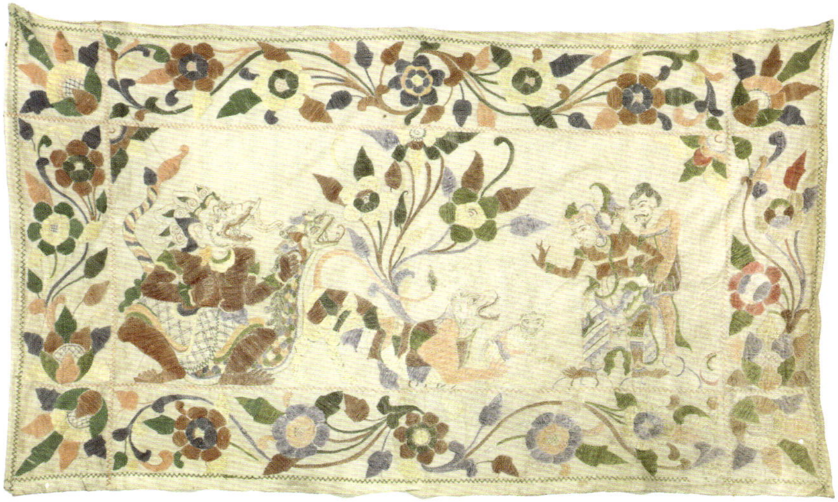

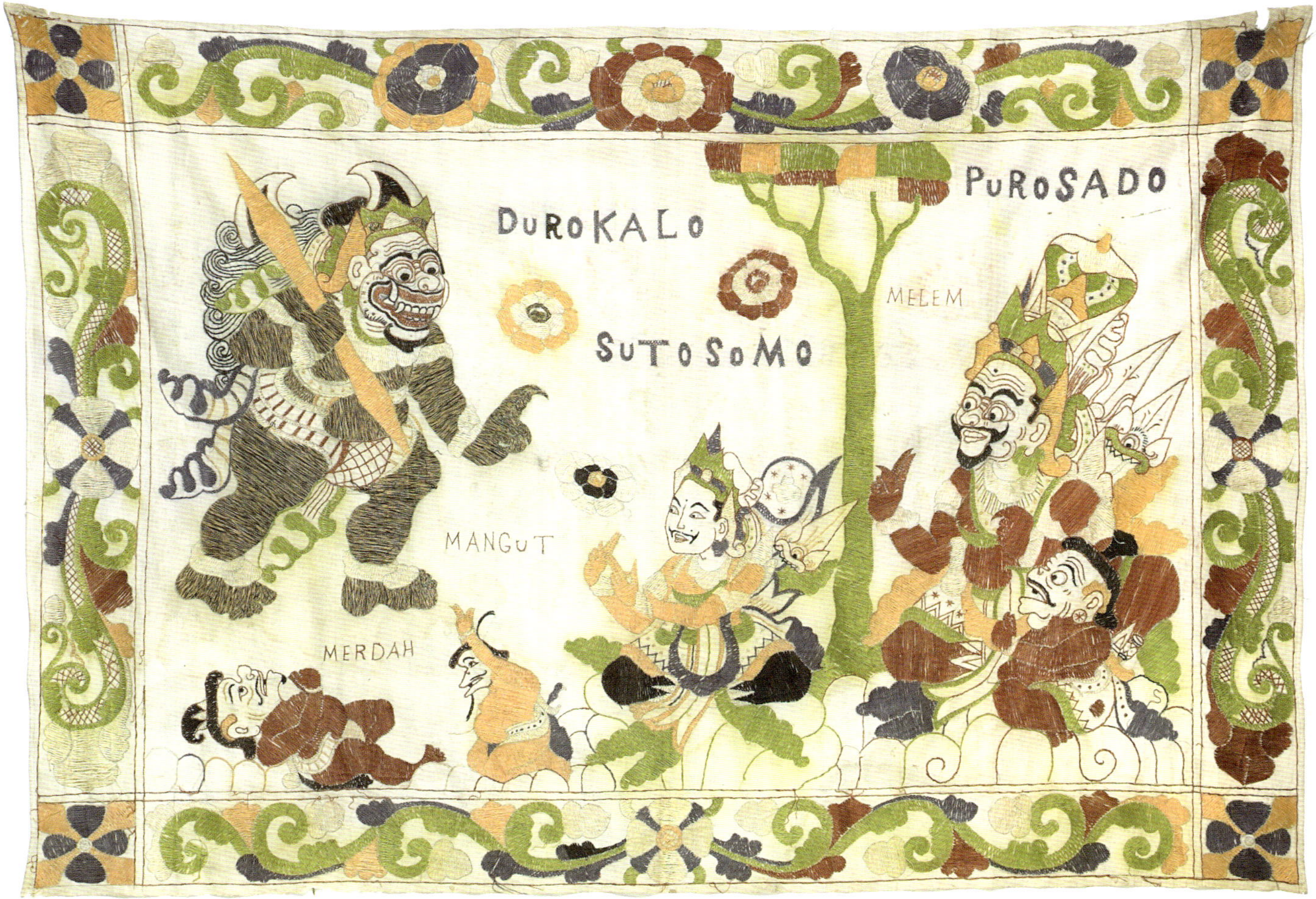

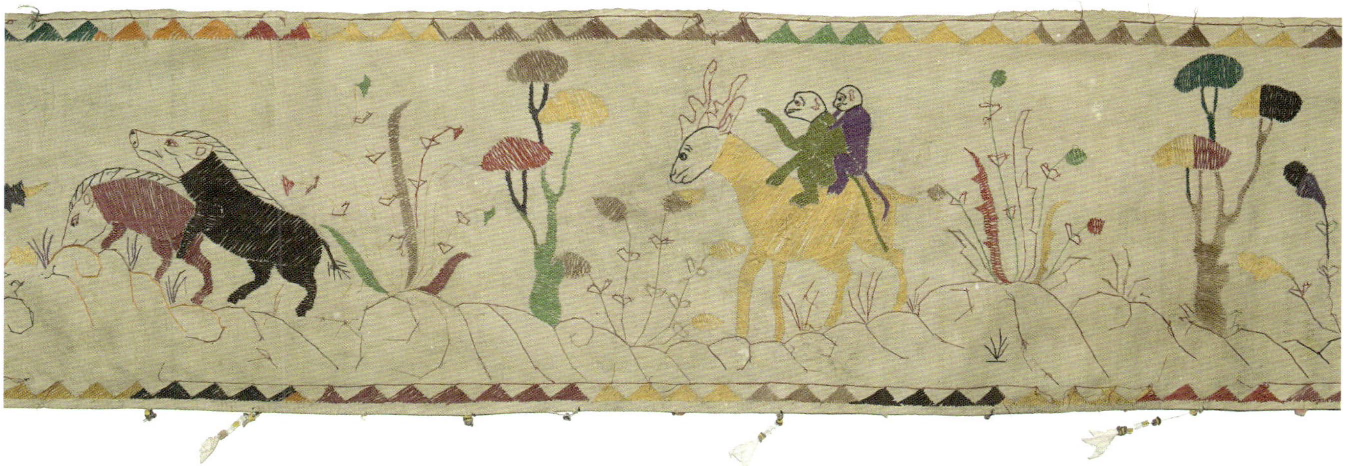

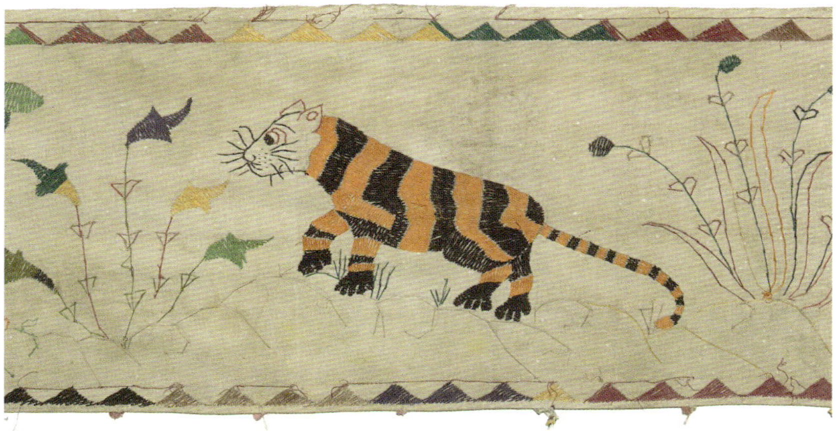

above: PLATE 78 **Negara.** *Ider-ider*, detail, 28 x 158. Two monkeys seated on a golden deer and two wild boars copulating.

left: PLATE 79 **Negara.** *Ider-ider*, detail, 28 x 158. A striped tiger.

below: PLATE 80 **Negara.** *Ider-ider*, detail, 23 x 206. *Ramayana.* A majestic multi-colored lion in the company of the seemingly unfrightened Sita.

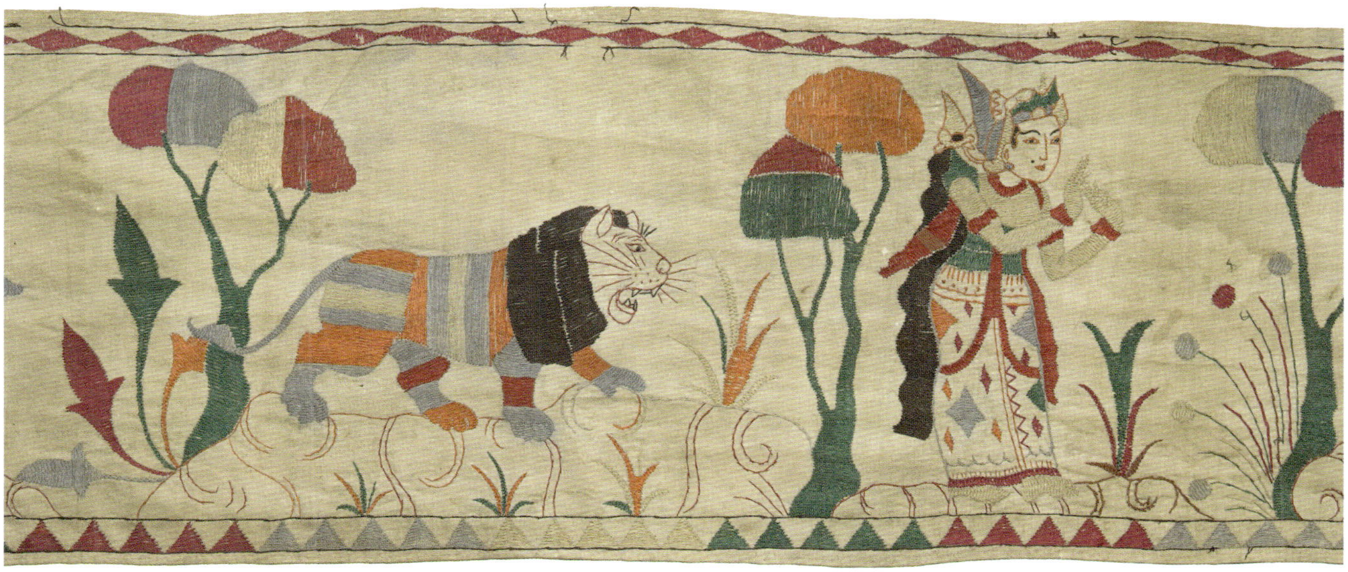

PLATE 81 Negara. *Ider-ider*, detail, 27 x 174. A typical animal scene of monkeys, birds, and fish inserted into the *Ramayana* by the embroiderer but with addition of the floating head of a *raksasa* (demon) and the White Monkey, Hanuman.

PLATE 82 Negara. *Ider-ider*, detail, 27 x 174. Four of the principal monkey/soldiers in the *Ramayana*: Anggada, Predjangga, Anila, and Hanuman.

and water buffalo. Some of the most striking renditions are of snakes, such as shown in PLATE 84. Clearly, both real and mythical animals are common in Balinese artistic and narrative traditions. Animals are, of course, one of the main subjects of folklore throughout the world. In Indonesia, aside from the ***Jataka*** tales, there are numerous animal fables, such as the ***Panchatantra*** and ***Tantri***, which came from India and are known in Bali.

Animals and humans are an intricate part of Balinese traditional culture, particularly in their folklore. Below the entrance to the mother Hindu temple in Besakih is a special stone marker dedicated to dogs. Visit any village or residential compound in Bali and you will find barking, dingo-like dogs. They are usually not regarded as pets, per se, but rather as guardians and as a part of country and urban life. So, it is not surprising to find so many of them in these embroideries.

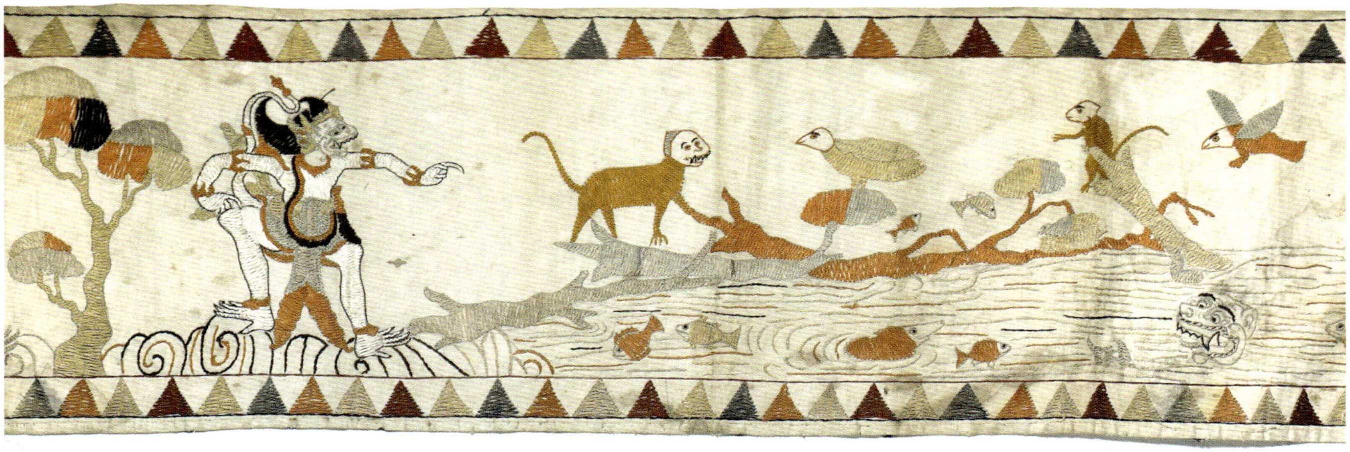

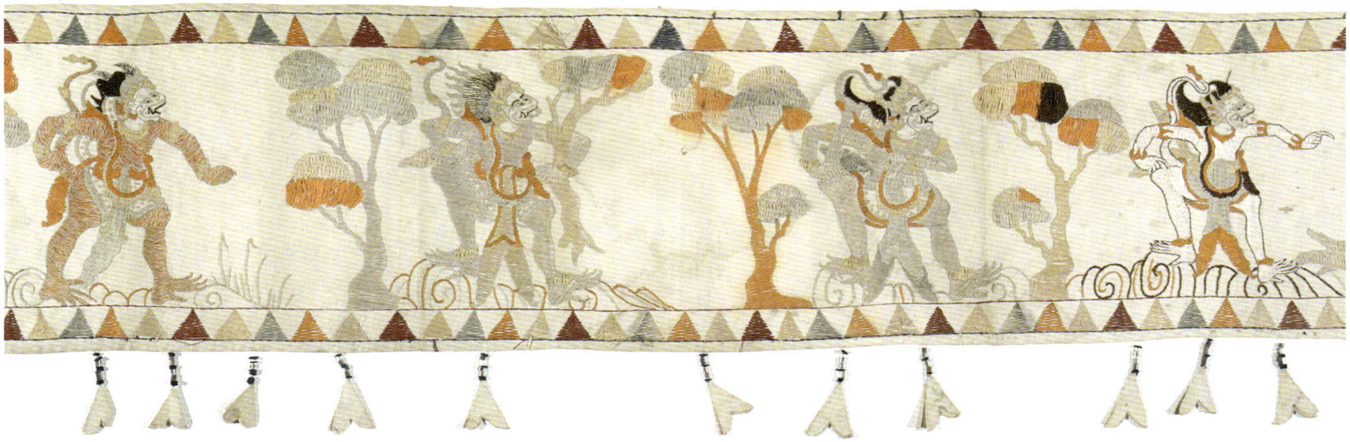

PLATE 83 **Negara.** *Ider-ider*, detail, 22 x 280. *Ramayana.* A wild boar, a deer, a ram, and a mongoose or civet cat run through the forest.

PLATE 84 **Negara.** *Ider-ider*, detail, 22 x 280. *Ramayana.* A grand snake and a bearded, almost human-like monkey.

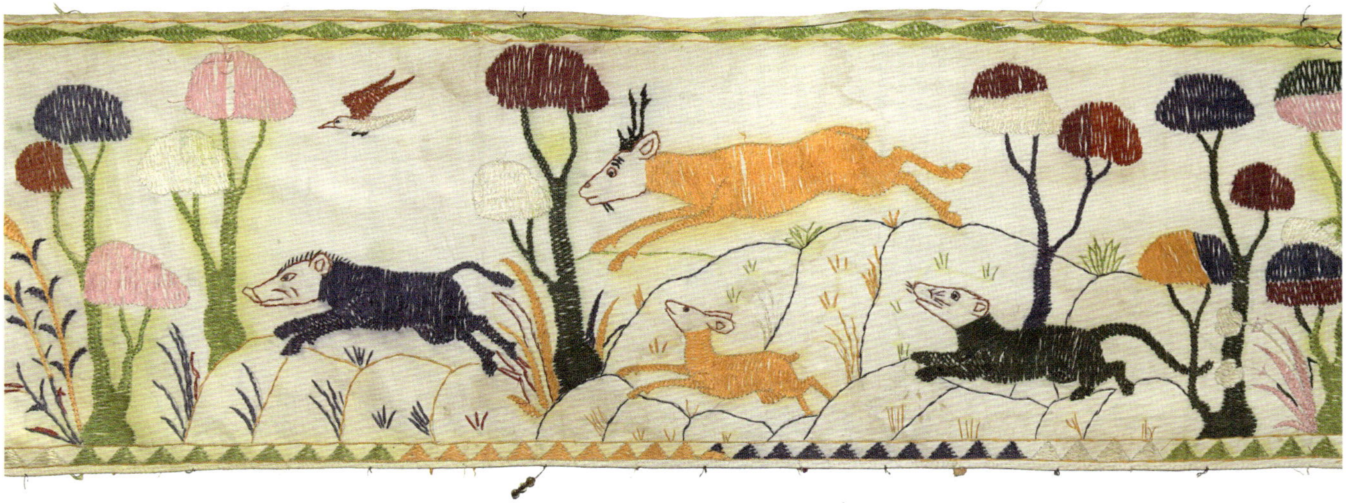

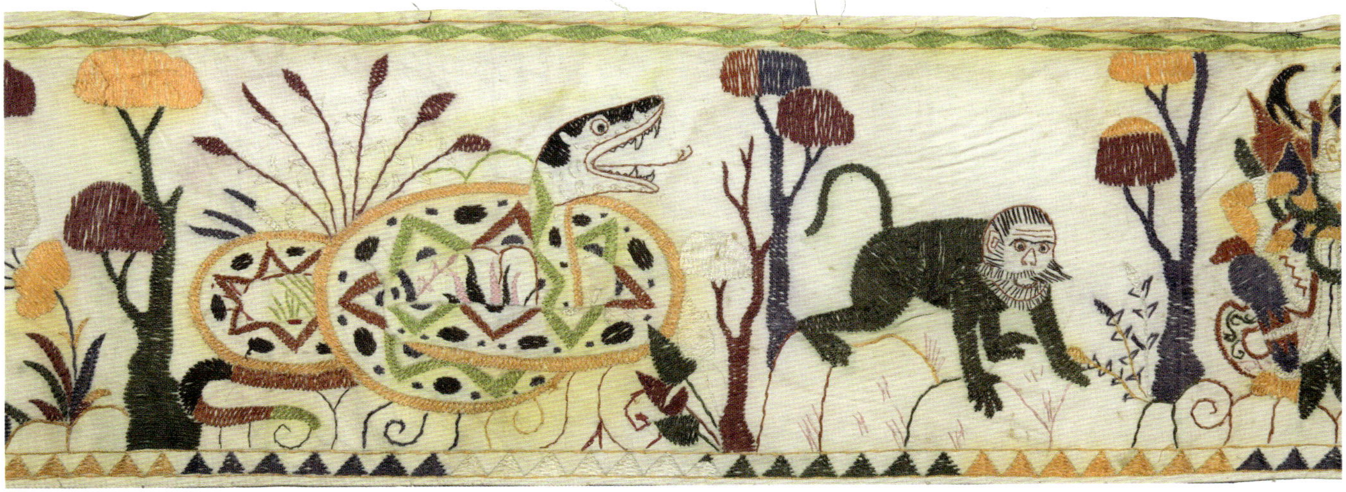

FOOTNOTES

1. Stella Snead, ***Animals in Four Worlds, Sculptures from India***, 5.
2. For a scholarly exposition of the ***naga***, see Vogel, "The *Nagas* in the Great Epic," 47–92, ***Indian Serpent Lore***.
3. My main source for this is P. J. Zoetmulder, ***Kalangwan: A Survey of Old Javanese Literature***, 329–341.
4. For a painting of Sutasoma offering himself to the tigress, see Höhn, ***The Art of Bali***, 183. (Note that the caption mistakenly identifies Sutasoma as a woman.)
5. For paintings of Indra bringing Sutasoma back to life, see ibid., 126 and 132–33. A summary of the entire Sutasoma story, including his many adventures after the tigress incident, is in Zoetmulder, ***Kalangwan: A Survey of Old Javanese Literature***, 329–341.

CHAPTER 5

The Mahabharata

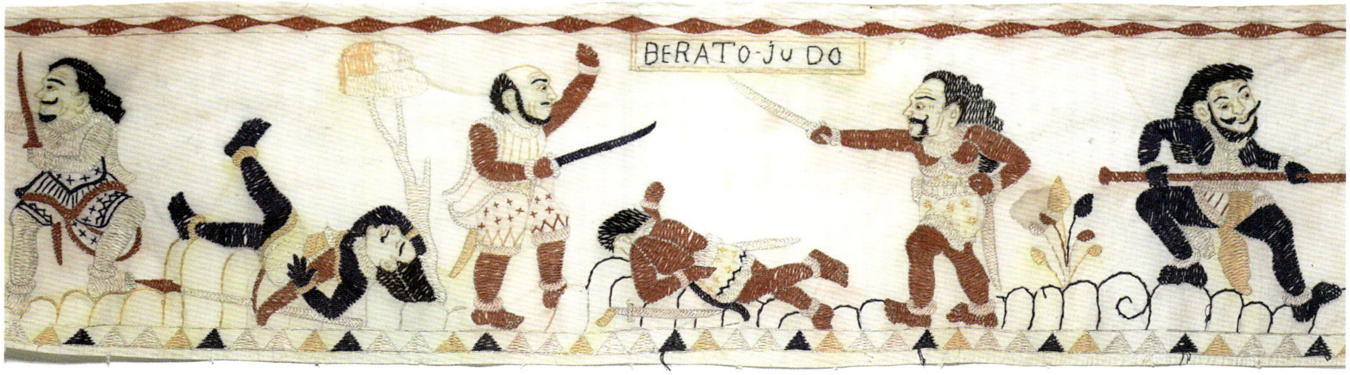

My first experience with the ***Mahabharata*** was in 1956, at a ***wayang kulit***—a nighttime shadow puppet performance in a small village just outside the city of Yogyakarta, Central Java. I was brought to the show by a Javanese professor who had been informally mentoring me about shadow puppets and the stories they encompassed. The host who paid for the performance was celebrating both the pending marriage of his daughter to a young man and the groom's graduation from law school. There were about thirty invited guests in the audience, as well as many more from the village, both adults and children. Tea, coffee, sugared peanuts, and sweetened rice cakes were served.

The performance was outdoors with a modest stage; there was a full moon and a hanging brass coconut oil lamp that shone a flickering light through the puppets, making clearly outlined images on a cloth screen. Behind the screen, the ***dalang*** (puppeteer) sat cross-legged for most of the evening, manipulating the puppets and their silhouettes, speaking all the dialogue, smoking an occasional cigarette, and from time to time drinking a cup of coffee.

The performance lasted from nine o'clock in the evening to six o'clock in the morning; I stayed all night and was kept awake by many, many cups of hot Java tea. The language spoken by the ***dalang*** was Javanese, so my friend had to translate for me. With so much going on that I did not understand, I decided to just concentrate on enjoying the manipulation of the puppets, the shadows that they cast, and the reactions of the people around me. Some were listening intently; others were eating, walking about, or sleeping.

The episode being performed involved Arjuna, hero of the ***Mahabharata***, on one of his long journeys to obtain wisdom, and his encounter with seductive nymphs sent by the gods to test his resolve. He was meditating in preparation for his role as eventual leader of his Pandawa family in

PLATE 85 **Negara.** *Ider-ider*, detail, 27 x 177. The *Berato Judo (Baratayuda)*, the great final battle in the *Mahabharata* between the victorious Pandawa and defeated Korawa families.

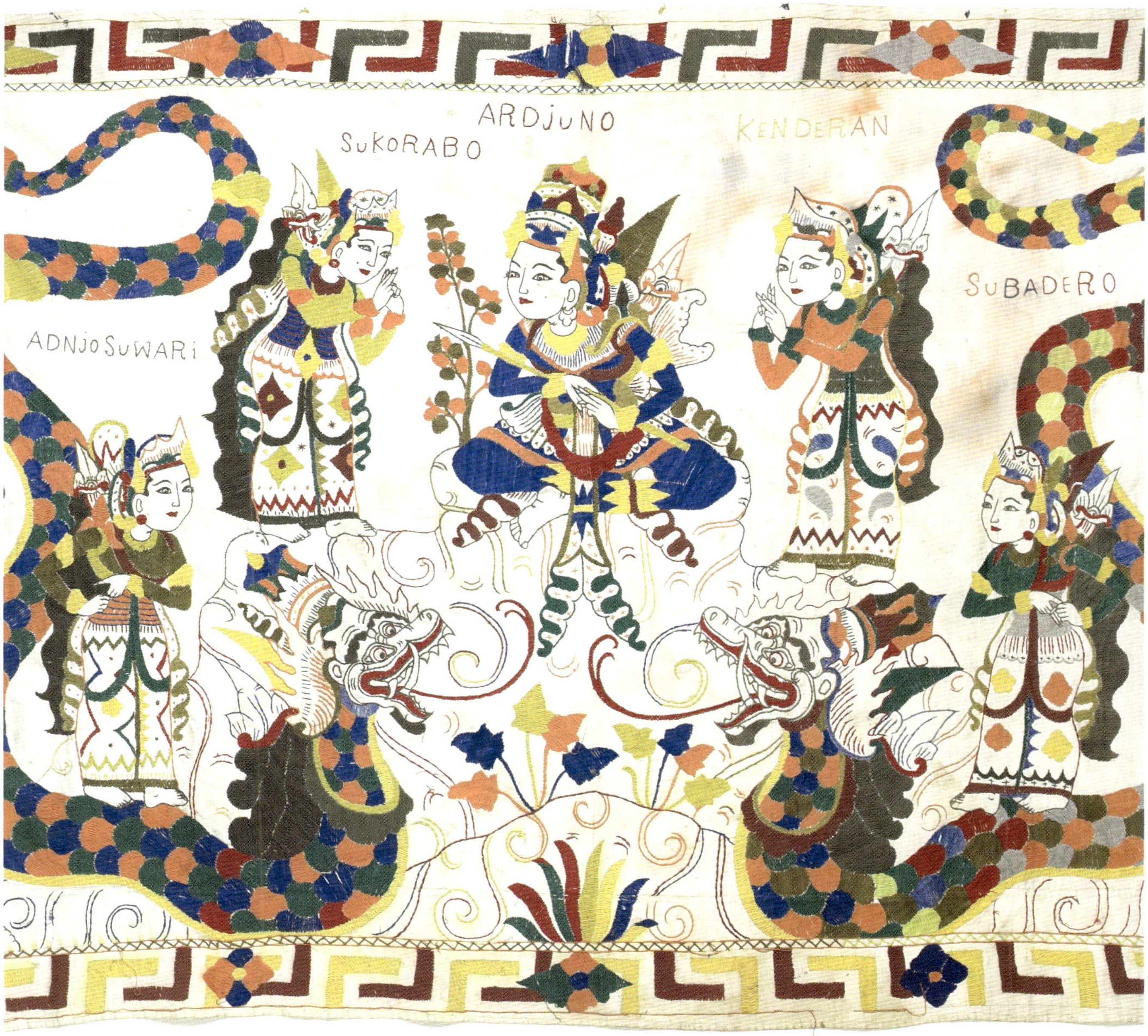

PLATE 86 **Negara.** *Tabing*, detail, 58 x 148. *Mahabharata*. Arjuno (Arjuna) surrounded by four of his wives, Sukorabo (Sukoraba), Kenderan, Subadero (Subadra), and Adnjosuwari, the latter two standing on *nagas*.

their victory over their Korawa enemies. At one point, I moved around to the back of the stage where the ***dalang*** was sitting as he moved puppets across the screen. The puppets appeared to be an extension of the ***dalang***'s arm as he became the voice of every character. It was a magical experience—one that at the time I enjoyed but did not fully comprehend.

Since that first evening, I have been enthralled with shadow puppets and the Indian epics they portray. Over the course of forty years, I have seen innumerable shadow plays and dance/dramas, all of them revealing parts of this great epic tradition, as well as others that are quite different. In Bali in July 2002, I saw a variation new to me: a daytime shadow puppet performance called ***wayang lemah*** that needs no screen and produces no shadows. It is performed only as a part of a traditional ritual and has no audience as such. The ***dalang*** brought forth his puppet characters and stuck their stick supports into the pliant trunk of a banana tree, where they stood upright while the ***dalang*** spoke their words. This ***Mahabharata*** path that I have been traveling for so long eventually led me—not by chance, I am sure—to discover this grand epic and its characters depicted in an unexpected place: on Balinese embroidered cloths in an antique shop.

POPULARITY & DISPERSAL

The ***Mahabharata*** is the longest epic in any language, with over 100,000 couplets, divided into eighteen sections and a supplement.[1] It originated in India in the eighth and ninth centuries B.C.; its reputed author is the sage Vyasa, and later additions were made by many diverse hands.[2] He intended it to be not just a heroic epic but rather a grand treatise on all life and the universe. The ***Mahabharata*** contains the ***Bhagavadgita***,[3] which is an essential text for practicing Hindus. Originally, as poetry, it was to be recited over the course of many days and nights. Over time, parts were added and changed and interpretations were made by many authors and scholars.

The ***Mahabharata*** has been compared to the ***Iliad*** and the ***Odyssey*** of Homer, but it is much longer, its scope much broader, and its characters and adventures far more numerous. It has been a major source throughout South and Southeast Asia for plays, dances, scholarly and popular books, religious cults, comic strips, modern stage adaptations, and television. The ***Mahabharata***'s continuing immense popularity over many centuries in India, Indonesia, and Thailand is reflected in the traditional dramas, puppet shows, and mask dances in these countries. In India several years ago, when it was featured on their national television as a kind of soap opera, it was reputed to have the largest audience in the history of television anywhere, with an daily audience of some 70,000,000 people over the course of a year. When the series ended, there were large street protests demanding its return, finally resulting in some reruns.

PLATE 87 Negara. *Lamak*, 27 x 86. *Mahabharata*. Kunti, the mother of three eldest Pandawa brothers, Yudistira, Bima, and Arjuna.

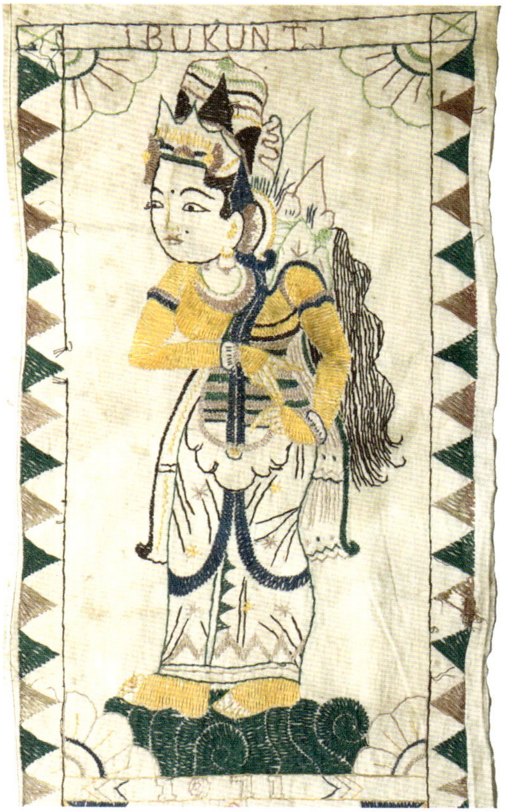

EPICS & HINDUISM

Even more significantly, the ***Mahabharata*** is closely connected to Hinduism and thus to Balinese culture. All the Hindu gods and many of its rituals and precepts, as well as the many ***Mahabharata*** characters and episodes, can be found in Bali. The major Hindu gods—with their Balinese names, Brahma, Siwa, and Wisnu—appear throughout the epic, alternately testing, challenging, and transforming royalty, heroes, lovers, villains, and each other.

CHARACTERISTICS & CONTENTS

The ***Mahabharata*** is a complex, sometimes confusing epic with constant philosophizing, complicated genealogies, many mysterious events and supernatural occurrences, and countless incarnations and reincarnations. Its plot twists include seductions, betrayals, gambling, contests, intrigues, battles, lies, and pilgrimages. Its various characters reflect an extraordinary range of personality traits and beliefs, including faith, loyalty, courage, devotion, honor, greed, lust, love, and justice. It contains events and descriptions that strain credulity. The roll call of characters includes almost every kind of person imaginable: gods, goddesses, kings and queens, princes and princesses, priests, shamans, warriors, dwarfs, giants, fortunetellers, clowns, servants, sages, ghosts, ogres, and witches. Many of these characters appear on the Balinese embroideries in this book. The animal world depicted on these cloths is just as diverse, including monkeys (the most numerous), roosters, birds, insects, water buffaloes, elephants, snakes, tigers, rabbits, boars, deer, dogs, cats, lions, and fish. The ***Mahabharata*** is a large canvas, encompassing the entire seen and unseen universe, in which all sorts of natural and supernatural events take place. The epic was clearly intended, in part, as a microcosm of human history. That it does this so splendidly, appealing to all levels of society, accounts for its survival over centuries and its continuing popularity in places like Bali.

In Bali, the ***Mahabharata*** is the most popular epic performed in dances, dramas, and shadow puppet plays. Its many famous characters, scenes, and symbols are subjects for painting, wood carving, weaving, and stone sculpture, and—obviously, for this book's purpose—embroidery. Images of Hindu gods and characters from the ***Mahabharata*** may be found as bas-reliefs on temples, on sacred ***lontars***, in the form of offering figures made of dough, in floral decorations for ceremonies, and on T-shirts and many tourist items.

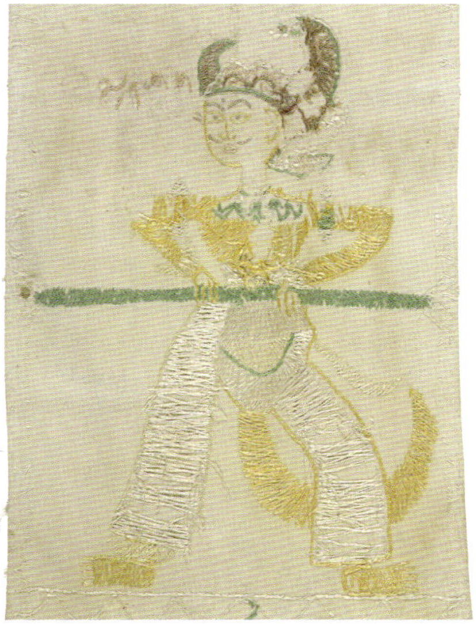

PLATE 88 **Negara.** *Lamak,* 20 x 54. *Mahabharata.* Sadewa, one of the Pandawa twins.

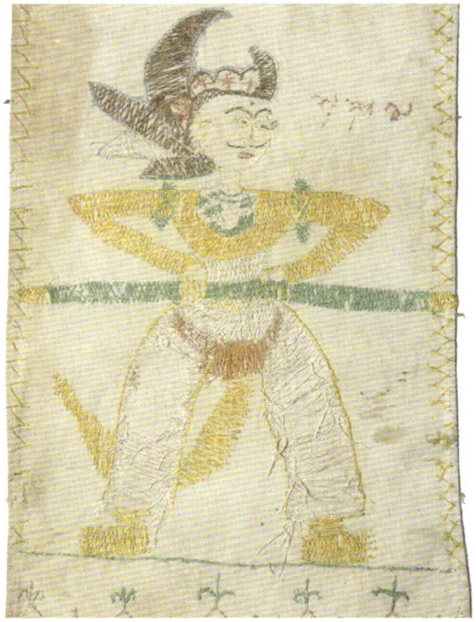

PLATE 89 **Negara.** *Lamak,* 22 x 53. Nakula, one of the Pandawa twins.

The central narrative of the ***Mahabharata*** begins in the ancestral region of a large clan in India, known most commonly as the land of Bharata. The last king whose succession is clear is Santanu, who has three sons. The firstborn is Bhisma, begotten from the king's union with the river goddess Ganges, and the legitimate heir to the throne. Serious complications arise from the king's second marriage to Satyavati, the daughter of the chieftain of a fisher tribe. This illustrates one of the most striking features of the ***Mahabharata***: the complexity of paternity and the ensuing conflicts over royal succession. Santanu's first alliance with a revered female deity and his second with a low-class girl result in a chain of troubles and intrigues throughout the epic. These seem to be the narrative basis for everything that happens.

Bhisma, the first son, decides to sell his birthright of succession so that his father, the king, can marry Satyavati. It is her father who demands this as part of the prenuptial agreement; it means that only her future sons can inherit the kingdom. This excludes any sons of the true heir, Bhisma, who in deference to his father does not contest the agreement. In any case, Bhisma is unambitious and mainly desires a quiet life, which also accounts for his acquiescence.

Satyavati gives birth to two sons. The first, Citrangada, dies unmarried, leaving no heir. His younger brother, Vicitravirya, marries two sisters (Ambika and Ambalika), but their offspring are girls—again, no male heirs. Here the whole succession issue is set in motion. It turns on the development that Bhisma evidently changes his mind about removing himself from royal politics. He makes Ambika (his younger brother's wife) pregnant; two sons are produced from this questionable union. The first, Dhrtarastra, is born blind, which excludes him from the succession. The second, Pandu, later actually becomes king and, through the magical intervention of the gods, fathers five sons with his senior wife Kunti (**PLATE 87**, see page 56) and his junior wife Madri. Kunti is the mother of Yudistira, Bima, and Arjuna (see **PLATE 98**, page 64). Madri produces twin sons, Nakula and Sadewa (**PLATES 88** and **89**, page 57). These five sons are the core of the Pandawa family clan. Their king, Pandu, falls under a heavy curse because he kills two deer while the animals are making love. Fearful of what might happen to him and his

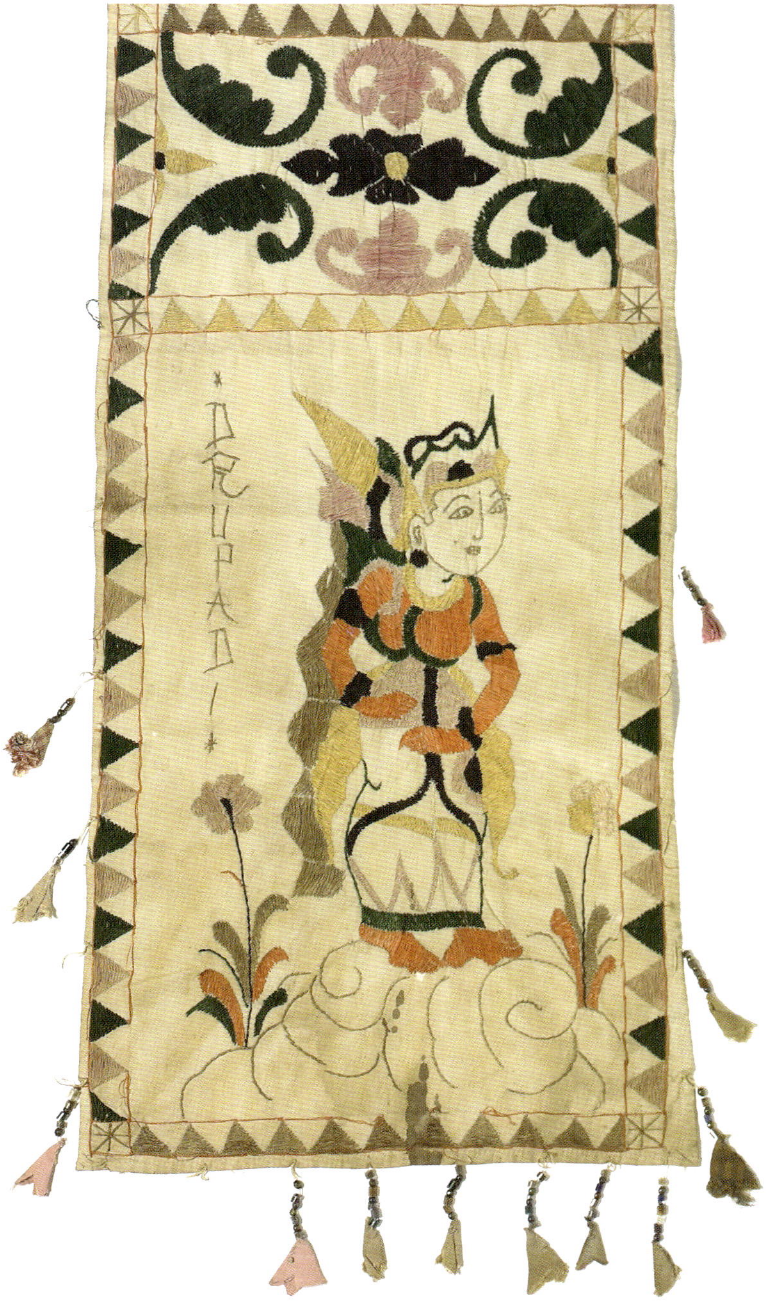

PLATE 90 Negara. *Lamak*, 30 x 90. Drupadi, wife of both Bima and Arjuna, in the *Mahabharata*.

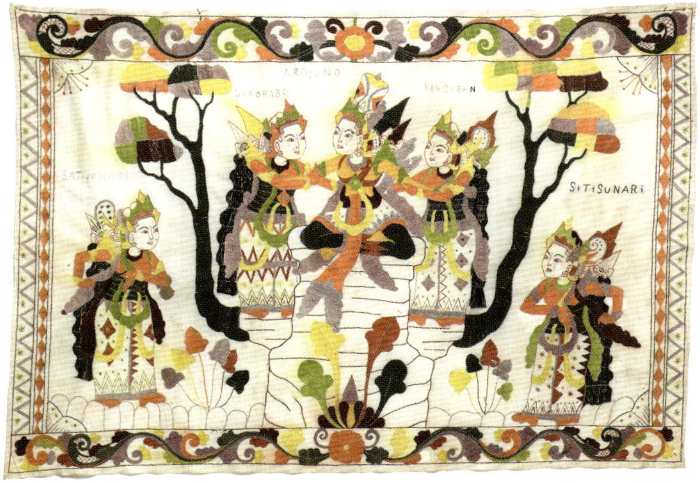

PLATE 91 Negara. *Tabing,* 58 x 125. *Mahabharata.* Arjuna with a crown symbolizing his godly status sits surrounded by his wives, Sukorabo and Kenderan, as well as two other admiring women, Satijowati (wife of Salya) and Siti Sunari (wife of Abimanyu).

family, he renounces his throne, retires to life in a secluded forest retreat, and dies not long thereafter. Yudistira, being the eldest son, ascends the throne, but by disposition he is ill prepared to reign.

Here the real conflict unfolds as Duryodhana, the son of the blind Dhrtarastra, after biding his time, enters the story to claim his right to the throne. He schemes to remove his cousins (the Pandawa brothers) and legitimate his own family clan, the Korawas. His assassination attempts fail and in semi-exile he plots to burn their house. The Pandawas discover the plot, leave substitute bodies as unrecognizable burned corpses, and escape with their mother Kunti. Duryodhana, however, is not deceived and continues to scheme against them. The story continues with an interlude.

The five Pandawa brothers, in disguise, appear at the court of King Drupada of Pancala, who has organized an archery tournament for the hand of his daughter, Drupadi (PLATE 90). Arjuna, who has through arduous training become the "best bowman in the world," wins her hand. This enables his Pandawa family to enter into an alliance with the Pancalas, whose domain borders Bharata, the kingdom in dispute. In an attempt to prevent war between the Pandawas and Korawas, a great council is held in the city of Hastinapura. The meeting fails because Duryodhana has become de facto king of Bharata and refused to negotiate or budge. An agreement of partition is reached, with the Pandawas accepting the poorer half of the Bharata domain but vowing not to give up their rights to the throne.

The Pandawas found the city of Indraprastha in their newly granted land. With great fanfare and some foreboding, Yudistira, with his shaky personality, is installed again as king. Soon Duryodhana, not satisfied with his triumph, challenges Yudistira to a winner-take-all game of dice. The unlucky and unwise Yudistira loses the Pandawa part of his kingdom; even more foolishly, he wages his wife Drupadi and loses again. However, all is not lost for the Pandawas, as a council of sages questions the legitimacy of such an outcome and the dice game's results are cancelled. Yudistira cannot be dissuaded; once again he challenges Duryodhana to a final throw of the dice and again he loses everything. As part of the unfortunate bargain, he and his family must go into exile for thirteen years. One could speculate at this point how the ***Mahabharata*** would have unfolded if Yudistira had won. In any case, it is clear that this gambling episode marks a turning point in the epic that has grave consequences and increases the interest of readers and listeners.

During the exile of Arjuna—the youngest, wisest, and most beautiful of the five brothers—he is ordered by the gods to begin a long journey of pilgrimage to seek knowledge and experience so that he will eventually be prepared to lead his family to victory after their exile has ended. He goes through many adventures and learns from all of them. One of the most famous is the *Arjuna Wiwaha*, in which the god Indra sends beautiful nymphs down from the heavens to distract or seduce him while he is meditating in the forest (PLATE 95, page 62). It is a test because Indra needs a strong human to kill the demon Nitwatakawaca. Arjuna steadfastly resists all temptation and eventually marries all seven nymphs. Through trials and travails, with great fortitude, Arjuna defeats the mighty demon and is ready for his future role as leader and hero.

RETURN FROM EXILE

After thirteen years, the Pandawa family returns to Bharata to reclaim their lost kingdom. They are, of course, rebuffed by Duryodhana and his Korawa clan. A fierce eighteen-day war called the *Berato Judo* ***(Baratayuda)*** begins (see **PLATE 85**, page 54). The battles are intense, blood runs like a flood, and bodies pierced with spears lie everywhere, along with the decapitated heads of men and animals. The Pandawa family is victorious and the dead members of the Korawas are given honorable burials because they were of similar royal lineage. Everything culminates in a great horse sacrifice, which supposedly symbolizes an end to all future wars. All of Drupadi's five sons are given the boon of immortality by the gods so they can live forever in heaven. The royal succession goes to Abhimanyu (a son of Arjuna) and later to other heirs, Pariksit and Janamelyaya. The entire ***Mahabharata*** story is retold by the ancient bards and finally the great epic ends.

ORIGINS

During the eleventh century in the reign of Dharmavamsa, the ***Mahabharata*** came to Java and was translated into the Javanese poetic form known as ***kakawin***, which was written in Sanskrit meters in the language called ***kawi*** that was used in the earliest shadow puppet plays in Java and Bali. Later, other parts of the ***Mahabharata*** were translated, but not the complete epic. The versions of the prose parts of the Sanskrit epic called *kidungs* were written in fourteenth-century Middle Javanese language but were mostly recorded by scribes in Balinese royal courts. Some of the most important parts of this preserved narrative tradition are:

- The *Arjuna Wiwaha* (his meditation, marriage, and triumphs over demons)
- The *Baratayuda* (the great war)
- Two parts of the *Adiparwa* (the Bharata story of magic and the ancestry of the Pandawas and Korawas and their lives up to Arjuna's marriage to Subadra after twelve years of exile)
- The *Wirata Parwa* (the sojourn of the Pandawas at the court of King Wirata and eight other ***parwas*** [stories])

Other important parts are the *Bima Swarga*, which relates the powers of Bima and his success in rescuing his mother Kunti and her husband from the torments of hell, and the *Bomakawya*, the tale of the monster Boma who destroys kingdoms and is finally defeated by Kresna.

There were few lasting connections to Hinduism in most of Java, except for East Java, whose Hindu/Javanism managed to survive, and many of whose adherents later fled to Bali to escape the impress of Islam. It is Bali and its court traditions of artisanship and scholarship that preserved the Indian epics that came to Java. The renowned scholar Zoetmulder has written:

> ***... all that remains of Old Javanese literature is to be found in copies and fairly recent ones at that. Of the works that originated in Java but were preserved in Bali, there is not one surviving manuscript that is not a Balinese copy written on Balinese material and in Balinese script.***[4]

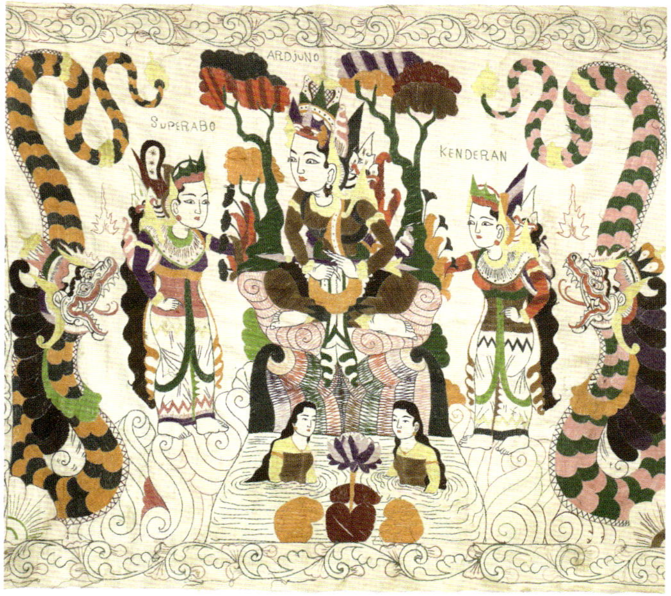

PLATE 92 Negara. *Tabing*, detail, 88 x 192. *Mahabharata.* One half of a large embroidery showing Arjuna with two nymphs in a pool below him and his two wives (Kenderan and Supraba) at his side. The entire scene is bordered by two colorful *nagas*.

He adds:

... why it is only Java of the countries with a similar past possesses an old indigenous literature of such proportions? No other country was fortunate to have its Bali to do the work of literary preservation.[5]

Kawi became the language used in the earliest shadow plays in Bali. It is a language that is mainly understood by ***dalangs*** *and literary scholars. The epic literature that formed the basis of both traditional performances and scholarly endeavors was preserved mainly on* ***lontars.***

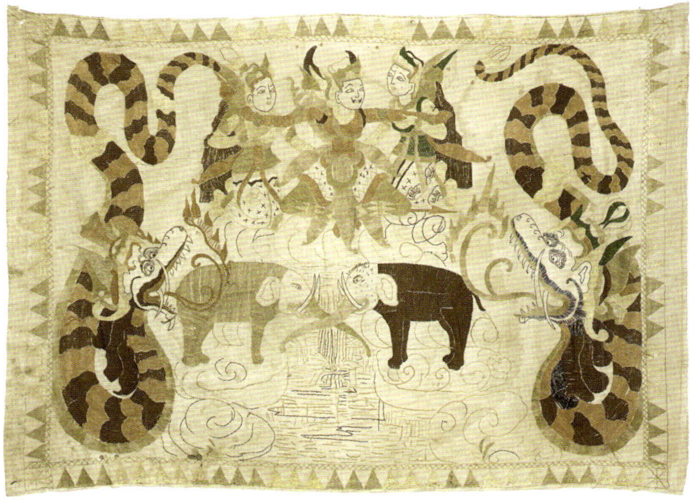

PLATE 93 **Negara.** *Tabing*, 58 x 120. *Mahabharata*. Arjuna, two of his wives, unusual elephant motifs, and two *nagas*.

The Balinese embroideries in my collection and the few others that I have seen obviously can reflect only a very small part of this immense epic, the ***Mahabharata***. In addition, these cloths were collected at random wherever I could find them. Systematic acquisition was not possible under such conditions. Even today, I do not know the complete parameters of this embroidery tradition. I only know that in terms of decoration, stitchery, and story their bounds have expanded every year since I began collecting them, in ways that I could not have anticipated. There are no documented museum collections and apparently no scholarly publications other than mine with which to compare.

One of the most popular ***Mahabharata*** scenes depicted in these Balinese embroideries is that of Arjuna serenely meditating, sitting cross-legged, surrounded by nymphs trying to seduce him or wives looking at him adoringly.[6] However, there are some differences from one cloth to another. In PLATE 86 (see page 55), Arjuna is seated in the center holding an arrow, a symbol of his archery prowess and wearing a crown symbolizing his godly status. He is looking toward his wife Sukoraba; one of his other wives, Kenderan, is on his right. Both wives have their hands extended and clasped in a traditional reverential position. On either side is a large ***naga*** with a crown signifying authority in the protection of Arjuna. Two other wives, Adnyosuwasi and Subadiro (Subadra) appear, each standing on a ***naga***. It is not unusual for ***nagas*** to be associated with wives, for they have their own spouses (see PLATE 72, page 47). The rendition and design in the ***tabing*** (PLATE 91, page 59) convey to me an image of Arjuna as a very self-assured man, revered by his wives who love him, and other wives who respect him. Such a scene seems to say that human perfection and unswerving loyalty are possible—and that the ***Mahabharata*** provides models in Arjuna and his wives.

A similar representation is shown in PLATE 92, with two of the wives named above and two young maidens sitting in a pond below Arjuna's feet. These latter may be nymphs who tried unsuccessfully to seduce him and later would also become his wives. The floral designs and the ***nagas*** are again typical. Arjuna is shown in PLATE 93 touching two of his wives, bordered by two ***nagas*** and below an uncommon motif of two elephants with crossed trunks. The muted brown and tan colors are most common in older cloths; most later examples tend to be much brighter. Arjuna is considered by the Balinese to be not only a hero but almost a godly figure, although he is not worshipped as such. Plate 48 shows Arjuna with a kind of halo, seated on Bomo his protector, with two of his wives and two ***nagas*** named Taksaka and Basuki. Bomo is a powerful symbol who descended from the god Wisnu's rape of the earth goddess Prthiwi or, as she is better known in Bali, Dewi Pertiwi.

PLATE 94 Negara. *Tabing, 88 x 105. Mahabharata.* Arjuna, with two of his wives nearby, sits on Bomo. The scene is bordered by two *nagas*.

PLATE 95 Negara. *Tabing,* 86 x 140. *Mahabharata.* Arjuna resists the seductions of two heavenly nymphs sent by the gods to test him. Two ordinary Balinese, a man and a woman, are present with offerings. The fish and the crab seem to be folk art decorations.

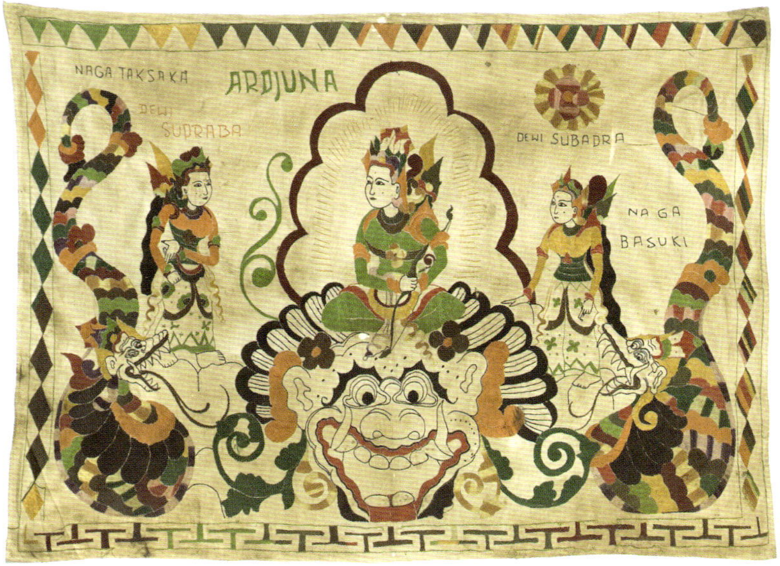

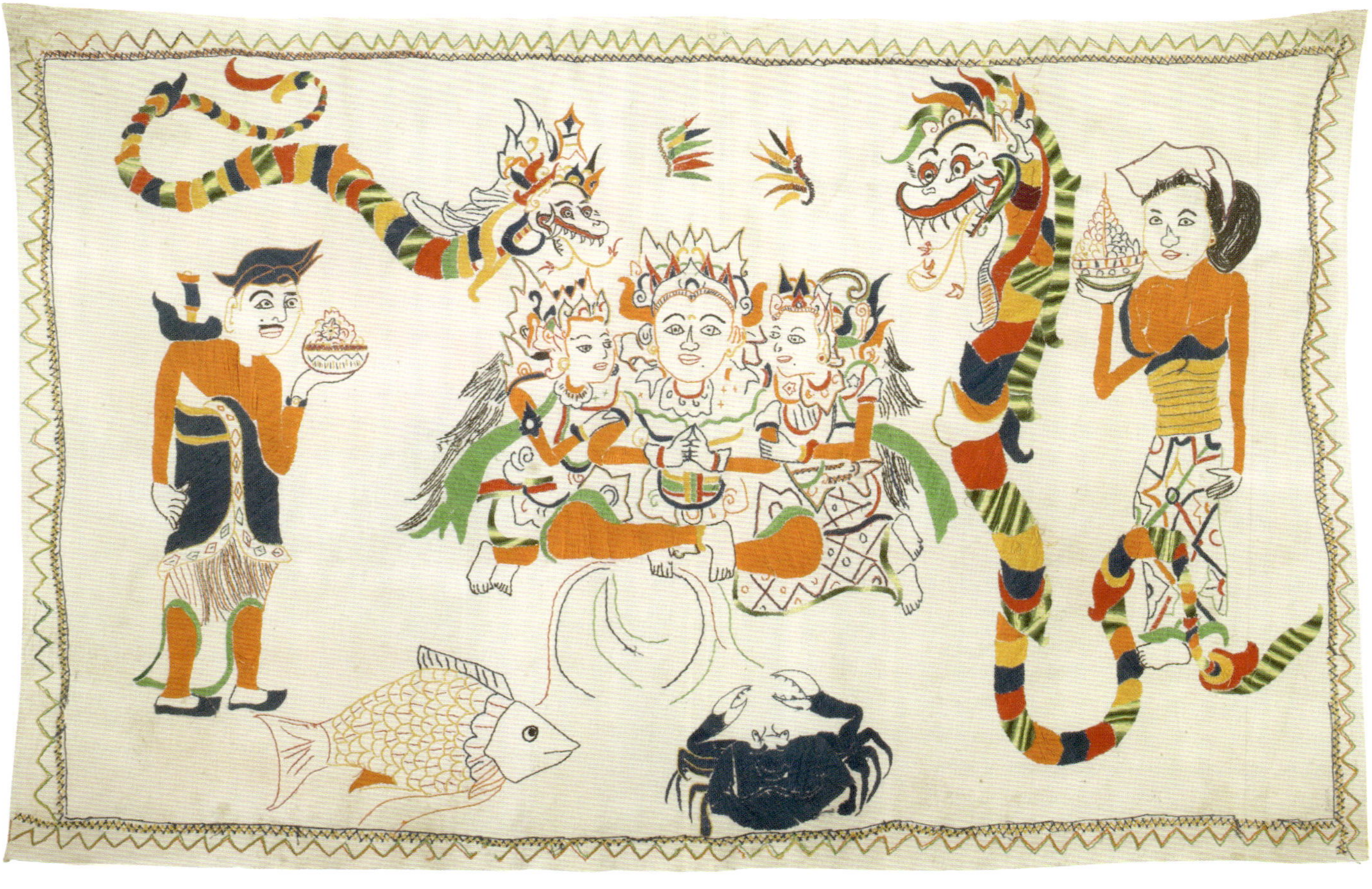

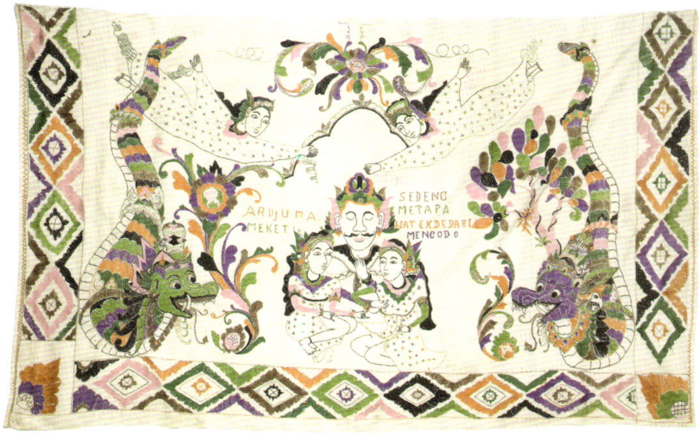

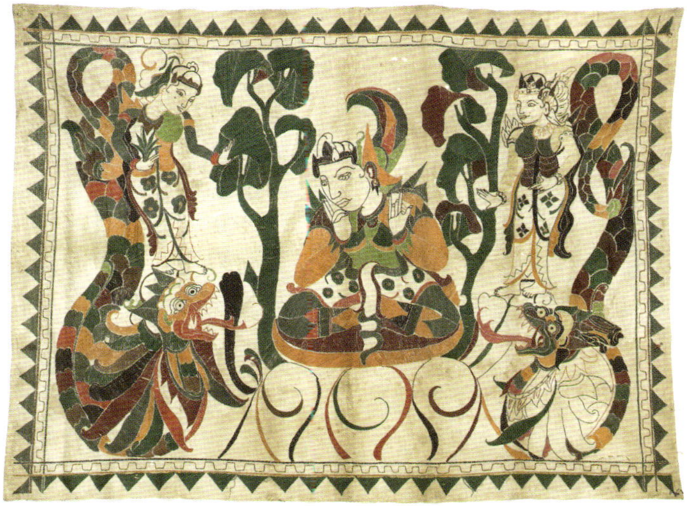

There is one general difference between the ***Mahabharata*** shadow puppet figures of Bali and and those of Java. Balinese puppets are regarded by the Balinese as being more realistic, with more true-to-life faces, than their Javanese counterparts. The reason for this is unclear. Some have suggested that unlike Islam, the primary religion of Java, Hinduism places no restrictions on depicting humans. A good example of this more realistic Balinese representation in an embroidery can be noted in **PLATE 95**, in which Arjuna and his two wives have simple, pretty faces, such as you might encounter in ordinary people. The two ***nagas*** are conventional and the man in Balinese dress holding an offering has an ordinary face. The fish and the blue crab are just unrelated folk-art decoration, though I have imagined that they may be paying homage to Arjuna.

PLATE 96 captures the beauty and simplicity of Arjuna in ***metapa*** (deep meditation), paying no attention to the ***sedeng*** (teasing) of the flying and seated nymphs. His face and those of his four consorts are naturalistic and there is a kind of naivete in all the expressions, particularly in that of Arjuna, with his unusually long, modern-looking mustache. Because he is meditating, Arjuna is wearing the ***meketu*** (headdress) of the god Siwa. Ordinarily he does not need such a crown, for his ***ksatriya*** (highest caste) status allows him to be so without it. The ***nagas*** and floral motifs are finely stitched and contribute to the overall refined aesthetic effect. Similar is the composition in **PLATE 97**, in which Arjuna is depicted with his regular curved headdress and a very lifelike, large face, with a wife and a ***naga*** on each side.

PLATE 27 (page 14) shows Arjuna and his wife Subadra. There are important traditional symbols in this cloth. The most significant one is a stylized tree of life with three lotus blossoms at its top. The first blossom signifies nature and earth, and thus fertility, which is so important in a rice-growing culture like that of Bali. I have included these several similar embroidered and varied depictions of Arjuna because it demonstrates that even within tradition there is considerable diversity in the way in which the same characters and scenes may be represented.

A different, but also popular Arjuna scene is shown

PLATE 96 Negara. *Tabing*, 84 x 136. *Mahabharata.* Arjuna in deep meditation *(metapa)*, ignoring four teasing *(sedeng)* nymphs, two of which are flying. Arjuna is wearing the headdress *(meketu)* of the god Siwa and has a realistic face. Two *nagas* and an uncommon diamond motif frame the scene.

PLATE 97 Negara: *Tabing*, 84 x 112. *Mahabharata.* Arjuna meditates and resists the seductiveness of two maidens sent by the gods to distract and test his resolve to resist.

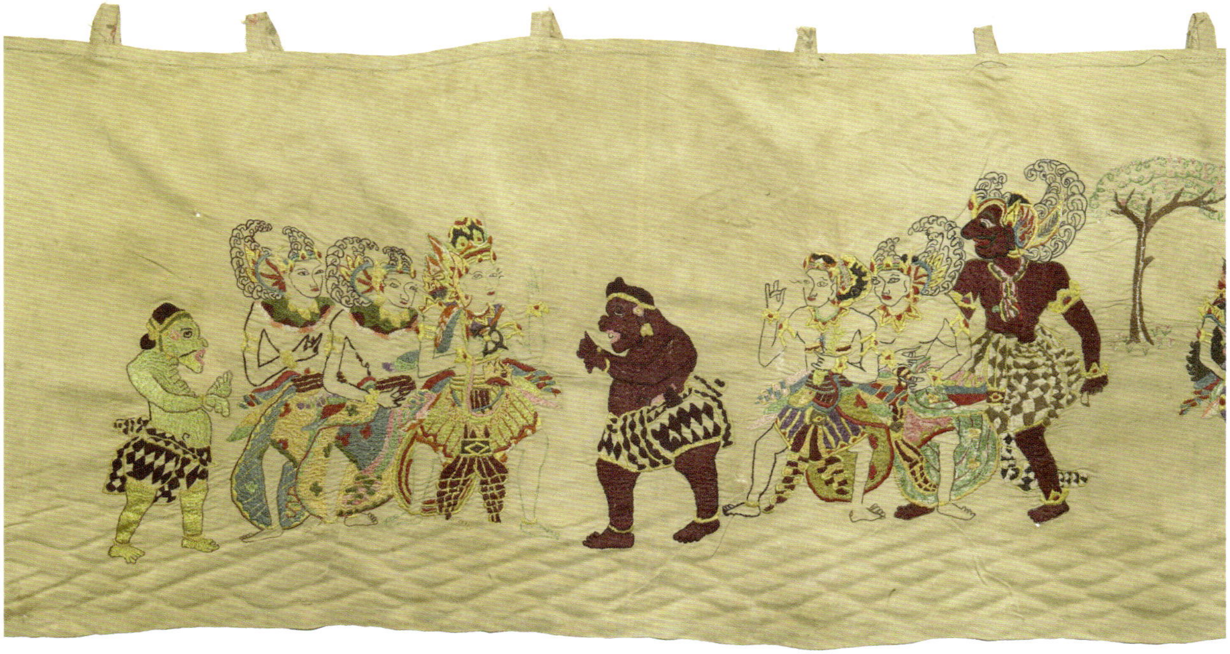

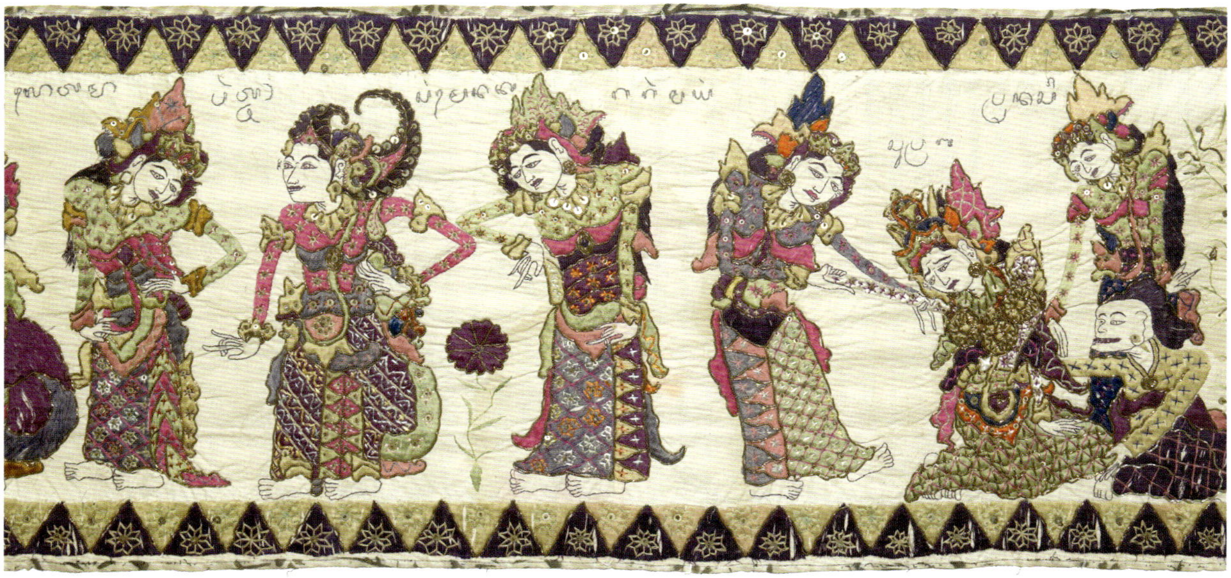

PLATE 98 **Buleleng.** *Ider-ider*, detail, 39 x 221. Silk threads. *Mahabharata*. On the right are Twalen (the clown) followed by Yudistira, Arjuna, and Bima (the three most important Pandawa brothers). On the left are other family members.

PLATE 99 **Buleleng**, *Ider-ider*, detail, 40 x 360. Silk threads, gimp, and sequins. *Mahabharata*. From left to right, Lotama (Wilotama), Parta, Sanang Menaka, Gagan Mayang, Supraba, and Pransil. Parta is a prince; the rest are heavenly nymphs *(bidadari)* who became wives of Arjuna.

in **PLATE 44** (page 27). On the left he is seated on a particularly fierce-looking ***naga***. Arjuna has his typical curved headdress, which means he is not an incarnation of any god. Facing him is the god Brahma, also sitting on a ***naga***; the two of them appear to be either contending or talking with each other. Bomo, the formidable protector, is in the center, guarding both of them or, perhaps, keeping them apart to show they must be respectful of each other. The tongues of the two ***nagas*** are entwined, which may indicate the strong connection with Brahma, one of the gods that helped Arjuna prepare to lead his Pandawa family.

THE WARRING FAMILIES

The Pandawas, who were eventually victorious over their enemies the Korawas, depended upon the character and strengths of the five brothers and the mother (Kunti). The three principal brothers in order of their importance were Arjuna, Yudistira, and Bima. They are shown in **PLATE 98** implausibly led by the clown Merdah, one of four clowns that the Balinese have added to the ***Mahabharata*** that do not appear in the original Indian epic. The three brothers may be off to visit their mother or to meet with other members of their family. Again, it is not possible to identify this scene as one that actually exists in the Balinese version of the epic. In addition, prominent members of both the Pandawas and the Korawas are related to each other and it is often difficult to ascertain who they are and what they are actually doing in a scene. This is true of many ***ider-ider*** and ***tabing*** cloths, on which many characters from both families appear. An example is an elegant ***ider-ider*** from Buleleng measuring some 360 centimeters long, shown in **PLATE 99**. There are twenty-seven characters, including a few Hindu gods arranged in sequences throughout the entire length of the embroidery that can be identified by name, but it is unclear why they are all together. Depicted in this scene are six women including a nymph, a princess, and wives of Arjuna. It is a kind of ***Mahabharata*** cosmos, with their names embroidered in Balinese script, leaving it up to individuals to unravel or imagine all the connections. This particular embroidery is very rare; I know of only two other examples. It illustrates all the elements of a fine north Bali (Buleleng) embroidery: tight stitching with carefully placed silk threads, integrated gimp and sequins, clearly defined borders and scenes, and elegantly adorned figures and names in Balinese script.

The god Indra and Duryodhana, the nasty leader of the Korawas, are shown in **PLATE 36** (page 21), as is Yama the God of Death. Next to Yama is Drona, the magician who was learned in the art of war. He was also a half-brother to the Pandawas and was killed by Bima because he sided with the Korawas. Because of his Brahman status and genealogy, his last rites were performed by both families.

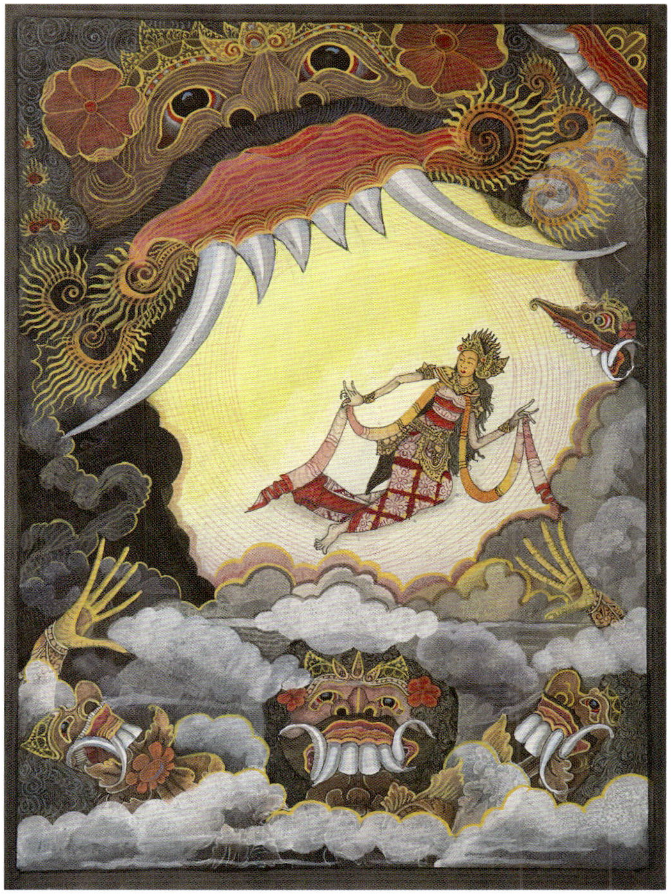

PLATE 100 *Kala Rauh Trying to Swallow the Moon Goddess, Dewi Ratih Causing an Eclipse*, 18 x 25 . c.1999, Balinese artist unknown. Acrylic on paper.

Also shown is Citrasena, one of the hundred sons sired by King Dhrtarastra. This is another indication of the immense extent of the Korawa lineage, which complicates relationships and intrigues in the struggle over succession. Other characters in the same cloth but not reproduced include Api Gana (the son of Siwa), three clowns, and various protagonists and servants. In terms of aesthetics, stitching skill, design, decoration, and authentic depiction, this Buleleng ***ider-ider*** has no equals in Indonesia and few in the world of traditional embroideries.

Another unusual embroidery, a ***tabing*** from Negara (PLATE 101), shows a melange of characters from the *Mahabharata*. Some appear to be marching, some are sitting, and some are just talking to each other. Perhaps they are just posing or merely gesturing. They are all depicted with bright colors and fine silk threads. A brown-bodied Kresna (Wisnu's personification on earth) is carrying a curved knife and a mace. Arjuna, in red with a black curved headdress, is pointing at someone. There are two demon soldiers in animated poses, one in blue and one in red; they have five claws and brandish machetes. Also shown are a Hindu priest, a king, and two court officials. It is as if the women who embroidered this cloth wanted to put into it as many characters as possible. From a distance, the scene looks like the end of a play in which all the characters appear on stage to take their bows.

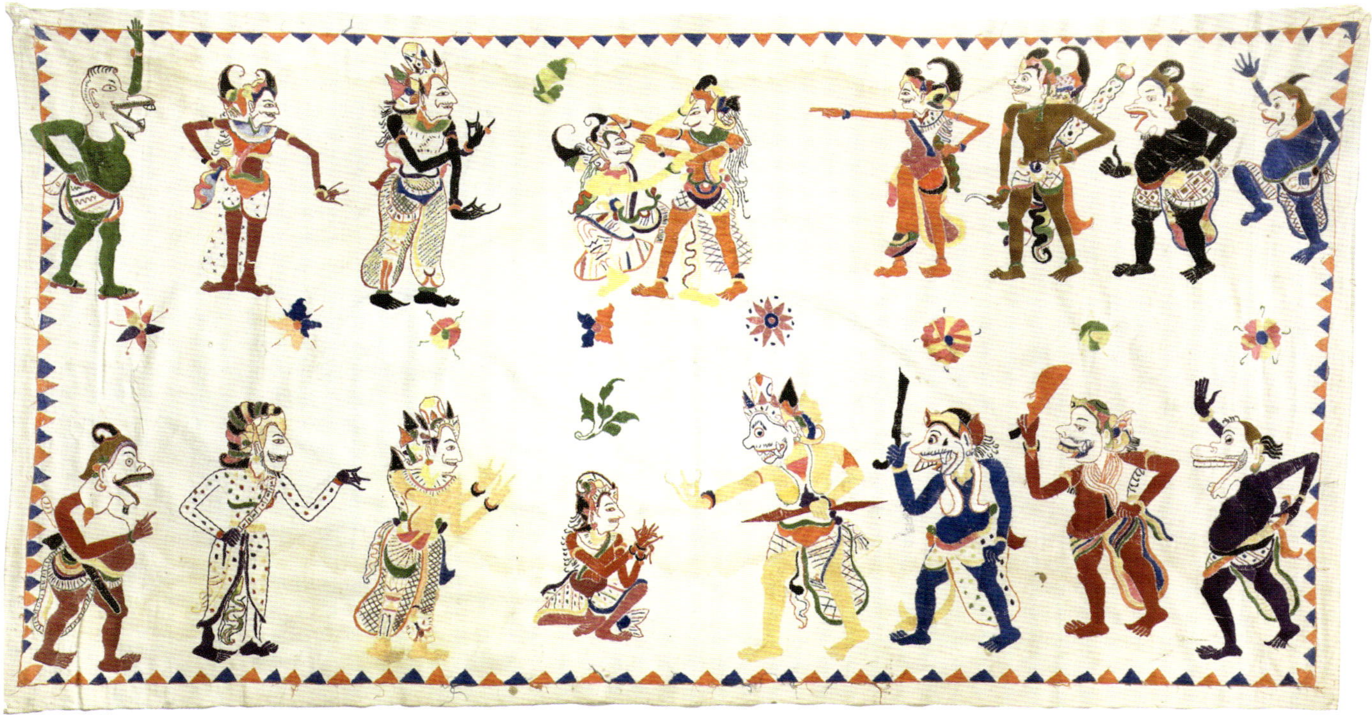

PLATE 101 **Negara.** *Tabing*, 97 x 165. A group of mainly *Mahabharata* characters including a brown-bodied Kresna carrying a knife and a mace, and Arjuna in red with a curved headdress just in front of Kresna. Behind Kresna is the black-bodied clown Twalen, a Brahman priest with a turban, one clown at each of the far corners, and various soldiers and royalty.

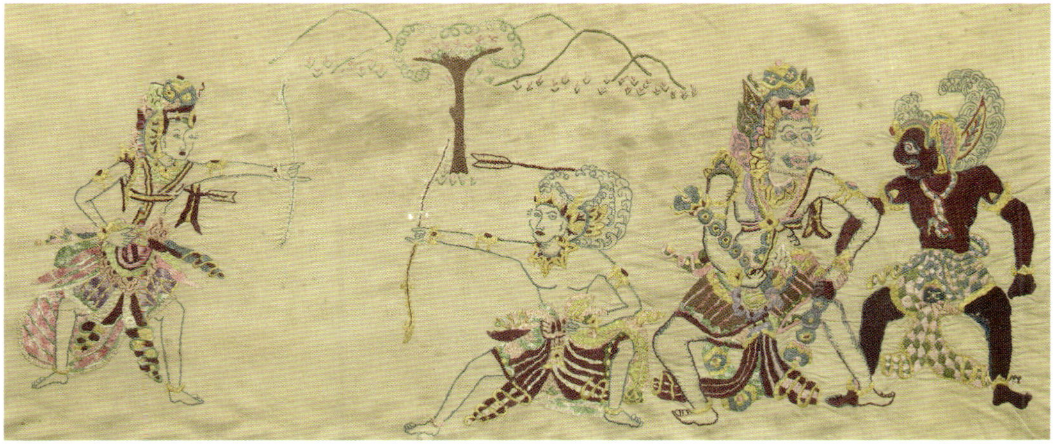

Eclipses and Myths

Eclipses are common; they occur in the heavens on the average of one every one and half years. They have been recorded in ancient calendars though without any scientific basis for their occurrence. They are clearly awe-inspiring events that were universal and required some cultural way of dealing with them. The eclipse is a strange and fearful phenomenon, particularly when one notes that the sun is four hundred times larger than the moon, yet it appears the same size during the event. Even without scientific knowledge, many traditional societies, both ancient and modern, viewed the sun as large and more powerful than the moon. It is understandable that so many myths have been concocted to explain and contend with eclipses—and the ***Mahabharata*** is no exception.

In many cultures, a common explanation held that the sun or the moon was being devoured by a monster in the sky.[7] This was recorded in the *Icelandic Edda* and believed by Lettish peasants in Latvia. The Buriats of Eastern Siberia believed that the monster Alka swallowed the sun or the moon but that the gods cut off his head and those heavenly bodies instantly reappeared. The Altaic Tartars believed that the monster was a vampire who lived on a star and had easy access to the sun or the moon. The Eskimos believed that the sun, Brother, and the moon, Sister, committed incest, causing an eclipse.

The ancient Armenians thought an eclipse was caused when two dark offspring of a primitive ox god got between the sun and the moon. Among some North American tribes, it was believed that an eclipse occurred when the sun or moon held a child in its arms. The Suma of Nicaragua sent arrows into the sky, built large fires and beat drums to chase away the huge black jaguar who symbolized the darkening eclipse.

One of the more frightening eclipse myths comes from Rhineland Germany.[8] A woman is visited by an unknown lover; because it is totally dark, to learn his identity she blackens her hands and leaves a mark on his back. Later she discovers the same mark on the back of her brother. She is horrified and runs away. She is symbolically the moon and her brother constantly searches for her. When he finally catches his sister, there is an ominous eclipse.

PLATE 102 **Buleleng.** *Ider-ider*, detail, 40 x 247. Silk threads. A battle scene including, from left to right, Duryodana, Arjuna, Dharmawangsa, and Bima.

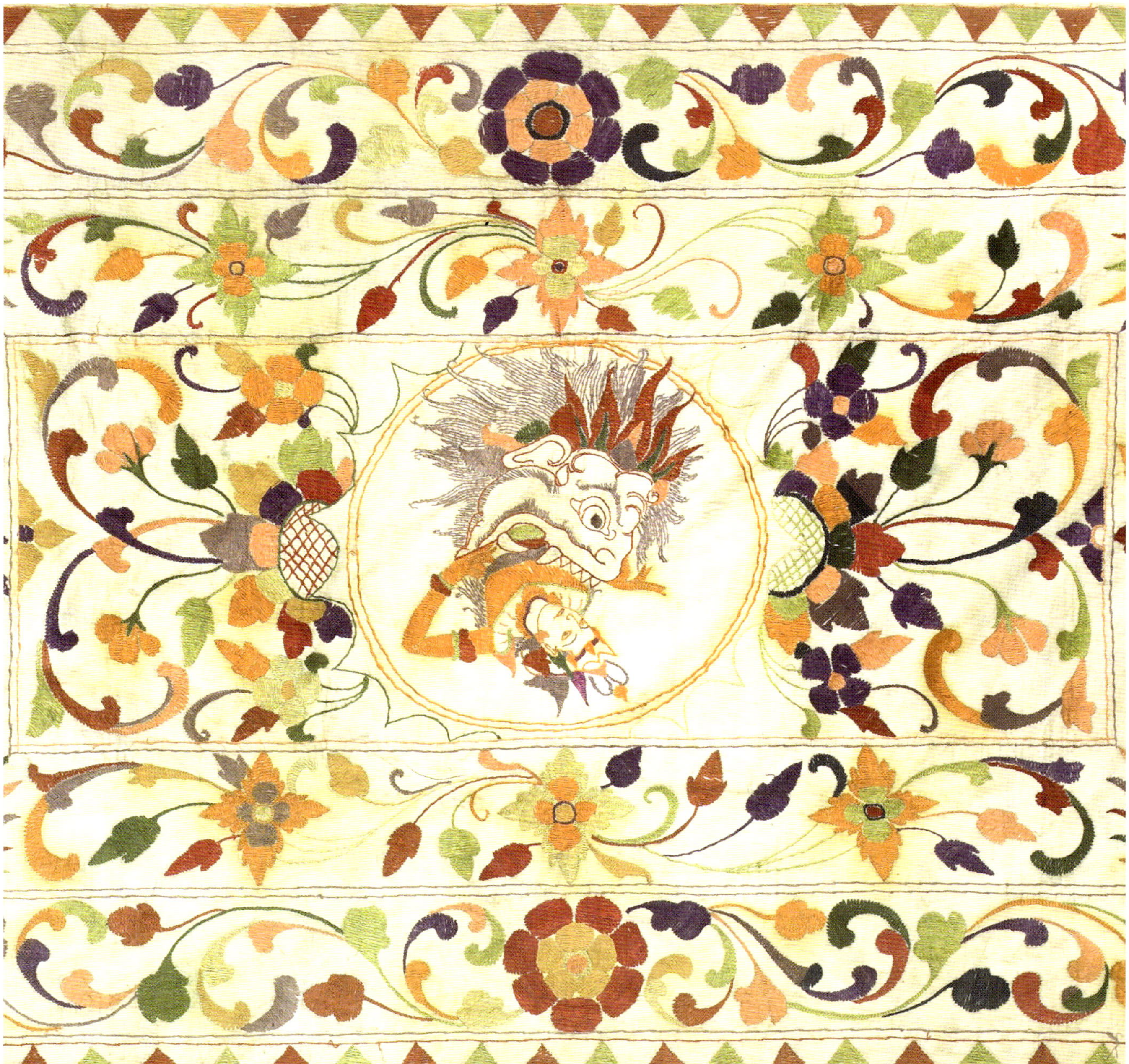

PLATE 103 **Negara.** *Tabing*, 58 x 143. *Mahabharata.* The sky monster, Kala Rauh, tries to swallow the Sun God, Surya, causing an eclipse.

The Monster Who Swallowed the Moon

A famous episode in the ***Mahabharata*** centers upon a giant monster in the sky, called Kala Rauh in the Balinese narrative tradition. It begins with the churning of the ocean and the theft by demons of the ***amerta*** (the Milk of Immortality).[9] The great gods hold a council, with Brahma and Wisnu presiding, to decide what to do to recover the ***amerta***. The most powerful of all gods, Siwa, hears about the meeting and comes to it. He proposes that his son Kumara lead an army against the ***daityas*** (demons) and it is agreed that preparations for war shall begin, with Kumara as general. In the meantime Wisnu, smarting because of Siwa's interference, pursues his own recovery plan. He assumes the form of a beautiful woman and arrives at the palace of the demon king Ratmaja, who has stolen the ***amerta***. The beautifully disguised Wisnu causes such a sensation that all other women in the court are "reduced to nothingness." The king is overwhelmed by this captivating creature and immediately falls in love with her. He is so enamored that he lets the "woman" hold the huge jar that contains the stolen ***amerta***. Wisnu reveals his true identity and slays Ratmaja with his ***cakra*** (a magical pointed discus). He temporarily possesses the ***amerta***—but not for long. The demon Kala Rauh, who was absent from the court when his father Ratmaja was killed, now seeks revenge. He finds Wisnu, seizes the ***amerta***, and begins to drink it. The gods are alarmed; they do not want such a monster to become immortal. The ***amerta*** reaches Kala Rauh's throat and arms. Immediately Wisnu throws his ***cakra*** and the giant's head is severed. However, the ***amerta*** has made Kala Rauh's head and arms immortal. Ever since then, this part of him, without the rest of his body, floats angrily about the heavens, determined to punish the gods for what they have done to him and his father. Whenever the sun or moon appears, Kala Rauh tries to swallow one or the other causing an eclipse. The earth darkens and people fear that the world may be ending.

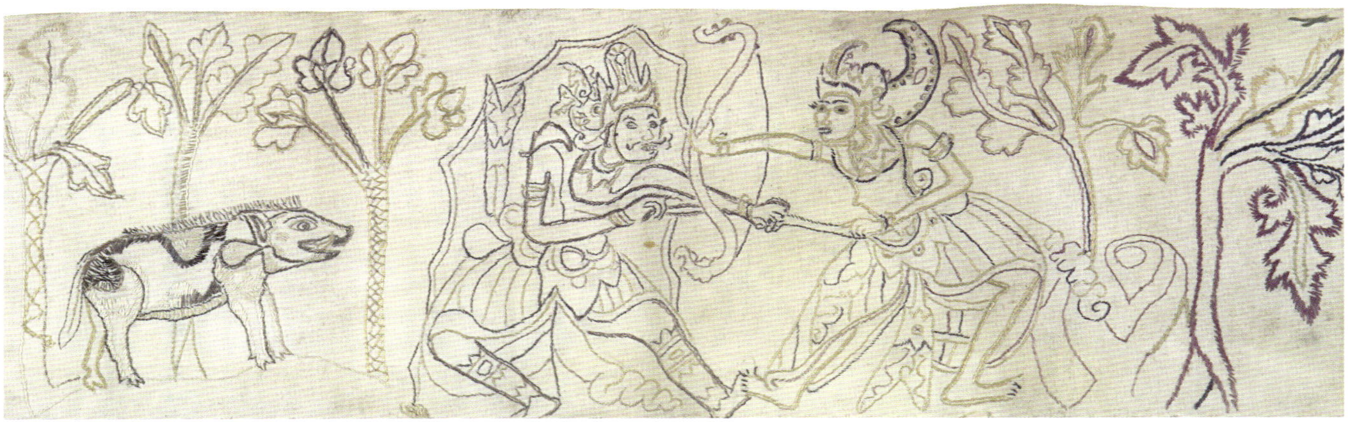

PLATE 104 Negara. *Ider-ider*, detail, 24 x 143. *Mahabharata.* The god Wisnu (on the left, disguised as a hunter) and Arjuna argue over whose arrow killed the wild boar. When Wisnu reveals his true self, Arjuna acquiesces.

The embroidery in **PLATE 103** (page 68) depicts the Sun God Surya about to be devoured by Kala Rauh. It is a Balinese tradition for people, particularly children, to rush out with all kinds of noisemakers hoping to chase Kala Rauh away. In a short time the sun or the moon reappears; the people's remedy has triumphed and harmony in the heavens has been restored. The depiction of Kala Rauh, though rare in embroideries, is very common in Balinese paintings on canvas and paper. The latter is seen most often in inexpensive miniature or small paintings sold in tourist shops in Bali, especially in the city of Ubud. See **PLATE 100** (page 65) for an example.

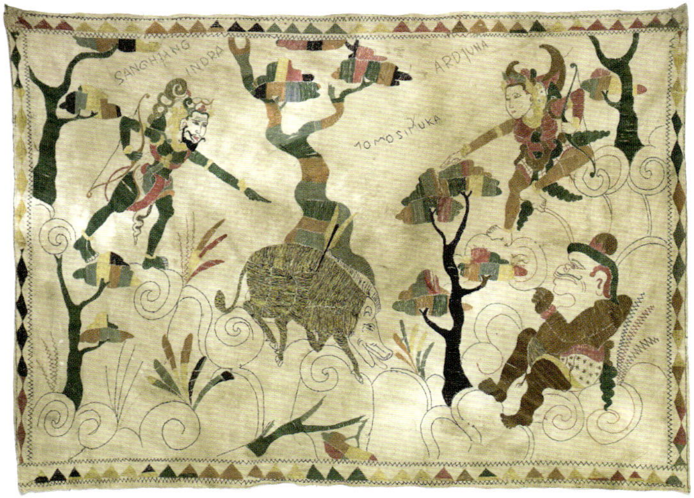

WHO KILLED THE BOAR?

A celebrated episode in the ***Mahabharata*** is the encounter between Wisnu and Arjuna. Arjuna is on one of his solo journeys in a forest, gathering local food and on occasion hunting animals. Wisnu, disguised as an old hunter, is intent on testing Arjuna's respect for the gods. Wisnu and Arjuna see a wild boar and both shoot their arrows. The boar is killed but only one arrow had reached its mark. Arjuna, being a great archer, is certain that it was his arrow that did the deed. Wisnu strongly protests, claiming it must certainly be his arrow. The argument between the two abruptly ends when Wisnu removes his disguise and reveals himself. In the face of such a mighty deity Arjuna quickly recants, saying indeed it was not his arrow. He kneels down and raises his hands in reverence. Arjuna passes the test that had been set for him and continues his forest journey. Wisnu returns to heaven with a favorable report about the encounter.[10]

PLATE 106 (page 72) is the detail of a small finely stitched ***ider-ider*** from Buleleng showing Wisnu on the left and Arjuna with their bows and one arrow in the dying boar. **PLATE 104** (page 69) shows a much simpler, almost colorless rendition in outline form. Wisnu and Arjuna have engaged their bows, while the boar looks on, not knowing his death is near. These two embroideries again illustrate the various ways in which the same episode may be rendered in a folk art tradition. However, sometimes mistakes are made or liberties taken. An example is shown in **PLATE 105**: ostensibly it is the same scene as noted above, but it depicts the god Indra instead of Wisnu holding a bow and pointing to his arrow in the boar. However, it has been suggested by one of my Balinese puppeteer friends that this may be an entirely different episode of an ogre (Bomosimuka) turning into a boar. I had been unable to find an explanation of this from any of the women embroiderers in Negara. For the time being it remains an open question.

PLATE 105 Negara. *Tabing,* 91 x 133. *Mahabharata.* Depicted are the god Sanghjang Indra and Arjuna arguing over whose arrow killed the wild boar (Bomosimuka). The clown Twalen observes the encounter. Indra is the incorrectly depicted god; it should be Wisnu.

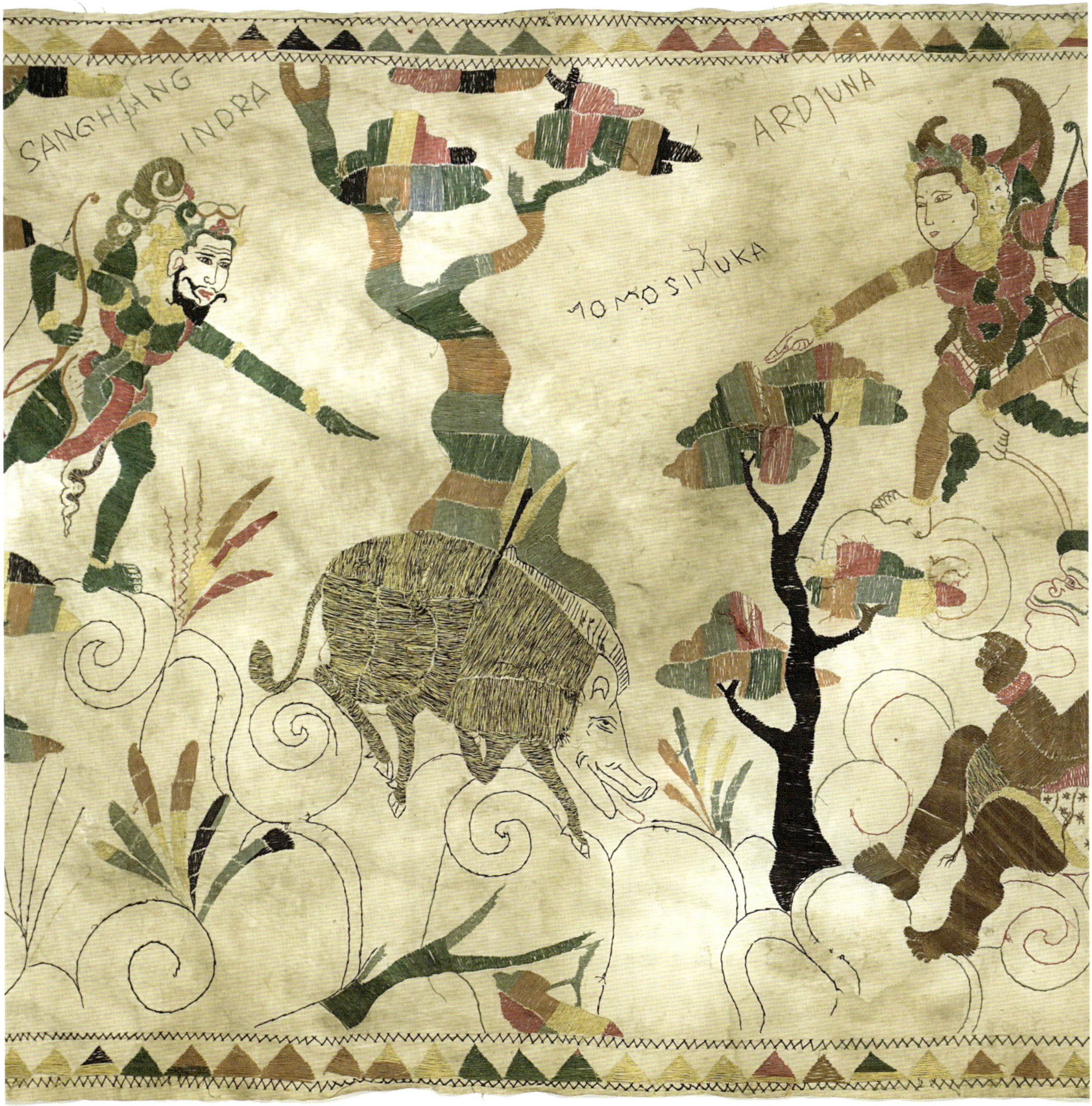
SANGHIANG
INDRA
ARDJUNA
MOMOSIMUKA

The *Lingga* of Indeterminable Length

The powerful gods of the Hindu pantheon (Siwa, Wisnu, and Brahma) often use their powers to intervene in the lives of many people. However, they are often distracted or consumed by struggles among themselves. Siwa, Wisnu, and Brahma often compete and contend with each other to demonstrate their supposed superiority. PLATE 107 depicts Wisnu and Brahma reacting to a great shaft symbolizing a penis that Siwa has sent down to earth. He challenges the two gods to find its length, which Siwa knows is indeterminable. No matter, the one that finds its true measurement will be forever supposedly regarded as the superior god. Both Wisnu and Brahma brag about their talents and readily accept Siwa's challenge. The ***lingga***, or shaft, is a symbol of virility and indeed, their manly powers will be tested but not in ways they expect.

Metamorphosed as a bird, Brahma is oriented in his search toward the heavens, which is his usual domain and he speeds upward to no avail. Wisnu, disguised as a wild boar, is bonded as he is to the earth and rapidly descends downward. Deep into the earth he still cannot find where the ***lingga*** ends. He is frustrated and the symbolic ***lingga*** has further aroused him. He is disguised as a wild boar. Then appears the beautiful Earth Mother Pertiwi (Prthiwi). Wisnu's sexual passion is so intense that he rapes Pertiwi. She later gives birth to the fierce animal-like Bomo who becomes a symbol in painting and sculpture for the protection of gods and temples. Because of his violent behavior, Wisnu loses face. Both he and Brahma have failed the challenge. Siwa remains secure in his superiority over his two powerful opponents.

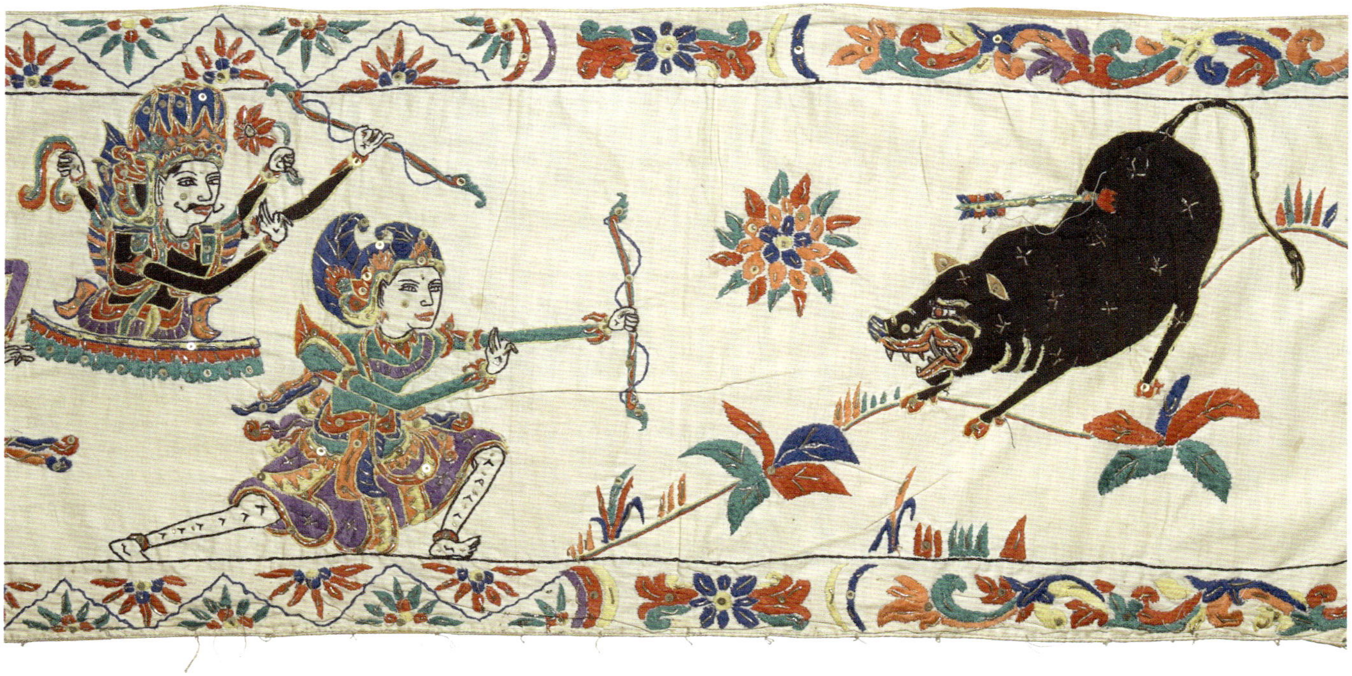

PLATE 106 **Buleleng.** *Ider-ider*, detail, 37 x 64. Silk threads, gimp, and sequins. *Mahabharata*. The god Wisnu (upper left) and Arjuna have shot a wild boar with an arrow. They argue about which arrow actually killed the boar. This is one half of the cloth, the other is a different scene. (See PLATE 34, page 19.)

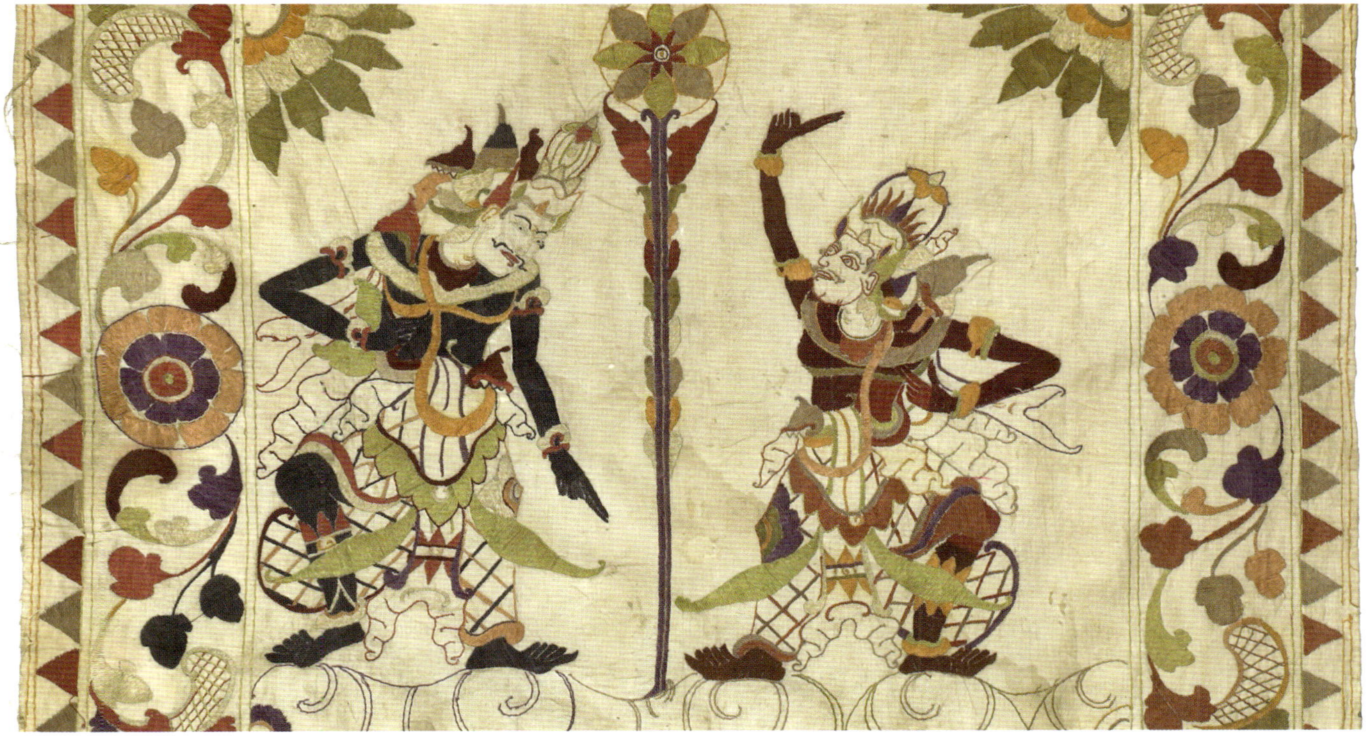

PLATE 107 **Negara.** *Tabing,* 90 x 115. *Mahabharata.* The god Siwa has sent down a *lingga*, or shaft, symbolizing a penis, and challenges the god Wisnu (on the left) and the god Brahma to find where it ends, deep down in the earth or high up in the sky. Neither god can find the end.

FOOTNOTES

1. A Javanese ***dalang*** once told me he could perform the ***Mahabharata*** nine hours an evening for seven days a week, fifty-two weeks a year, and never repeat an episode, so vast is the narrative.
2. The major English translation of the ***Mahabharata*** is by J. A. B. van Buitenen, ***The Mahabharata***, 3 volumes. This represents about one-third of what will eventually be translated. Some other, much shorter versions are: William Buck, ***Mahabharata***, and Chakravarthi V. Narasimhan, ***The Mahabharata***. An illustrated edition is Stanley Rice, ***Tales from the Mahabharata***.
3. A useful translation is: Kees Bolle, ***Bhagavadgita: A New Translation.***
4. P. J. Zoetmulder, ***Kalangwan: A Survey of Old Javanese Literature***, 437–438. This is the authoritative work in English.
5. Ibid., 50.
6. For a painting of the seduction, see Höhn, ***The Art of Bali***, 92.
7. For a review of various myths of the eclipse, see Maria Leach, editor, ***Standard Dictionary of Folklore, Mythology and Legend***, 337–338 and 393–394, and Janet McCrickard, ***Eclipse of the Sun: An Investigation into Sun and Moon Myths.***
8. For general scientific information and some mythological information about eclipses, see J. B. Zisker, ***Total Eclipses of the Sun.***
9. A description of both events is given in Heinrich Zimmer, ***The Art of Indian Asia***, vol. I, 228–229. See also Alain Danielou, "The Seizer (Rahu)," in ***The Gods of India***, 315–316, and John Emigh, (Dealing with the Demonic), ***Masked Peformance***, 60–104.
10. For a painting of Wisnu and Arjuna depicting the argument over whose arrow killed the boar, see Höhn, ***The Art of Bali***, 106. Note that the caption is incorrect.

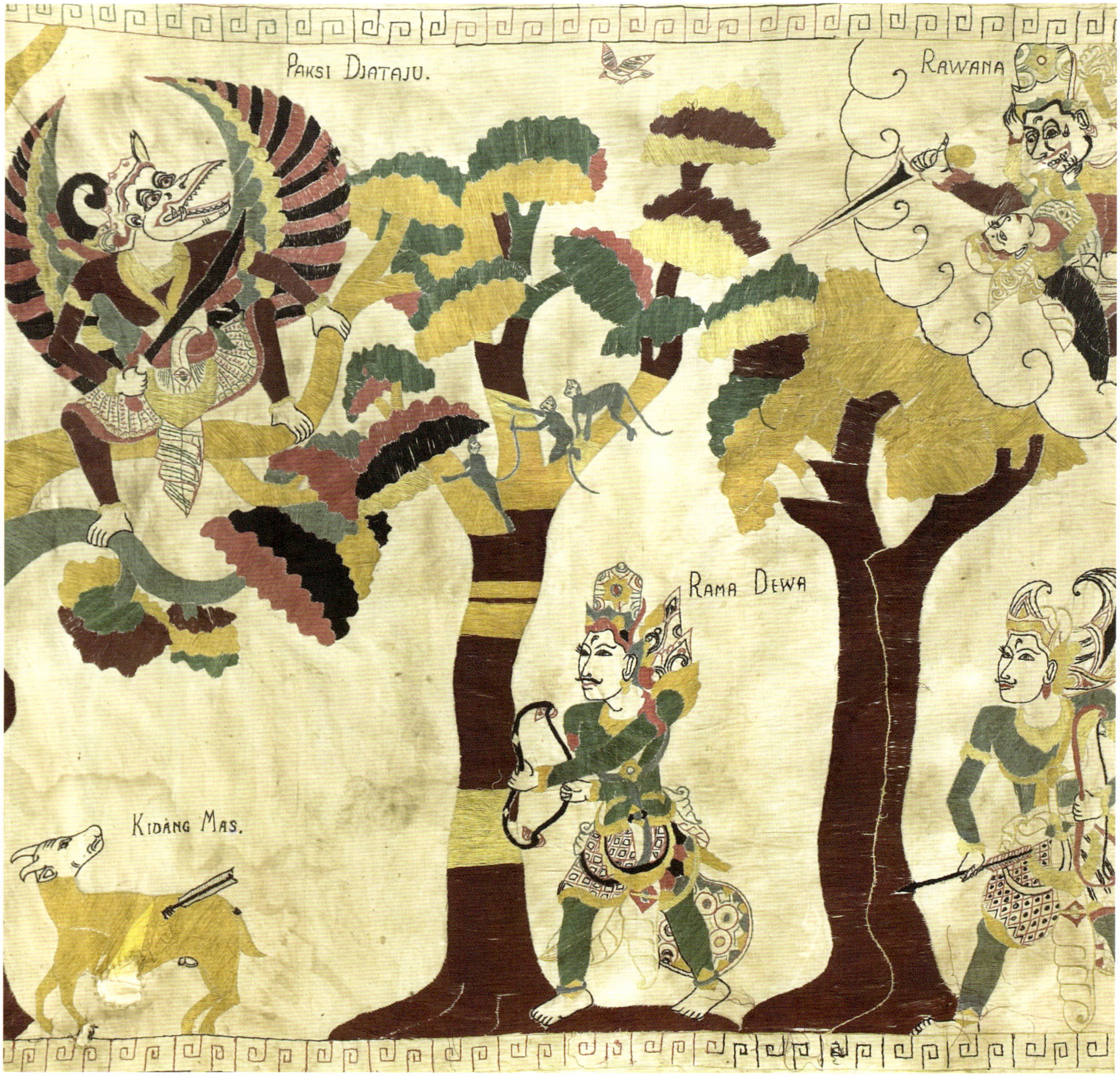

PLATE 108 **Negara.** *Tabing,* detail, 98 x 128. A famous *Ramayana* scene showing Rawana kidnapping Sita while Rama and Laksmana have been lured into the forest by the ogre Marica disguised as a golden deer *(kidang mas).*

Chapter 6

The Ramayana

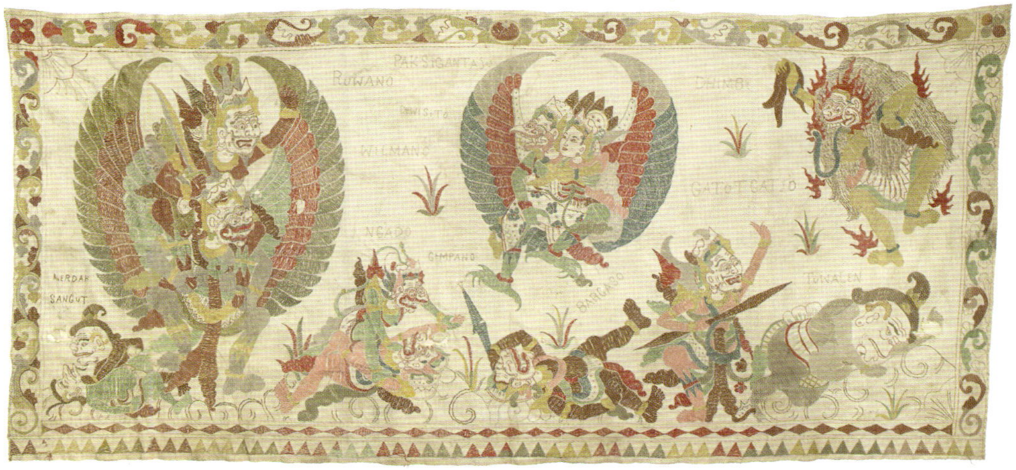

As long as the mountains and rivers shall endure upon the earth,
so long will the story of the Ramayana *be told.*
—Valmiki

Few works of literature produced in any place at any time have been so popular, influential, imitated, and successful as the great ancient Sanskrit poem, the Valmiki Ramayana*... For at least the last two and a half millennia, the tragic tale of Rama and Sita... has entertained, moved, enchanted, and uplifted untold millions of people in India and much of Southeast Asia for countless generations.*[1]

The Ramayana *is neither one story nor one text—it is an epic universe that has deeply influenced the religions and cultural life of India and Southeast Asia for thousands of years. It has been told, retold, and transmitted in poetry, prose, folk song and learned commentary for millennia. It has been illustrated... in various media—stone, wood, paint, palm-leaf, and clay.*[2] *In the beginning of the epic, the poet and author Valmiki asks the sage Narada:*

"Is there a man in the world today who is truly virtuous? Who is mighty and yet knows what is right and how to act upon it? Who exemplifies proper conduct and is benevolent to all creatures? Who is learned, capable, and a pleasure to behold? Who is self-controlled, having subdued his anger? Who is both judicious and free from envy? Who, when his wrath is aroused in battle, is feared even by the gods? His name is Rama... All men know of him, for he is... mighty, radiant, steadfast, and masterful." [3]

PLATE 109 **Negara.** *Tabing*, 86 x 192. Characters from both the *Ramayana* and the *Mahabharata*. Shown are Rawana on his bird vehic e, Wilmano, about to kidnap Dewi Sito (Sita) who is being protected by the bird Paksi Gantayu (Jatayu). Ngado (Anggada), the son of the fallen Subali, is fighting Gempano, one of Rawana's minions. Also in the scene are Dhimbi (Arimbi), the wife of Bima and her son Gatotgatjo (Gatokaça) Three clowns, Merdah, Sangut, and Twalen, are up to their usual tomfoolery.

The ***Ramayana*** has beguiled, intrigued, and gratified me since I first witnessed a version of it performed in Yogyakarta, Indonesia, forty years ago. I was captivated by this very long tale (twenty-four thousand verses in seven books) of a near-perfect but tragic prince, his loyal but unfortunate wife, their high-flying magical monkey companions, the ten-headed demon king, and a fierce, brave giant warrior. It differs sharply from the ***Mahabharata*** in timeframe, location, style, and content and, very significantly, in its view of the universe. The ***Ramayana*** is called ***kavya*** (poetry); it is "full of family loyalties, adventure, love, loss, and mythic renewal" and as such has a definite piety. In contrast, the ***Mahabharata*** is called the ***itihasa*** (history) of what has been said and is characterized more by violence, greed, and moral uncertainty, as well as much philosophizing.

To me, the most attractive aspect of the ***Ramayana*** is its cast of clearly defined main characters, who sustain the narrative and its telling throughout and make for compelling drama. Its overall plot appears relatively simple; its winners and losers are plain to see. The way it is written, one can sympathize with both. It contains narrative complexities, with a mixture of realistic events and supernatural occurrences, but the central story of royal love, kidnapping, rescue, tragedy, and redemption is always in the forefront.

ORIGINS

The oldest text of the ***Ramayana*** in India dates from the ninth century A.D. Its authorship is always ascribed to the poet and sage Valmiki. The epic is divided chronologically into seven major books or ***kandas***.[4] These describe the major events in the life of Rama from his birth to his death. They deal with his disinheritance, his exile, the kidnapping and rescue of his wife Sita, the defeat of King Rawana (the kidnapper), Rama's regaining of the throne, and the eventual tragedy in his family.

The ***Ramayana*** came to what is now Indonesia, first to Java and much later to Bali. Its transmission dates from about 930 A.D.; it is the only poetry from this time that has been preserved in Indonesia. It was translated from the Sanskrit by the great Javanese poet Yogiswara and rendered into a verse form known as ***kakawin***. The ***kakawin*** poems formed "such a conspicuous part of Old-Javanese literature, that the language in which they were written was called ***kawi*** after them."[5] This poetic narrative, along with the ***Mahabharata***, became the basic literary tradition in both Java and Bali, where ***kawi*** was used as the language of manuscripts and shadow plays. Today in Bali it has fallen into disuse except for its use by a few scholars and ***dalangs*** (puppeteers).

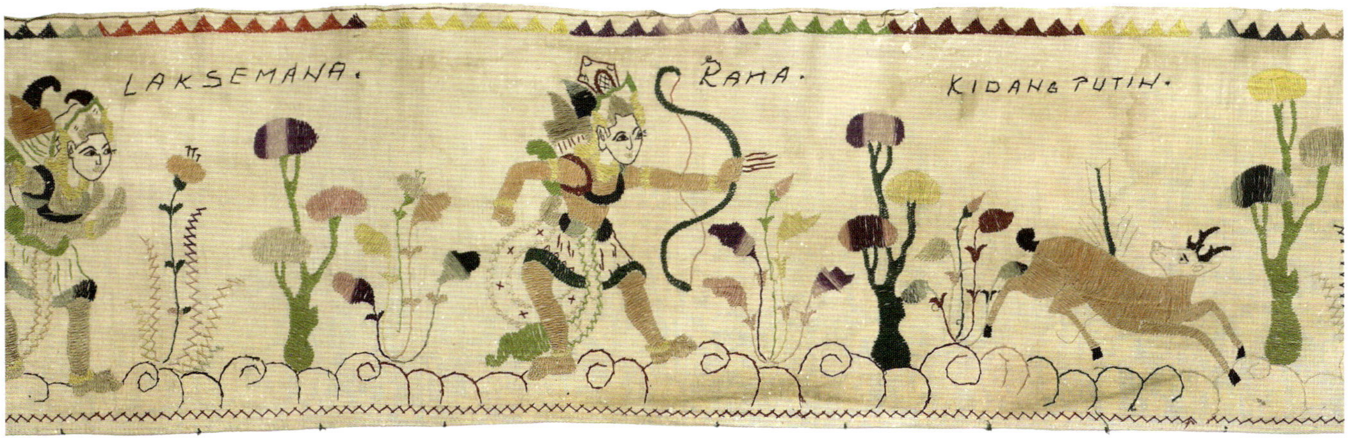

PLATE 110 Negara. *Ider-ider*, detail, 29 x 265. *Ramayana.* Rama has killed the ogre Marica who is disguised as a white deer *(kidang putih)* sent by Rawana to enable him to kidnap Sita. Laksemana, Rama's brother, identified the ogre.

PLATE 111 Buleleng. *Ider-ider*, detail, 44 x 343. Balinese script. Silk threads and sequins. A famous scene showing Rawana on his vehicle-bird Wilmano while Jatayu is carrying and trying to protect Sita from Rawana.

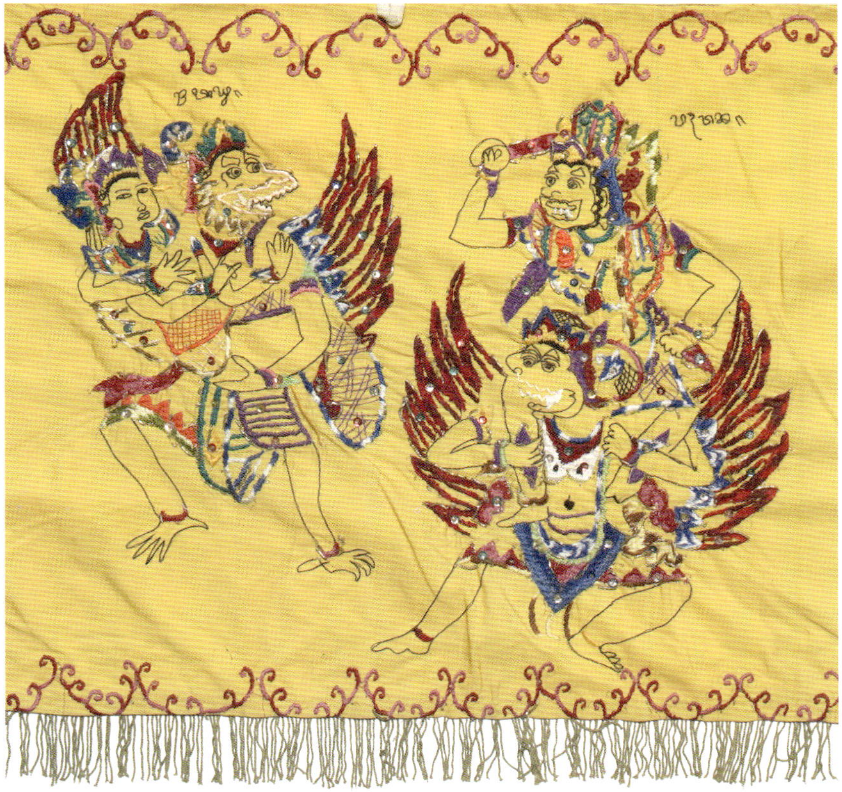

The ***Ramayana*** epic begins with a king and problems over succession to his throne.[6] Dasartha, king of Kosala, lives within the walled city of Ayodhya in India; he has no son and thus no heir. He arranges a grand sacrificial ritual so that he may have offspring. From three of his wives, four sons are born. There is great jubilation in the palace, but troublesome questions arise. Kausalya, the first wife, gives birth to Rama, the eldest. Bharata, the second son, is birthed by Kaikeyi, who later schemes to make her son the king's successor. Sumitra is the mother of the two remaining sons, Laksmana and Satrughna. Right at the outset, many complications over who shall inherit have begun. Both Rama and Bharata are considered to embody portions of the god Wisnu, for it was he who provided the magical power in the sacrifice that allowed them to be born. No real troubles arise while the two brothers are still young, and as they grow into manhood they become close friends. At this time, the revered sage Wiswamitra asks Rama's help in defeating a whole tribe of ***raksasas*** plaguing his forest hermitage. King Dasartha reluctantly gives permission to his sons Rama and Laksmana to go on this dangerous mission. Because Rama was endowed with supernatural powers, he defeats all the demons, including their ugly and treacherous chief, Marica.

ARCHERY CONTEST

The grateful sage suggests that, as a reward, the brothers should go to Mithila, where Janaka, king of Videha, is holding a tournament in which the winner will become the husband of his daughter, the beautiful Sita. The king possesses a mighty, unyielding bow; whoever can master it will win Sita. Rama takes the bow and with his magical strength bends it until it breaks in two. King Dasartha invites all the participants and royalty to attend a grand wedding ceremony, and two kingdoms are united in the marriage of Prince Rama and Princess Sita.

ROYAL STRUGGLES

After the ceremonies, King Dasartha returns to his home city of Ayodhya with Rama, Sita, and Laksmana. Elaborate preparations begin in anticipation of a new succession ordered by the king. Dasartha abdicates the throne and Rama is crowned king. Complications arise immediately when Kaikeyi reminds the old king that he made a promise long ago that her son, Bharata, would succeed him. Ancient tradition holds that a king's vows cannot be revoked and Dasartha is compelled, unwillingly, to honor his promise. Bharata ascends the throne and Rama, Sita, and Laksmana go into voluntary exile, beginning a long journey through forests and mountains. The saddened King Dasartha is so grief-stricken that he dies of a broken heart and is cremated in a solemn ceremony. However, despite his mother's strong desire, Bharata has absolutely no interest in being king, preferring instead to lead a peaceful and contemplative life. He decides to find Rama and persuade his disinherited brother to return and take over their father's kingdom.

Bharata finds Rama on Mount Citrakuta and urges him to return to Ayodhya. Rama has to refuse, since he believes he must live out the terms of exile to which he had agreed. He convinces Bharata to govern in his place and gives him his golden sandals as a symbol of kingship. After receiving lengthy instructions from Rama on the rights and obligations of being king, Bharata departs.

Rama, Sita, Laksmana, and their servants leave to go to the wild Danaka forest and find a peaceful ashram. They settle down to a life of moderation and meditation and use their powerful weapons only to protect the hermits and their serene community. Their peace is soon disrupted when Supranakha, the ugly sister of King Rawana, suddenly appears. While roaming about the forest, she sees the handsome Laksmana. Instantly infatuated with this unmarried and desirable prince, she transforms herself into a beautiful and seductive woman. She offers herself to Laksmana as a future wife but he adamantly refuses this unseemly proposal from someone he doesn't know. Supranakha's desires are not so easily thwarted, however, and she turns her attention to Rama. She has heard about his powers and virtues and demands they become husband and wife. Rama merely points to his beloved wife, Sita; his refusal is clear. Supranakha is put off again, but this time Laksmana recognizes who she really is and cuts off her nose. Bloodied and screaming, she flies away and calls for her demons to besiege the hermits and Rama and his family. Many skirmishes take place but without resolution.

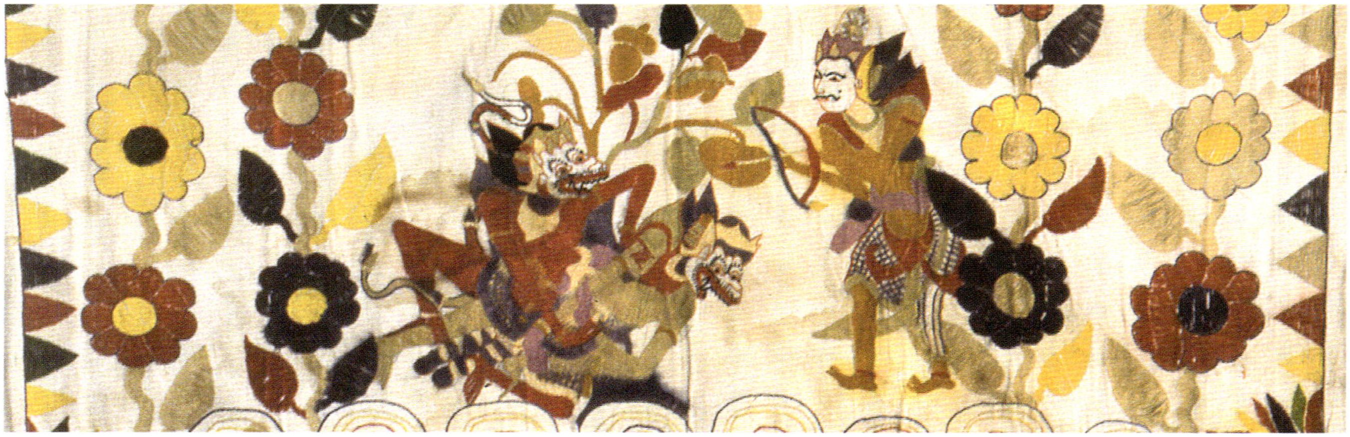

PLATE 112 **Negara.** *Tabing,* 70 x 126. *Ramayana.* Sugriwa (in red) fights with his brother, Subali. Rama waits with his arrow to kill Subali.

THE KIDNAPPING

Supranakha returns to her home in Langka and immediately goes to her brother, King Rawana, to complain. She tells him of her bad treatment and points to her much shortened nose. She urges him to interrupt his eating and drinking and order his demon soldiers to avenge her insults. Rawana is not eager to do this until he hears his sister describe Sita's inordinate beauty; he then decides to kidnap her. He sends the demon Marica disguised as a shining golden deer to lure Sita. Marica, fearful of Rama's awesome power, at first refuses to go. The king insists and threatens her, so she reluctantly sets forth

At the first sight of the golden deer, Sita is fascinated; she asks Rama to follow it into the forest and capture it for her Rama kills the golden deer with an arrow and it emits a loud scream (PLATE 110, page 76). Sita thinks Rama is shouting for help and urges Laksmana to go to him. Laksmana does not want to leave Sita alone, but the great mythical bird Jatayu, is protecting her (PLATE 109, page 75). At Sita's frantic urging, he goes to Rama's aid and sees through Marica's disguise for the demon she really is. Laksmana and Rama realize they have been fooled and hurry back to Sita, but it is too late to save her. Rawana, disguised as a priest, has approached Sita, then reveals his true self and carries her off into the sky in his bird vehicle, Wilmano (PLATE 110).[7] PLATE 111 (page 77) depicts a similar scene: Rawana with a raised sword riding on the back of Wilmano with Jatayu holding Sita. The valiant Jatayu tries to prevent her abduction but cannot do so. He is severely wounded by Rawana and just before dying he tells Rama what has happened. PLATE 108 (page 74) depicts both the killing of the golden deer and the abduction of Sita.

The embroidered words ***Kijang Mas*** mean golden deer; *Rawana Merebut Dewi Sita* denotes the kidnapping. Also present in the scene are Rama, Laksmana, and Jatayu. Rama vows to get Sita back, but it will be difficult, for Rawana has carried her away to far-off Langka (present-day Sri Lanka). The grieving Rama does not forget to honor the slain Jatayu, who is cremated in a solemn ceremony appropriate to his death as a hero.

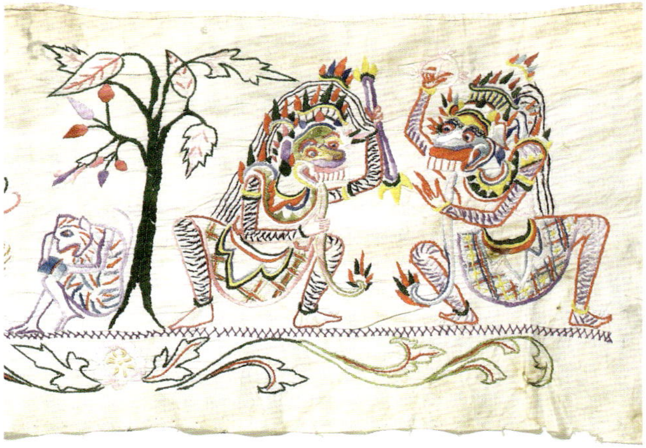

PLATE 113 **Negara.** *Ider-ider,* detail, 33 x 235. Minimal use of threads. *Ramayana.* Monkey brothers, Sugriwa (with club) and Subali fight.

PLATE 114 **Negara.** *Ider-ider,* detail, 26 x 343. The two enemy brothers, Sugariwa and Subali, are about to hurl trees at each other while Rama is ready to shoot one of the twins if he can distinguish between them. Finally, Subali is killed.

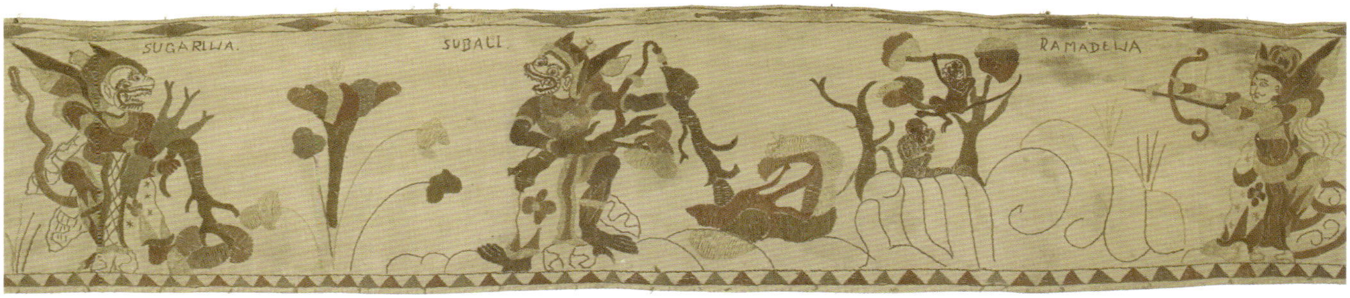

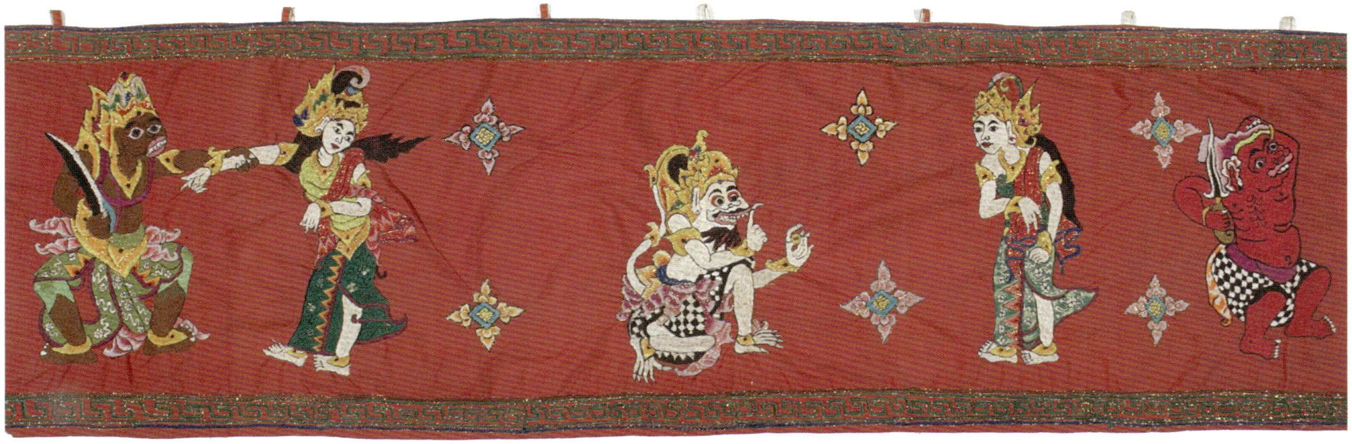

PLATE 115 Buleleng. *Ider-ider*, detail, 40 x 375. Silk threads and gimp on red satin cloth. In the scene in the center, Hanuman, the Great White Monkey and hero of the *Ramayana*, shows Rama's ring to Sita (who is in captivity) to identify himself as a friend. The other scene shows the kidnapped Sita refusing the advances of the lusting Rawana who holds a sword.

In their grief, Rama and Laksmana seek solace in a beautiful, serene forest. Here by chance they meet the son of the Rice Goddess Dewi Sri, who, after learning of the tragedy, advises them to seek out and secure the help of Sugriwa, king of the monkeys. Coincidentally, Sugriwa has been searching for Rama to ask his aid in defeating his enemy brother Subali. Sugriwa had dispatched Hanuman, the White Monkey warrior, to find Rama; once he does, they all meet together to discuss plans. At first, Sugriwa is uncertain whether Rama is powerful enough to defeat Subali. To prove his strength and magic, Rama shoots one arrow that goes through the trunks of seven palm trees. Sugriwa is duly impressed and agrees that if Subali is defeated he will aid Rama in his quest for Sita. They all depart for Kiskindha Cave, Subali's guarded abode.

After they arrive, Sugriwa and Subali begin to fight (PLATE 112, page 78), with Rama looking on. Rama raises his bow to shoot Subali, but he is confused about which monkey he is because the brothers look so much alike (PLATE 113, page 79). PLATE 114 (page 79) shows Sugriwa and Subali about to hurl trees at each other while Rama waits to shoot his arrow. Sugriwa urges the uncertain Rama to do something as he had promised. Rama manages to place a wreath of leaves around Sugriwa's neck to distinguish him from his enemy brother. In the midst of the struggle, the haughty Subali chastises Rama's behavior as ridiculous and not worthy of his royal status. Rama points out that it is not his character that is questionable, but that of Subali, who had abducted and had a sexual affair with Tara, his brother's wife. It is clear that Subali deserves punishment. He readily confesses his guilt, dies truly repentant, and therefore receives a full royal funeral. Homage is paid to Subali, and his son, the virtuous Anggada, succeeds his father.

Cupa Manik Astagina

A side story in the Ramayana *tells how two human brothers, Sugriwa and Subali, were turned into two monkeys, though still with some human features. They were the sons of Resi Gautama and Lady Andradi, who also had a daughter named Anjani. The three siblings coveted a beautiful, magical* cupu *(box) that their mother possessed and cherished. They believed that the box would give them great magical power. They constantly quarreled and squabbled over who was entitled to receive it. Their father, exasperated by his children's bickering and antics, took the box himself and, to his dismay found within it a love letter from the Sun God, Surya, to his wife Andradi. Resi Gautama became enraged by this discovery and cursed his wife. (He transformed her into a*

PLATE 116 Negara. *Ider-ider*, detail, 27 x 217. *Ramayana*. Hanuman purposefully allows himself to be captured by Indrajit so he can be brought to face and defy Rawana.

PLATE 117 Negara. *Tabing*, 86 x 105. From a side story in the *Ramanyana* called *Cupu Manik Astagina*. Resi Gautama holds a magic box, while his wife Andraci kneels beneath him. Their two sons (upper left) are transformed into monkeys (lower center). Two *nagas* frame the scene.

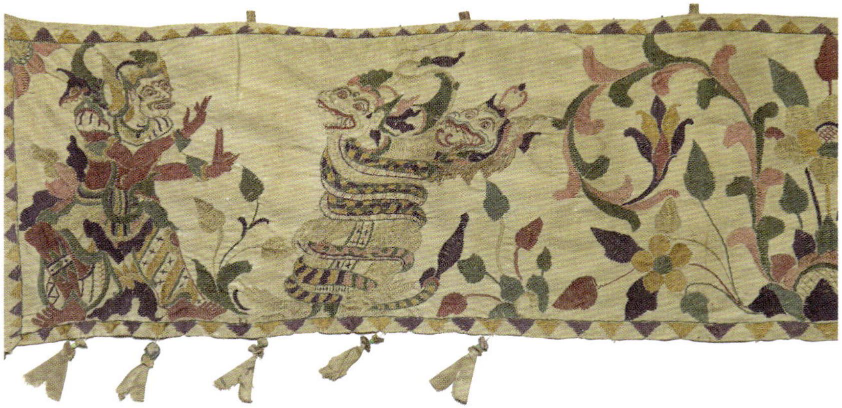

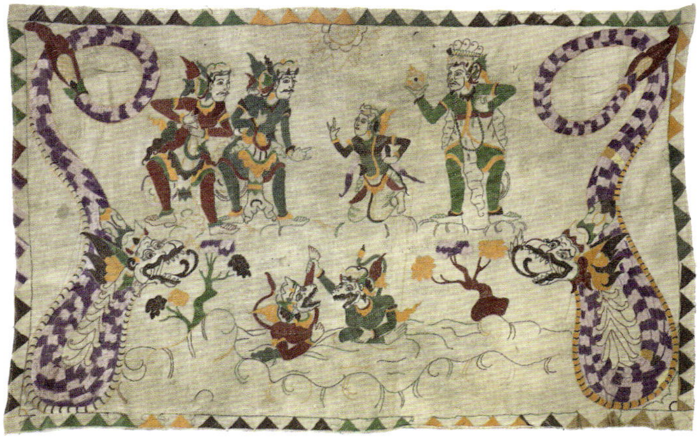

rock, but she was later restored by Rama.) In his anger he threw the box high into the air and it split in two. When the parts landed, two beautiful lakes were instantly formed, as if by magic. The three siblings plunged into one of the lakes to retrieve the sinking box. Anjani could not swim and, frustrated, she stays in the water but cannot pursue the box. Her brothers continued to struggle for the box, splashing about and diving for it, but without success. But because of their bad behaviour, something drastic had happened to them: all three had been transformed into monkeys and as such they didn't even recognize each other when they emerged from the lake.

Their father eventually forced his three children into a long penance to redeem themselves. However, the god Siwa noticed all that had happened and became especially attracted to Anjani, despite her monkey features. He became so aroused that he dropped his manik *(semen) into one of the lakes in which Anjani was still immersed. She accidently swallowed the floating* manik*, became pregnant, and later gave birth to Hanuman, the Great White Monkey Warrior.*

During his penance of prolonged meditation, the unworthy Subali was able to learn a powerful magic formula. He later met Rawana, to whom he divulged it in exchange for a great cave. This gave Rawana extraordinary wicked power, which enabled him eventually to kidnap Sita and wage war against Rama and the monkey army led by Sugriwa.

This is essentially the story as told in Java, particularly the wayang golek *(rod puppet) tradition of Sunda (western Java).*[8] *However, the Balinese version is different in one important aspect: the box does not contain a love letter from Surya; instead, when Resi Gautama removes the lid magically he can see the whole world in all its four directions (*astagina*) at a single glance. The significance of this and how it originated in the Balinese mythos is unclear. Otherwise, the Balinese plot—the transformation of Sugriwa and Subali into monkeys and Anjani's birthing of Hanuman—is the same. This* Ramayana *story is well known in both Bali and Java. This once again illustrates the vicissitudes of some of the folktales as they are told and retold in different cultures.*

PLATE 117 is a *tabing* showing Resi Gautama holding the *cupu* while his wife Andradi kneels beneath him and gestures to Surya. His two transformed sons, Sugriwa and Subali, are fighting. The entire scene is framed by two giant *nagas*.

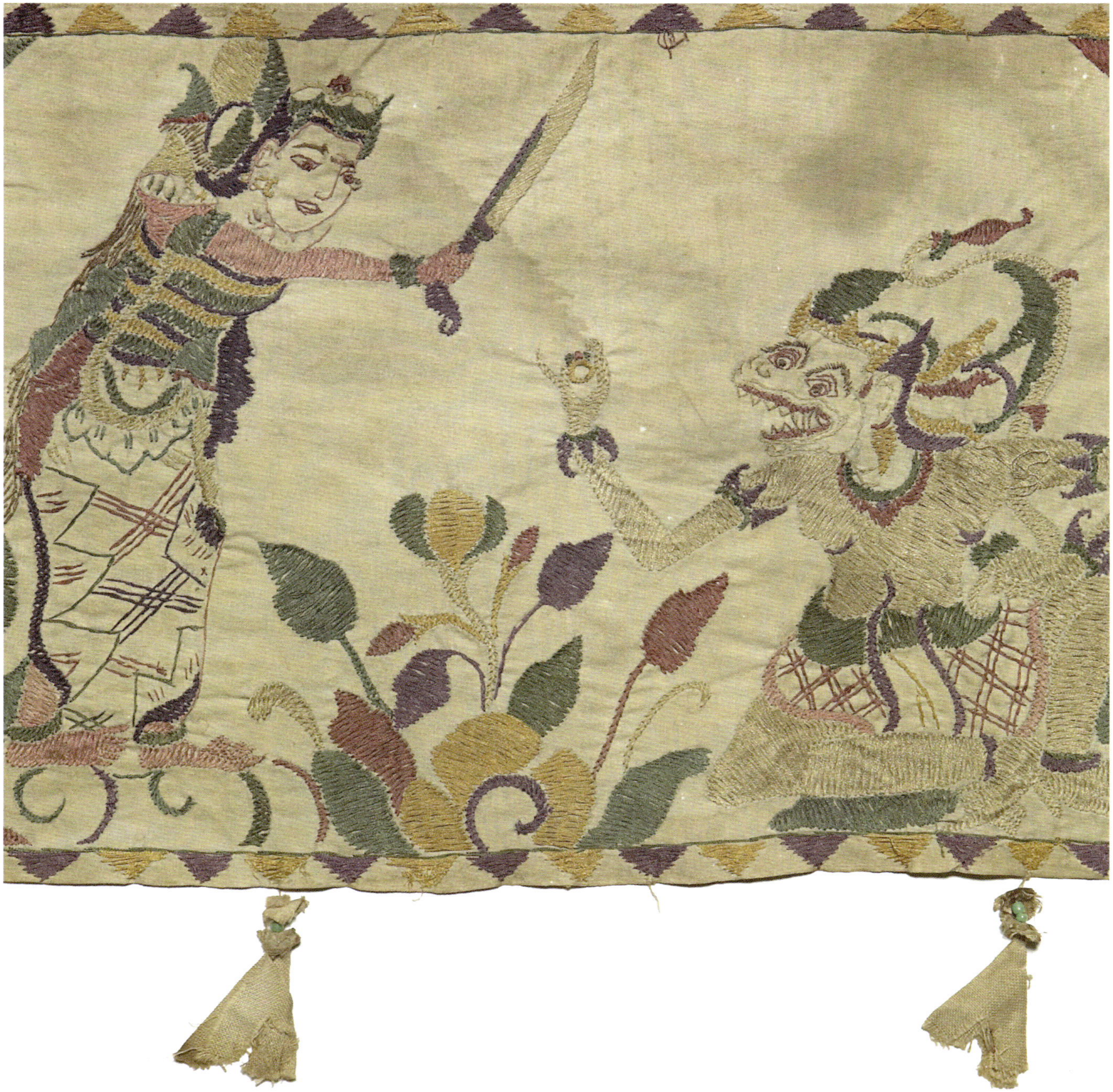

PLATE 118 **Negara.** *Ider-ider*, detail, 27 x 217. *Ramayana.* Sita in captivity raises her sword against Hanuman because she fears that he is an enemy. She eventually learns he has come to rescue her.

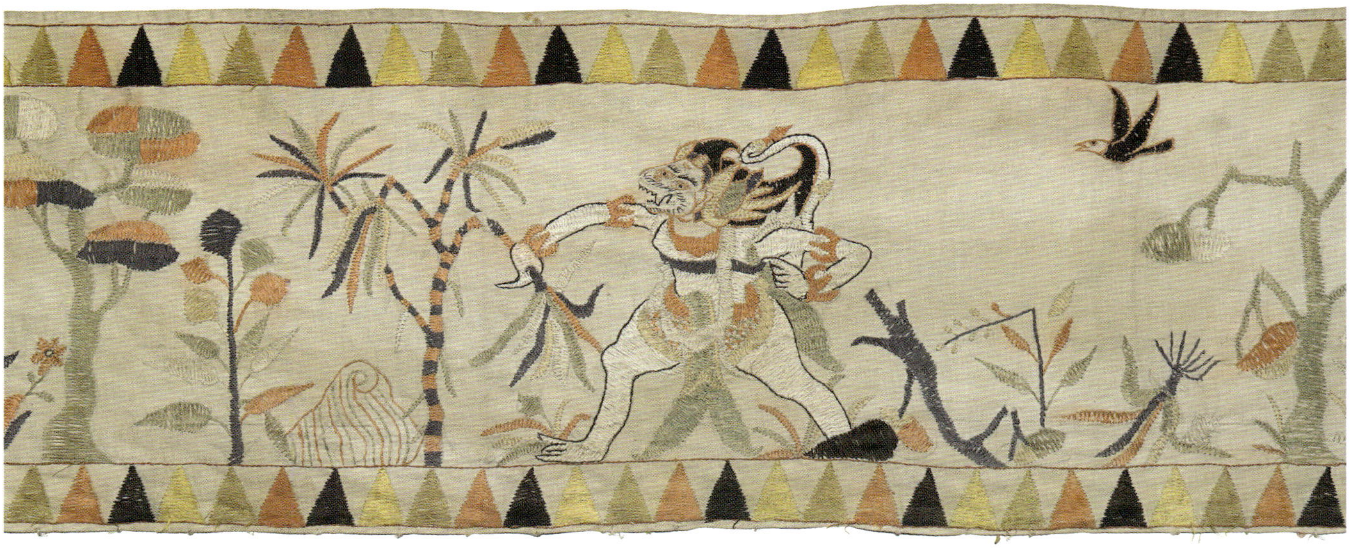

PLATE 119 **Negara.** *Ider-ider,* detail 25 x 290. *Ramayana.* Hanuman breaks the branches off of trees to show his strength.

PLATE 120 **Negara.** *Ider-ider,* detail 35 x 442. *Ramayana.* Hanuman carries a large boulder to use as a weapon.

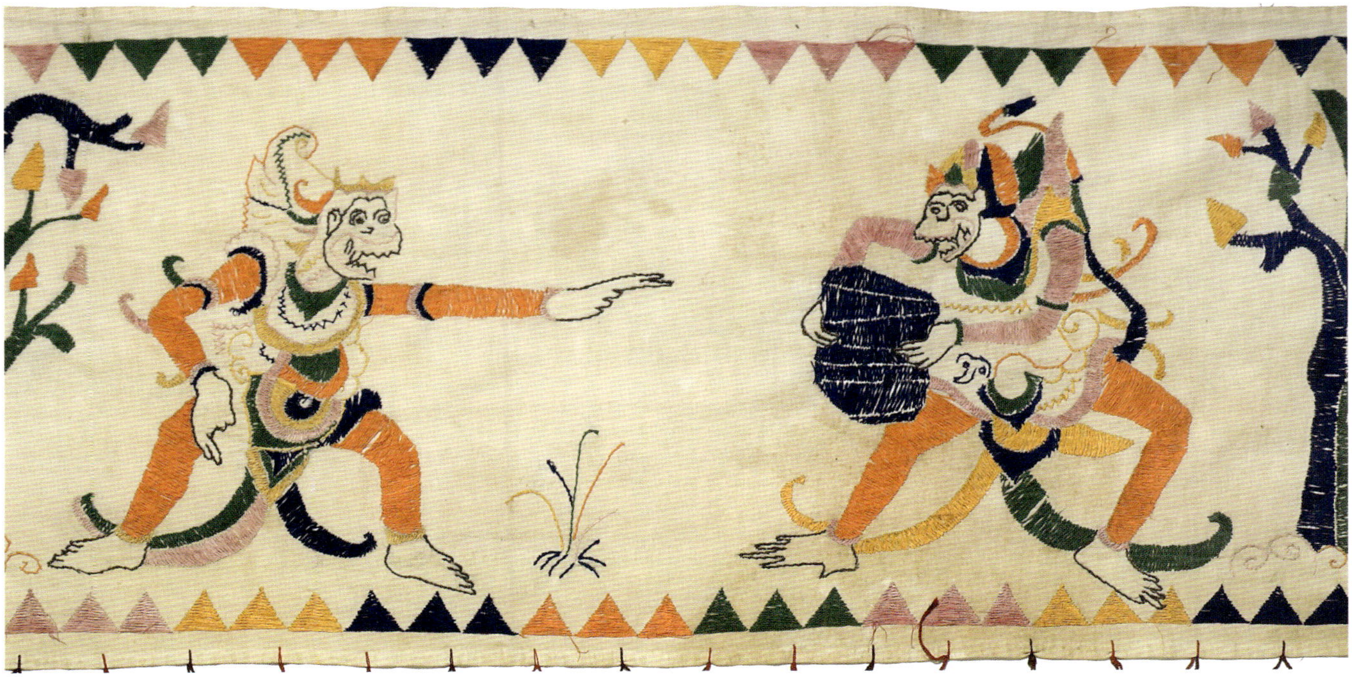

THE SEARCH FOR SITA

The coming of spring and then the summer rains find Rama still grieving and anxious to find his beloved Sita, but he has not yet heard from Sugriwa. His brother Laksmana goes to Kiskindha and meets with Sugriwa, who finally orders his monkey army to prepare for battle. He plans his war strategy with Hanuman and two other monkey officers, Anila and Anggada. The monkey army, fully mobilized, marches southward; they are lured into a glittering cave where a spell is cast over them, causing them to sleep for thirty days. The eagle Sempati, brother of the fallen Jatayu, awakens Hanuman and his followers and tells them how to reach Rawana's kingdom in Langka. Hanuman decides to first reconnoiter the city and assess the strength and disposition of the enemy forces. After some harrowing adventures, he magically transforms himself into a tiny rabbit so he can enter Langka unnoticed. When he finally discovers Sita, she is crying and distraught. He witnesses Rawana's demand that Sita become his wife and sees her firm refusal (PLATE 115, page 80). She angers Rawana even more by praising her husband and saying that Rama is superior to him in every way. Rawana threatens her with a dagger and then leaves, commanding his servants to harass her. Hanuman resumes his normal appearance, jumps out of his hiding place, and presents himself to Sita, who has never seen him before. She is frightened and raises a sword to protect herself (PLATE 118, page 82). Hanuman holds up Rama's wedding ring to identify himself (PLATE 115, page 80) and assures Sita that his presence is not a trick and that he has come to rescue her.

To do so, Hanuman must first confront Rawana; he purposely allows himself to be encoiled by a snake manipulated by Indrajit, the king's son (PLATE 116, page 81). Hanuman is brought before the king, who orders him to be killed. Wibisana, Rawana's brother, urges the king not to do this because Hanuman is an official emissary and so, according to convention, must not be harmed. Rawana will have none of this and orders his ***raksasas*** to set fire to Hanuman's tail (PLATE 121). But the gods had endowed Hanuman with the boon of immortality; he is the destroyer who cannot be destroyed. Hanuman leaps away, setting the whole city ablaze with his tail.

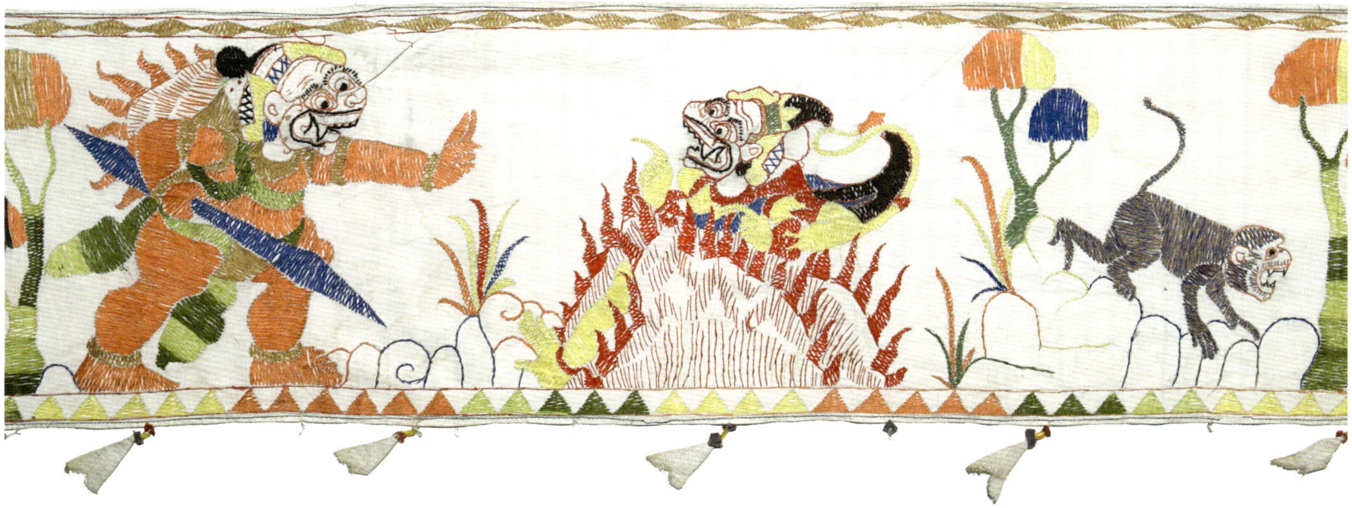

PLATE 121 **Negara.** *Ider-ider*, detail, 20 x 330. *Ramayana.* One of Rawana's soldiers has set fire to Hanuman in order to destroy him but fails, as Hanuman cannot be destroyed.

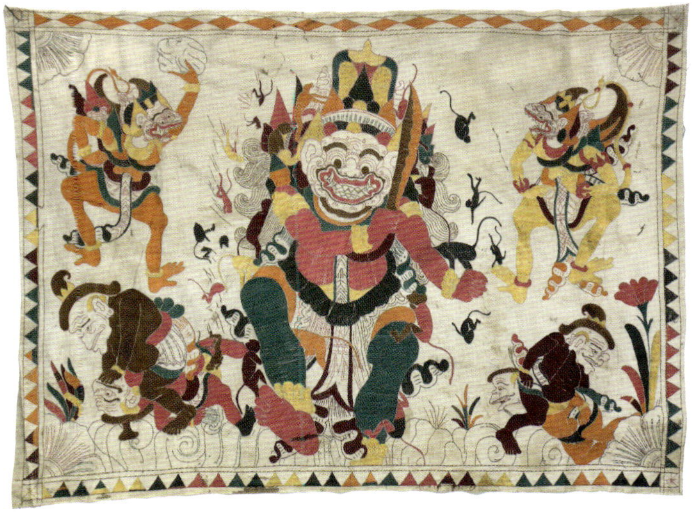

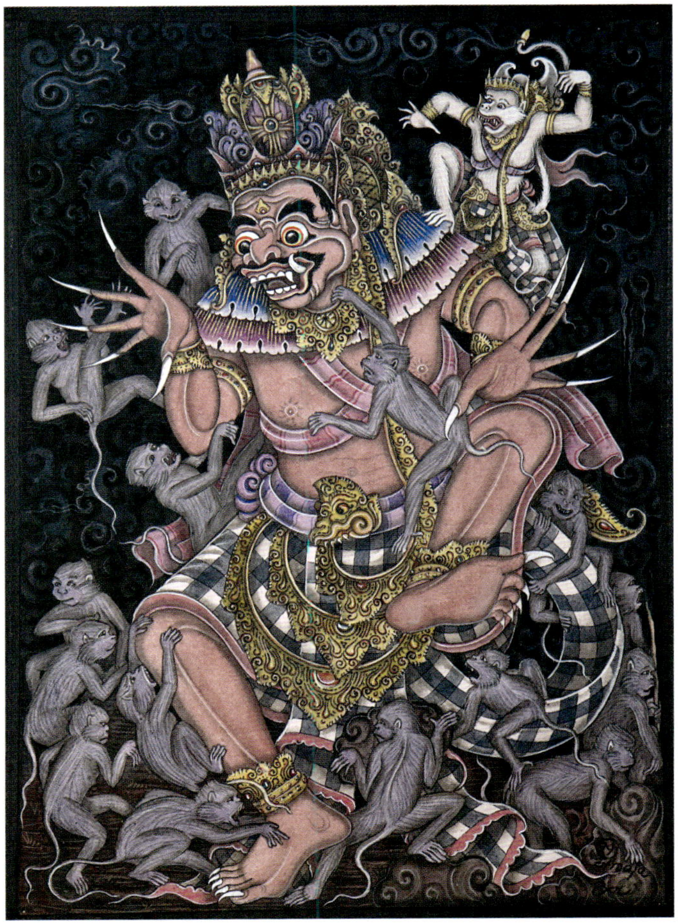

WAR

King Rawana is determined to go to war against Rama and his monkey army. His reluctant but loyal defender is his powerful giant brother, Kumbakarna, who has been awakened from a long sleep. Violent battles begin between the ***raksasas*** of Rawana and the monkey army of Rama. Giants, demons, monkeys, and men struggle against each other, (see **PLATE 34**, page 55). Hanuman hurls a tree and an ogre with a bulbous head bites a monkey while two others attack him. Another embroidery shows a whole assortment of characters in one beautifully embroidered ***ider-ider***, including Rawana, Hanuman, four clowns, ***raksasas***, monkey soldiers, and various other warriors. It is a kind of "who's who" of ***Ramayana*** contenders. (See **PLATE 9**, page 3, and **PLATE 62**, page 39.)

Kumbakarna looms large in this battle; he is literally the largest person and as brave as he is ferocious. He is shown in all his might in **PLATE 122**, wielding a sword, with monkeys falling around him. Sugriwa is on the left, threatening; Hanuman is hurling a boulder, which he is frequently depicted doing on many ***Ramayana*** embroideries. Three clowns (Twalen, Merdah, and Sangut) are ridiculously entwined with each other, while another clown (Delem) attacks a monkey soldier (Anila). **PLATE 123** is a painting of Kumbakarna beset by fifteen biting monkeys and also attacked by Hanuman.

In another cloth (**PLATE 15**, page 7), Kumbakarna carries Sugoriwo (Sugriwa) away and buries him under a mountain. He later escapes and comes back to bite off the nose of his giant captor. Rama and Laksmana attack Kumbakarna with many arrows and pierce his body armor. The giant emits a terrifying groan that can be heard over the entire world, then dies.[9] The earth shakes when his body falls.

PLATE 122 Negara. *Tabing*, 89 x 116. The giant Kumbakarna in the *Ramayana* battles blue monkeys. Hanuman is on his left, and Anggada throws a rock. In the left corner Twalen wrestles with Delem while in the other corner Merdah wrestles with Sangut. These antics are unrelated to the story.

PLATE 123 Mengwi. Kumbakarna, 19 x 26. Acrylic on paper, by Atmoja, dated 1999. The giant brother of Rawana is attacked by Hanuman (the White Monkey) and other lesser monkeys in the *Ramayana*.

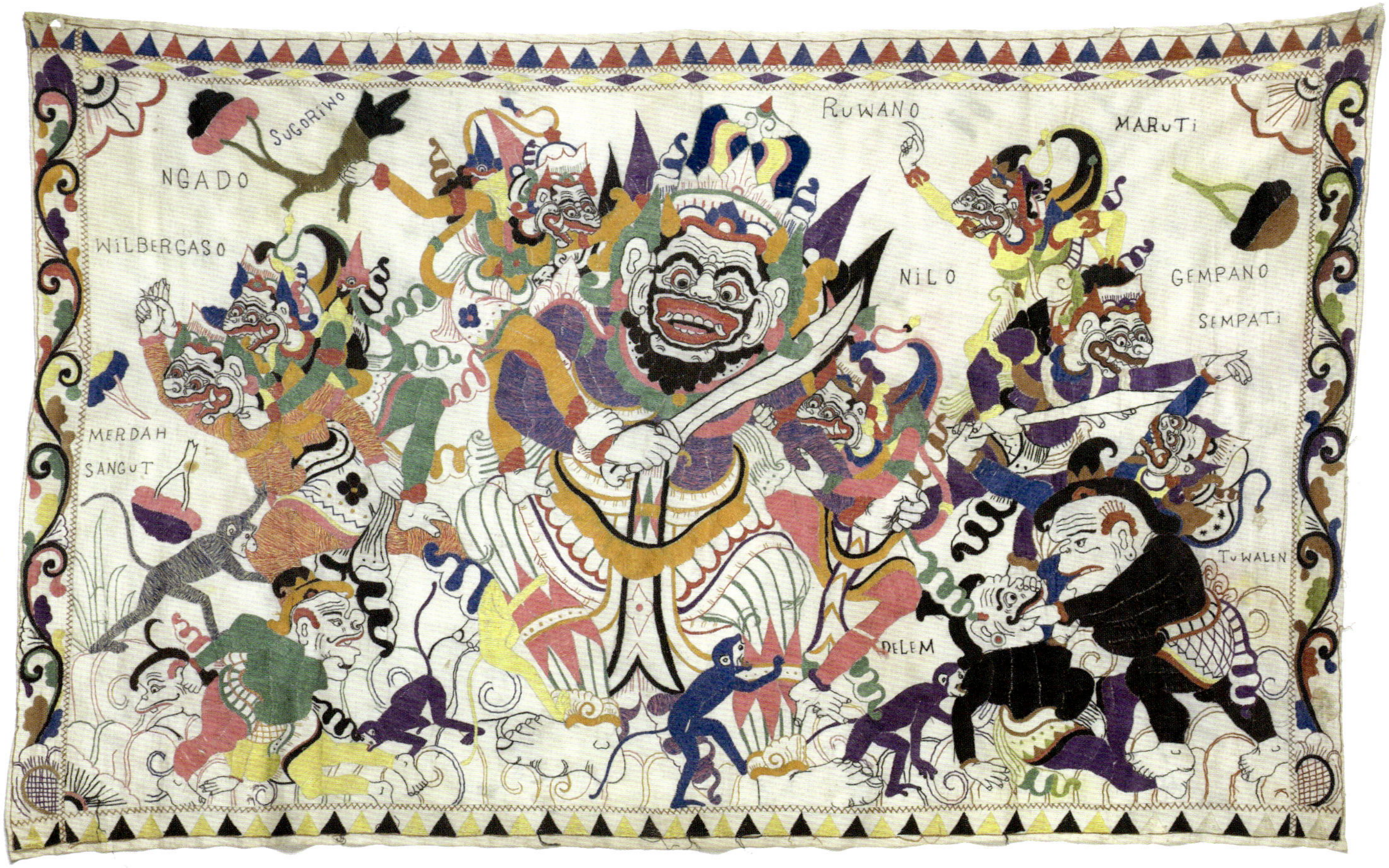

PLATE 124 Negara. *Tabing.* 60 x 120. The final battle in the *Ramayana* with the victory of Rama and his army including Ngado (Anggada), Sugoriwo (Sugriwa), Nilo (Anila), Sempati, and Maruti (Hanuman). The losers are Ruwano (Rawana), Gempano, and Wilbergaso.

DEFEAT OF RAWANA

Rawana and his forces are losing the battle. His son, Indrajit and his seven wives lie dead on the battlefield; four of his other sons have also been killed. Rawana knows he cannot win; he is besieged by Sugriwa's army but still fights on, bravely slashing at any of his enemies.

The final struggle is vividly depicted in PLATE 124, with the defiant Rawana in the center and all the main monkey soldiers attacking him, including Maruti (Hanuman), Nilo (Anila), Sugoriwo (Sugriwa), and Ngado (Anggada). Small monkeys are biting and scratching everyone. The four clowns (Delem, Twalen, Merdah, and Sangut) are engaged in their usual antics. Still, Rawana has not been defeated.

Rama has received a deadly magic arrow and commands a chariot given to him by the god Indra. He rides off to engage Rawana in what is to be the final mortal combat. The fighting is so intense that the whole world trembles. Rama's arrow kills Rawana in one shot. Because of his bravery and his royal lineage, the king is given a royal cremation. All the monkeys that had fallen in battle are restored to life by Indra's magic milk. Wibisana becomes king of Langka and the city is restored. Sita will at last be released from her captivity. It appears that a happy ending has resulted, but, as always in such complex epics, nothing is quite so simple or final.

TRIALS OF SITA

Sita prepares herself to meet Rama, donning a splendid costume that signifies her virtues and faithfulness. In contrast, Rama, worn down by battle and dressed shabbily, is not really ready to properly meet his wife. In addition, he clings to a conventional ethos, which assumes that a kidnapped woman could not possibly have been faithful, especially after a long captivity. His family and advisers also have doubts about Sita's behavior. In the end Rama foolishly rejects Sita, even though Hanuman vouches for her fidelity. Sita is forlorn and appears to lose her faith in the world, but she agrees to a test by fire provided by the god Agni to determine her truthfulness. Her ordeal is watched by Ramo Dewo (Rama), Laksmana, Maruti (Hanuman), Sugoriwo (Sugriwa), Ngadc (Anggada), and the clown Merdah (**PLATE 127,** page 89). She steps into the flames, which form a golden lotus beneath her, a symbol from the gods that she has indeed been faithful (**PLATE 126,** page 89). Rama is overjoyed, but some of his followers are still doubtful. They all return to their home in Ayodhya. Rama settles in with Sita and reestablishes his rule in the now peaceful kingdom. However rumors and gossip about Sita's supposed sexual infidelity still exist among members of Rama's court. He believes in his heart that the accusations are false, but he gives in to the doubts of his supporters and foolishly banishes Sita from the kingdom. The *Ramayana* gives no really plausible explanation of such a drastic act; however, it dramatically sets in motion the tragedy that is to follow.

SITA'S BANISHMENT

Sita finds refuge in a distant forest and discovers she is pregnant. Unbeknownst to Rama, she gives birth to two sons, Kusa and Lava. They are all sheltered in the ashram of the great sage and poet Valmiki, the author of the *Ramayana*. Years pass and Sita's two sons mature into fine, handsome adults. Rama still does not know they exist. One year, Rama as king organizes an elaborate sacrifice initiated by a poetry contest. Contestants come from all over the kingdom to read traditional poetry. Two young bards appear and eloquently recite parts of the *Ramayana*. Their skill in recitation, their handsome stature, and their physical likeness to Rama proclaim that they are the king's sons, Kusa and Lava. Rama is elated, for now he can redeem himself and atone for his exiling of the faithful Sita. His sons tell their father of their mother's life of struggle and pain and her enduring love for Rama. Rama weeps with remorse and immediately sends for Sita. It is all in vain, for Sita has been seriously ill and cannot travel. She is tired of her life now, without her sons and being alone for so many years without her beloved husband. She calls on the Earth Mother, Dewi Pertiwi, to end her suffering. The earth opens up to receive her and she disappears forever.

The news of Sita's tragic end reaches Rama. He is distraught; he cannot be consoled and cannot bear his grief. He gives up his throne and divides his kingdom between his two sons. Rama gives up his life by entering the waters of the Sarayu River, then rises to heaven incarnated as the god Wisnu. The great epic has ended.

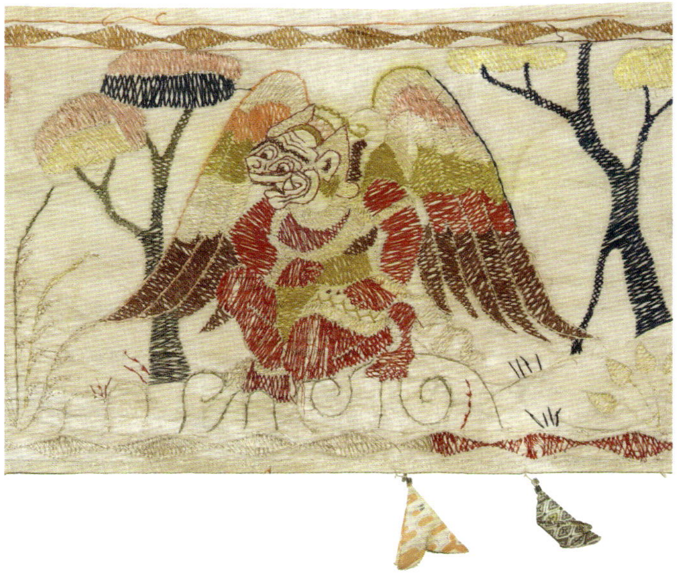

PLATE 125 **Negara.** *Ider-ider*, detail, 28 x 540. *Ramayana.* Wilmano, the mythical bird vehicle for King Rawana.

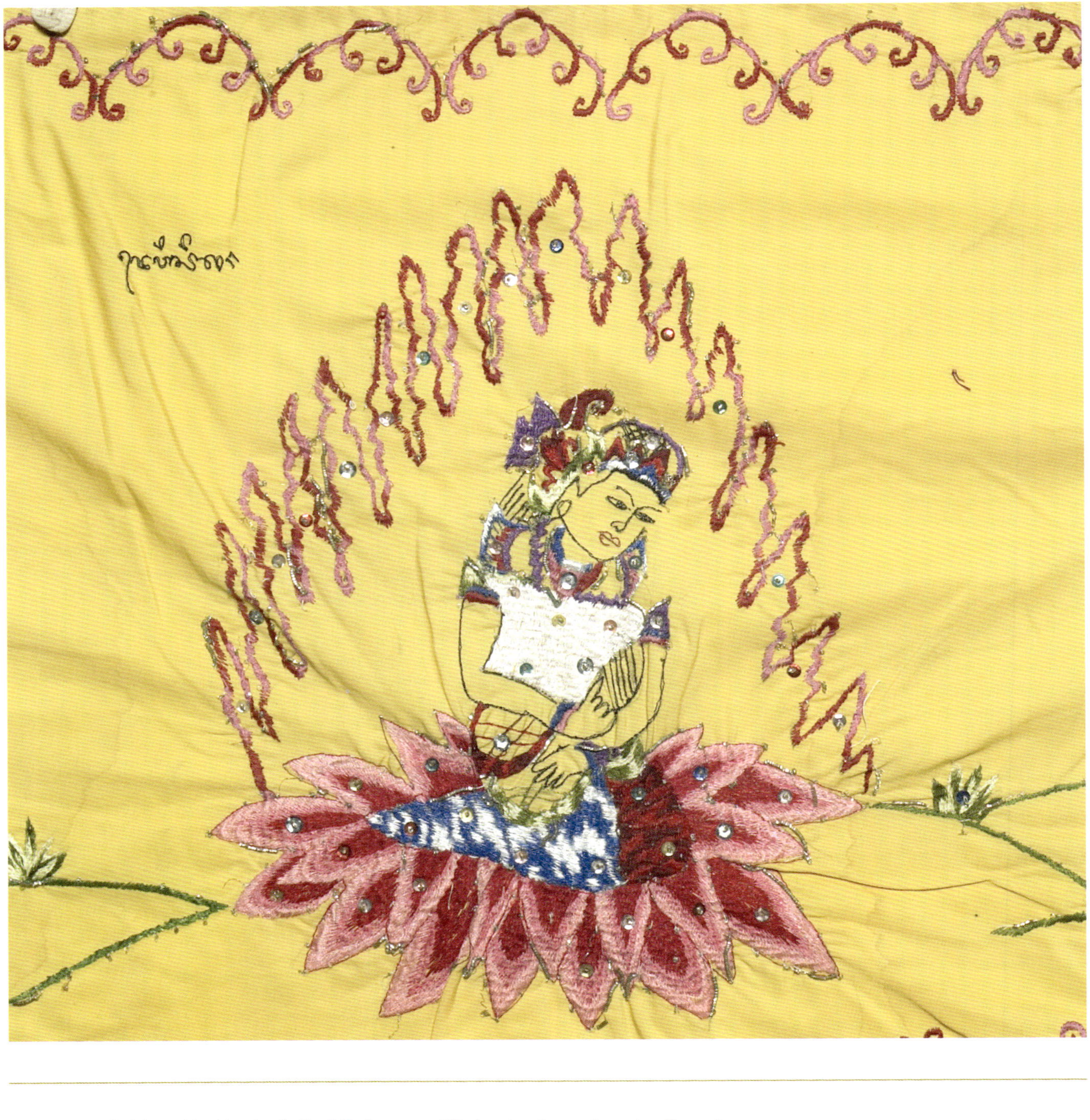

PLATE 126 **Buleleng.** *Ider-ider*, detail, 44 x 343. *Ramayana*. Silk threads, gimp, and sequins. The end of Sita's trial by fire in which she sits on a lotus flower sent down by the gods to symbolize her utter faithfulness while in captivity.

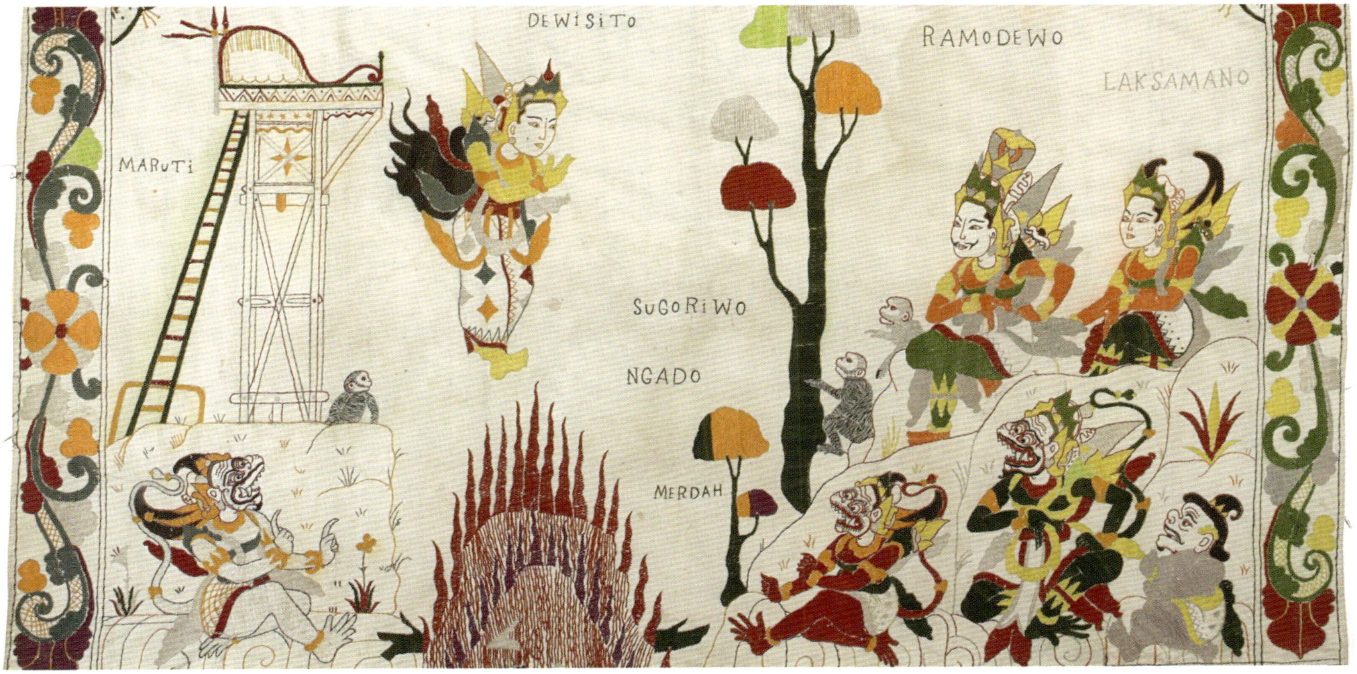

PLATE 127 **Negara.** *Tabing,* 91 x 127. *Ramayana.* Sita undergoes a trial by fire to prove her fidelity to Ramo Dewo (Rama) when she was a captive of Rawana. Witnessing are Laksamano (Lakesmana), Maruti (Hanuman), Ngado (Anggada), the clown Merdah, and three monkeys. The high structure reached by a long ladder has at its top a wooden throne from which Sita jumps into the fire but is not harmed. The gods have seen to it that Sita is vindicated.

FOOTNOTES

1. Robert P. Goldman, translator, ***The Ramayana of Valmiki,*** vol. I, 3.
2. Barbara Stoler Miller, "The Universe of Rama, Valmiki's Epic Poem," in Vidya Dehejia, editor, ***The Legend of Rama,*** 14.
3. Goldman, ***The Ramayana of Valmiki,*** vol. I, 121–122.
4. The standard translation in India is by Hari Prasad Shastri, ***The Ramayana of Valmiki,*** 3 vols. The most recent but not yet complete translation in the United States is by Goldman, ***The Ramayana of Valmiki,*** 5 vols.. Many popular short versions have been published; examples are Aubrey Menen, ***Rama Retold,*** and William Buck, ***Ramayana***. There are several heavily illustrated editions, such as Ranchor Prime, ***Ramayana, A Tale of Gods and Demons,*** and ***The Illustrated Ramayana***. There is a marvelously illustrated edition for children by David Weitzman, ***Rama and Sita***.
5. C. Hookyaas, ***The Old-Javanese Ramayana Kakawin,*** 6.
6. I am relying here in part not only on the main translations noted above but also on the Dutch scholar and Javanist, P. J. Zoetmulder, in his ***Kalangwan: A Survey of Old Javanese Literature,*** particularly 217–220.
7. Another version has Laksmana drawing a circle arount Sita and demanding she stay in it when he goes to help Rama. Rawana disguised as a beggar appears and extends his hand asking for alms. The kind Sita reaches out; Rawana grabs her hand, pulls her out of the circle and carries her off.
8. My source for this version is Kathy Foley, "Cupa Manik Astagina", in Mimi Herbert, ***Voices of the Puppetmasters: The Wayang Golek Theater of Indonesia,*** 220–225.
9. In the Javanese and Balinese modern performance version, Kumbakarna is sometimes burned to death.

Chapter 7

Hanuman: The Indomitable White Monkey

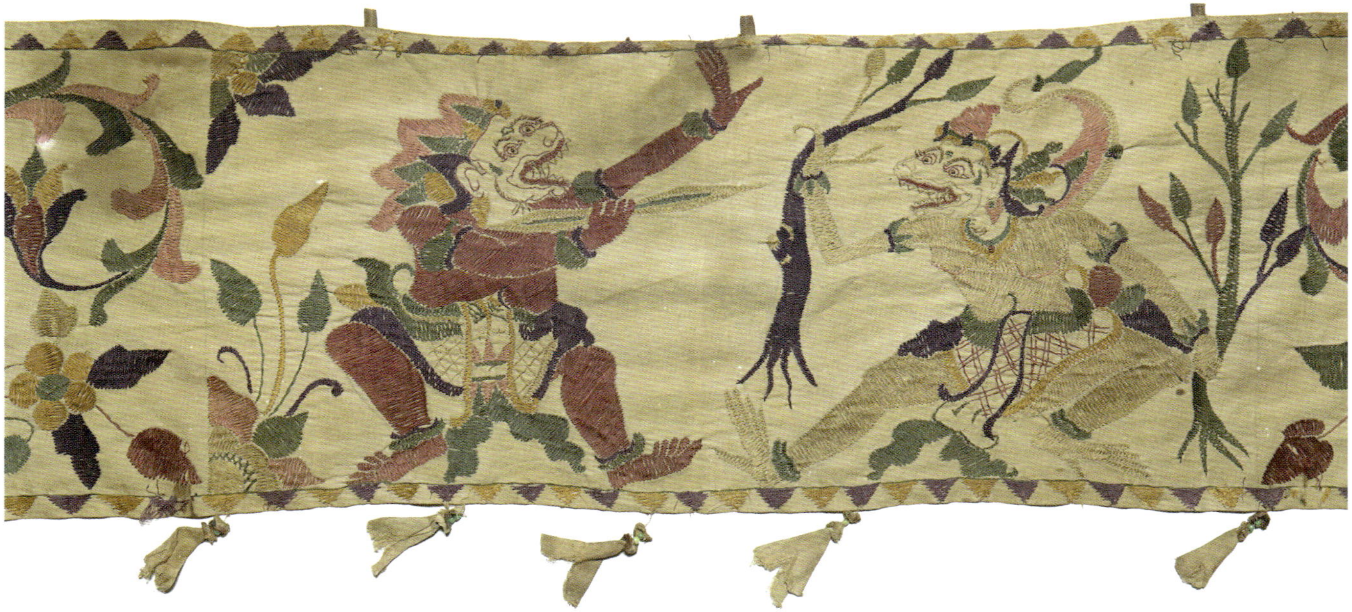

If adulation, longevity, and continuing popularity are any measures of greatness of mythological figures in South and Southeast Asia, then Hanuman surely should be placed first. He is the common people's adored folk hero whose images are placed everywhere. In Bali he may be found on stone temple walls, in paintings on canvas and paper,[1] in woven textiles, as a bronze or stone statue, on household wooden panels, as children's toys, and as tourist carvings. He is a major character in Balinese masked dance/dramas and shadow puppet plays. His face may appear on a store logo, on good-luck charms, on shopping bags, on a restaurant menu, on jewelry, as a tattoo and, of course, on the embroideries featured here. In fact, Hanuman is so popular and so prominent in these embroideries that I thought it fitting he should have his own small chapter.

Hanuman is the Great White Monkey Warrior, a son of the awesome god Siwa and adopted son of Bayu, God of the Wind. He uses his extraordinarily long tail as a powerful weapon; it enables him to fly at will about the heavens and escape from all enemy pursuers. He can jump over mountains in a single bound, hurl boulders the size of a house, and effortlessly pull up the largest trees.

PLATE 128 **Negara.** *Ider-ider,* detail, 27 x 217. *Ramayana.* Hanuman uses an uprooted tree as a weapon against a warrior.

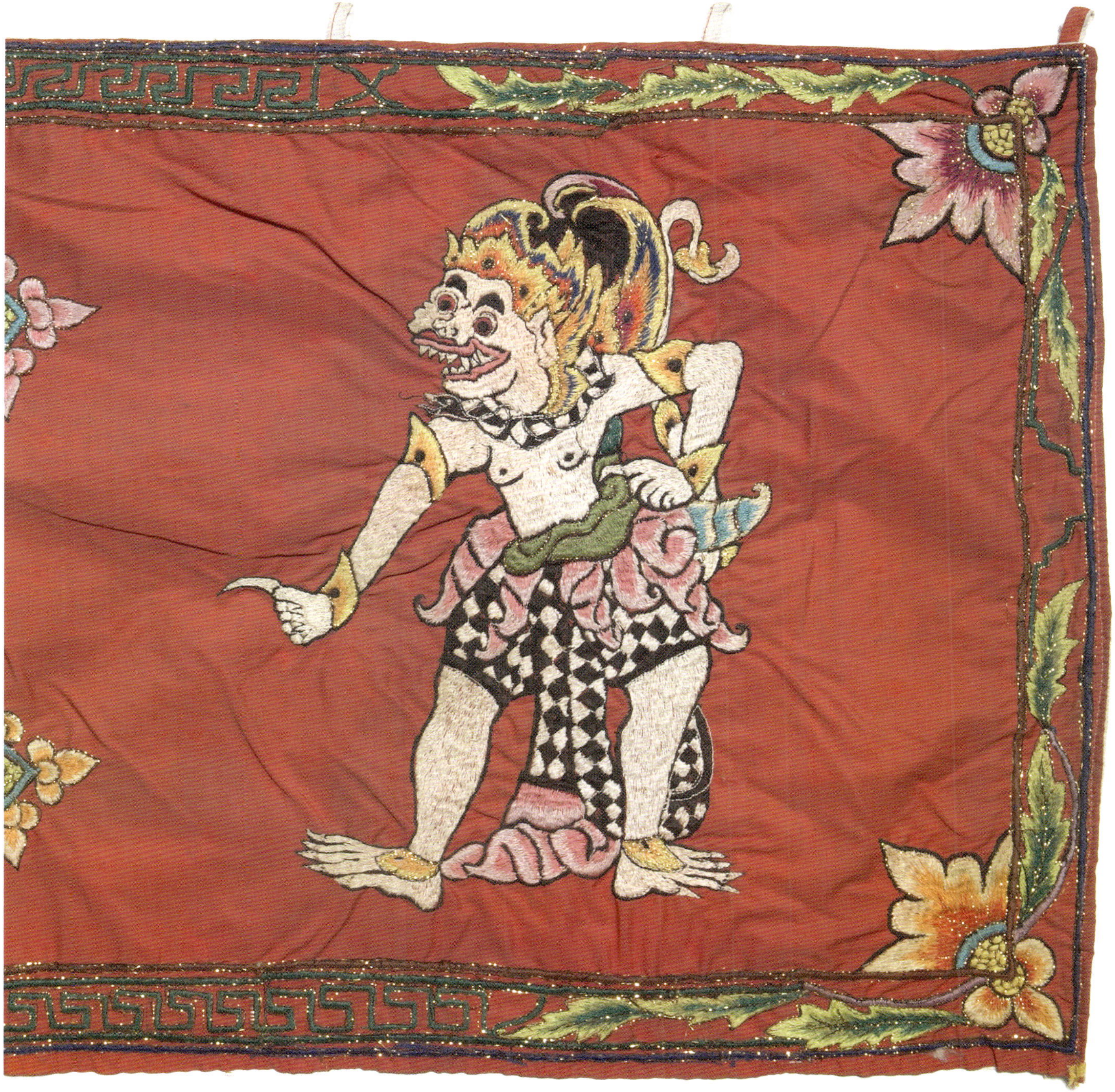

PLATE 129 **Buleleng.** *Ider-ider*, detail, 40 x 375. Silk threads and gimp on red satin cloth. Hanuman, the Great White Monkey hero of the *Ramayana* in full dress and adornment.

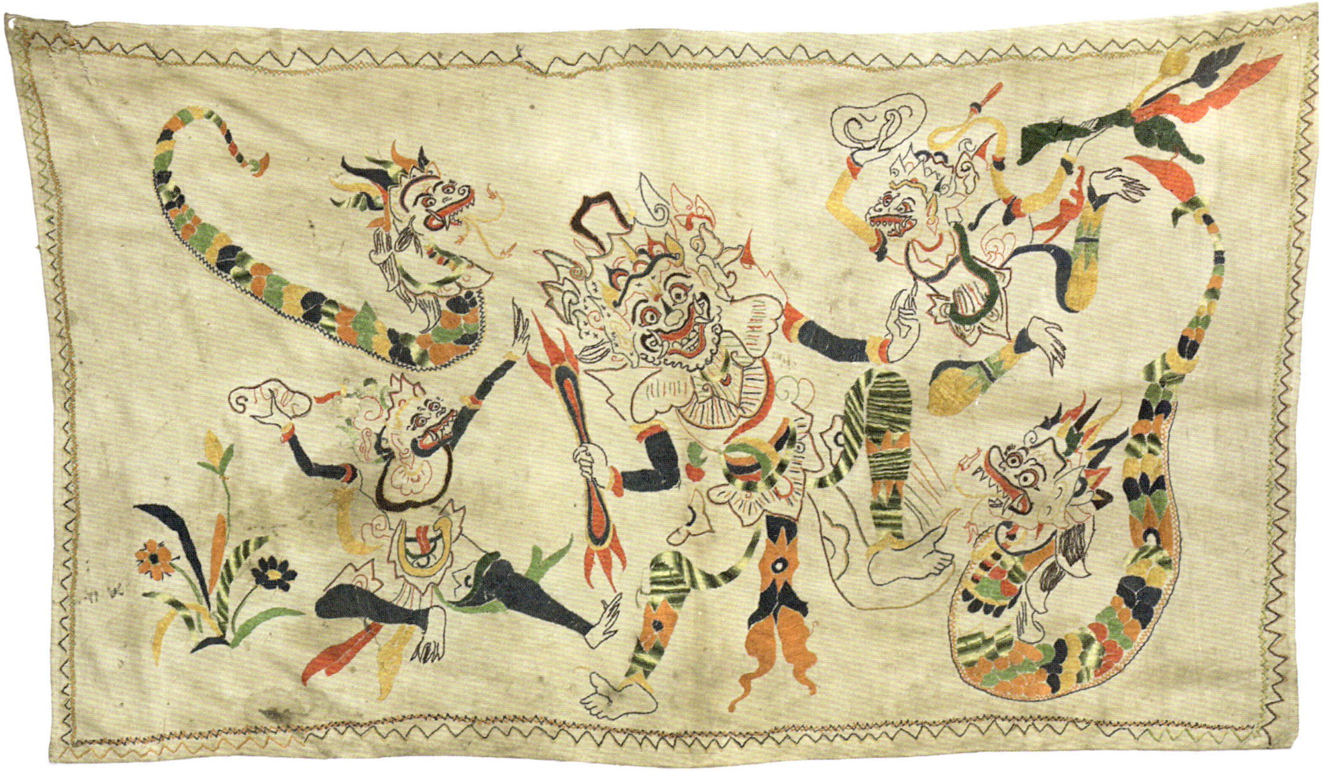

PLATE 130 **Negara.** *Tabing*, 98 x 128. *Ramayana*. Hanuman (upper right) hurls a rock and his tail throws a large bush, all aimed at the giant Kumbakarna. Another monkey (Anila) also throws a rock. Also present are two *nagas* depicted in uncommon, asymmetrical positions.

He cannot be hurt or killed; he is invincible in all his endeavors. Hanuman is at once a grammarian, a healer, a warrior, a spy, and a servant.

He is extremely clever and full of artful tricks. For example, in one ***Ramayana*** episode Hanuman confronts Surasa, the evil mother of the ***nagas***, who tries to swallow him. To prevent this, he makes his body larger and larger, but she stretches her mouth until it is a hundred leagues wide. Hanuman quickly changes his tactics and shrinks himself to the size of a thumb, whereby he escapes through her ear.[2]

His loyalty to Rama is absolute and he is obedient to the commands of his army general, Sugriwa. He is quick to anger but fair in his actions. His nature is that of a super animal but he clearly has significant human qualities. His hero status may appear exaggerated at times, but tradition has it that he has no character flaws. In Bali he became the folk hero of heroes, part animal and part human, and this image endures. His fame derives mostly from his amazing exploits in the ***Ramayana*** but he also appears, albeit as a lesser figure, in the ***Mahabharata***.

His extraordinary popularity in Bali and many other parts of Asia is difficult to fully explain. It may be that being a monkey with superhuman traits sets him apart and makes him more admired by people who also marvel at his successful exploits. Also, in the ***Ramayana*** he is the leader among other monkeys with similar human traits, such as Anggada, Anila, and Predjangga. In addition, monkeys have a semi-sacred status in India and many Southeast Asian countries. They are revered and protected in all Hindu and Buddhist countries, especially when they live on or near sacred sites.

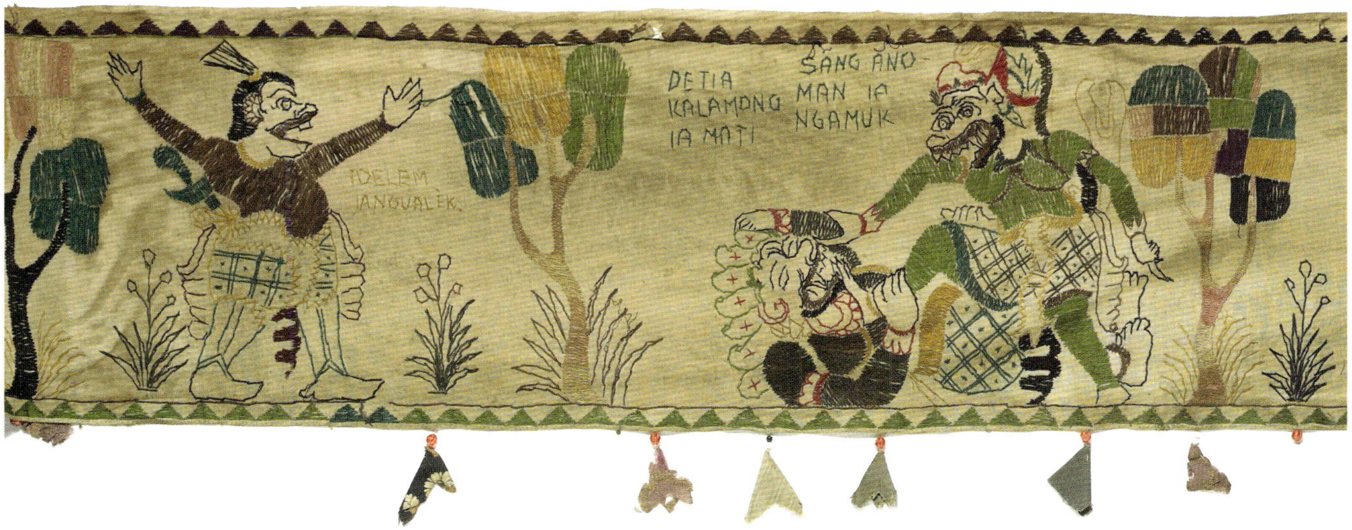

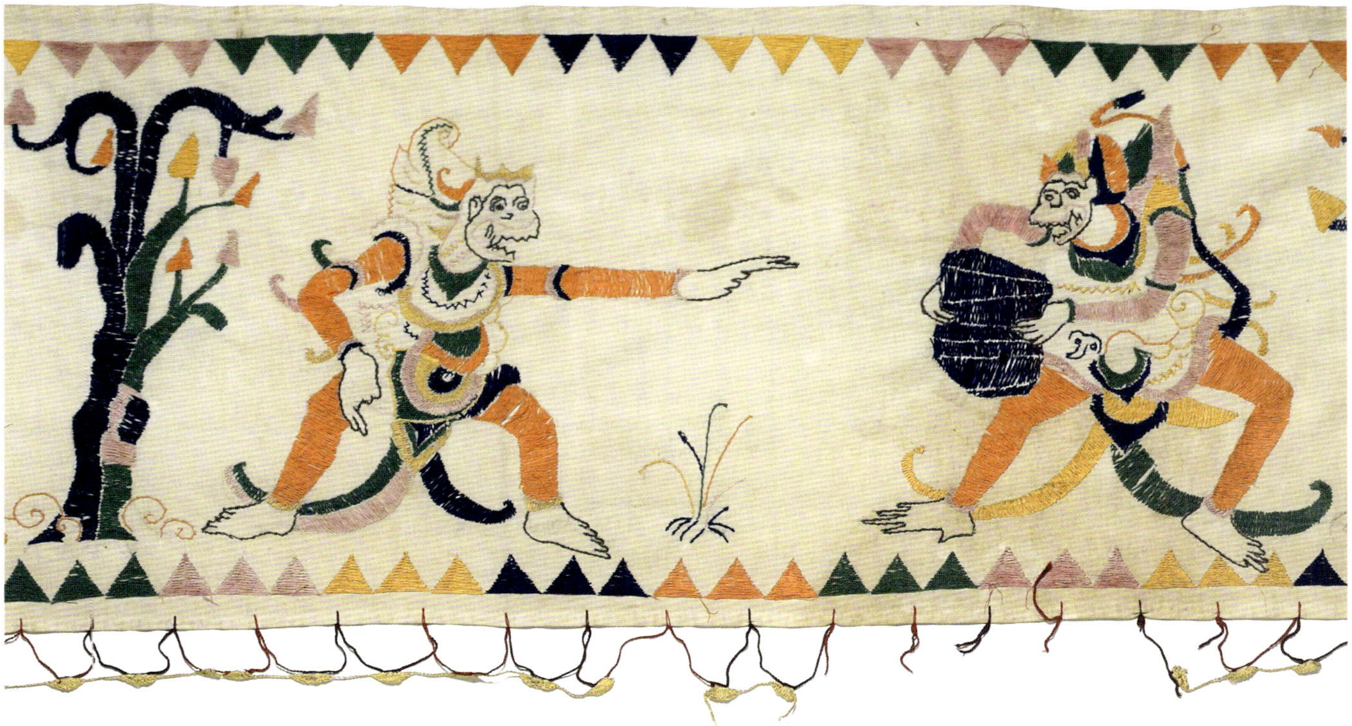

PLATE 131 Negara. *Ider-ider*, detail, 28 x 183. *Ramayana.* Sang Ano-Man (Hanuman) kills an enemy while the clown Delem rejoices at the outcome.

PLATE 132 Negara. *Ider-ider*, detail, 35 x 442. *Ramayana.* Hanuman carries a large boulder to use as a weapon.

The fact that monkeys in general are highly regarded further bolsters Hanuman's prestige and popularity. He appears often in the Balinese embroideries, as do other mythical monkey soldiers. The general of Rama's army, Sugriwa, is a larger-than-life monkey, as was his vanquished brother Subali. Ordinary monkeys are commonly depicted, particularly in battle scenes; they also appear as observers or witnesses, or as mere decorations. ***Ider-ider*** cloths from Negara are full of monkeys; in many scenes they often outnumber clowns and warriors.

HANUMAN'S EXPLOITS

Hanuman is shown often, mostly as a fighter or a messenger. Typical examples are in **PLATE 58** (page 37), in which he is killing a giant ***raksasa***, and in **PLATE 132** (page 93), in which he's carrying a large boulder as a weapon. In **PLATE 130** (page 92) he is throwing a rock with one hand while his tail is grasping an uprooted bush. In these embroidery depictions, Hanuman seems to never tire of using rocks and trees as weapons (see **PLATE 128**, page 90).

In what may be Hanuman's most famous and oft-depicted scene, he is a messenger, using Rama's ring to identify himself as Sita's rescuer. In **PLATE 118** (page 82), Sita raises her sword against him because she is not yet sure that Hanuman has been sent by Rama. When he shows her a ring that she recognizes as Rama's, she is reassured (see **PLATE 115**, page 80).

The clearest and most elegant image I have of him is shown in **PLATE 129** (see page 91). Here he is in all his finery: a black-and-white checkered sarong, a crown-like headdress, golden cuffs on his arms and ankles—all set against white fur covering his body. His pose is typical Hanuman: feet splayed, his left arm bent at the elbow and his right arm gesturing outward. His non-monkey feet have long toenails; a single talon sticks out from each hand.

For me, Hanuman symbolizes the close animal/ human connection and the fact that simians may be as great a source of humanity as *Homo sapiens*. Hanuman seems irresistible. I can only be impressed at the glowing description of him in various traditional narratives.

He is fortunate, destructive as a thunderbolt, swift as an eagle, and excelling in wisdom.... He is a hero of boundless energy, equal in size to elephants or mountains; and incarnate. In haughtiness and might he is equal to the tiger and the lion.... He is skilled in every kind of weapon, can remove the largest mountains, pierce the stoutest trees, cause rivers to overflow, seize clouds, and cause birds to fall to the ground.[3]

He is the ideal perfect servant, the servant who finds full realization of manhood, of faithfulness, of obedience—the subordinate whose glory is in his own inferiority.[4]

"Hanuman's ultimate reward is the boon of immortality given to him by the god Indra."[5] From time to time, I dream of him hopping about the universe, searching for a new master, and in this dream I fantasize meeting him some day—but then someone reminds me that I am mortal and he is not. However...

FOOTNOTES

1. For depictions of Hanuman in Balinese classical paintings, see Forge, ***Balinese Traditional Paintings***, cover and **PLATES 17–20**. For a painting of Hanuman in the so-called Batuan style, see Höhn, ***The Art of Bali***, 40. To compare with traditional Indian representations of Hanuman, see Aryan, ***Hanuman in Art and Mythology***, **PLATES 1, 8, AND 12**. For very different and almost modernistic renditions, see Balraj Khanna, ***Kalighat***, **PLATES 14 AND 15**.
2. John Dowson, ***A Classical Dictionary of Hindu Mythology***, 310.
3. Ibid., 116.
4. P. Thomas, ***Epics, Myths, and Legends of India***.
5. K. C. Aryan and Subhashini Aryan, ***Hanuman in Art and Mythology***, 19.

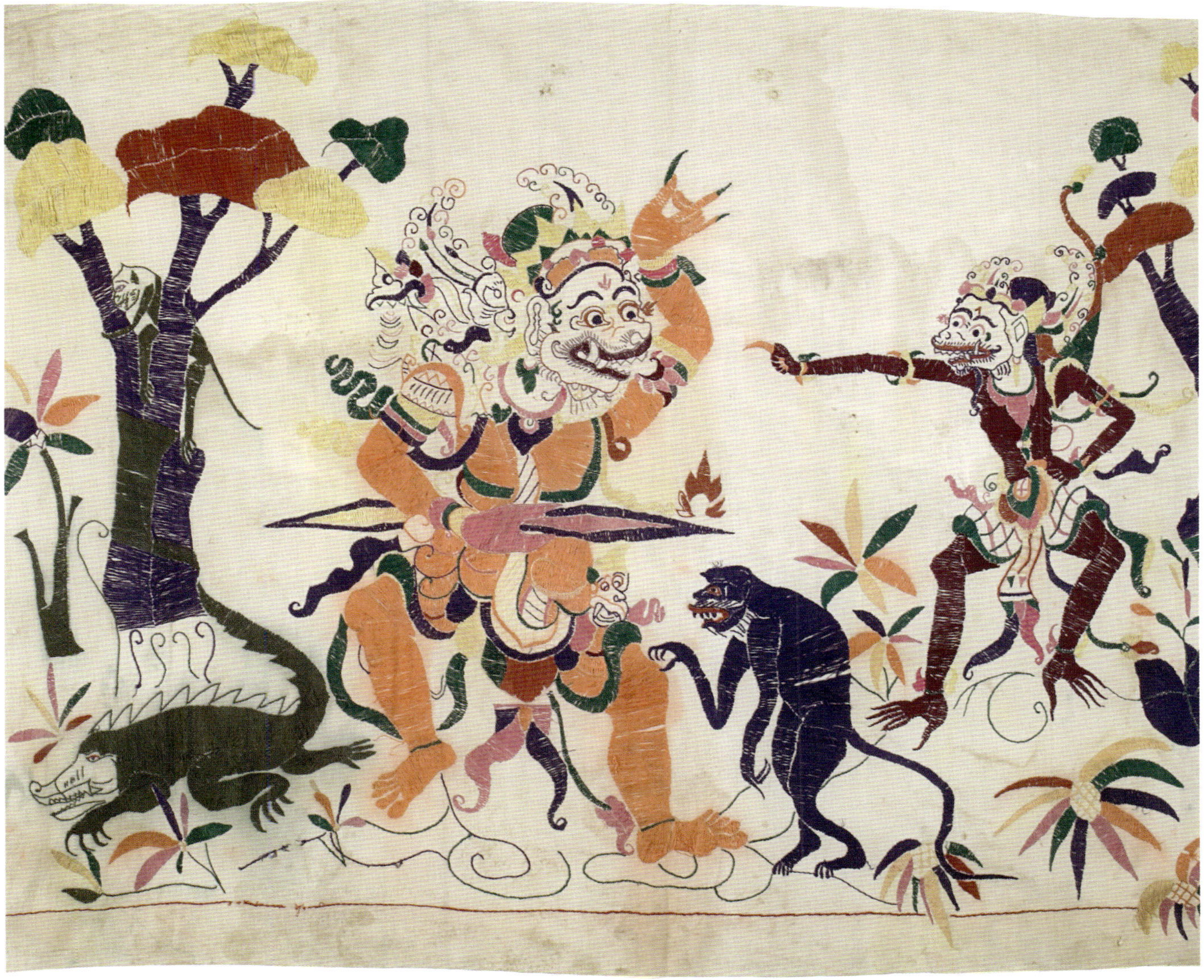

PLATE 133 **Negara.** *Tabing*, 90 x 124. *Ramayana.* The giant Kumbakarna, carries a double-pointed spear tipped with a flame. He is challenged by a red monkey soldier from Rama's army (most likely Anggada), and a purple monkey. A crocodile lurks, undisturbed, in the corner. Notice the tiny monkey-like face peeking out from behind the giant.

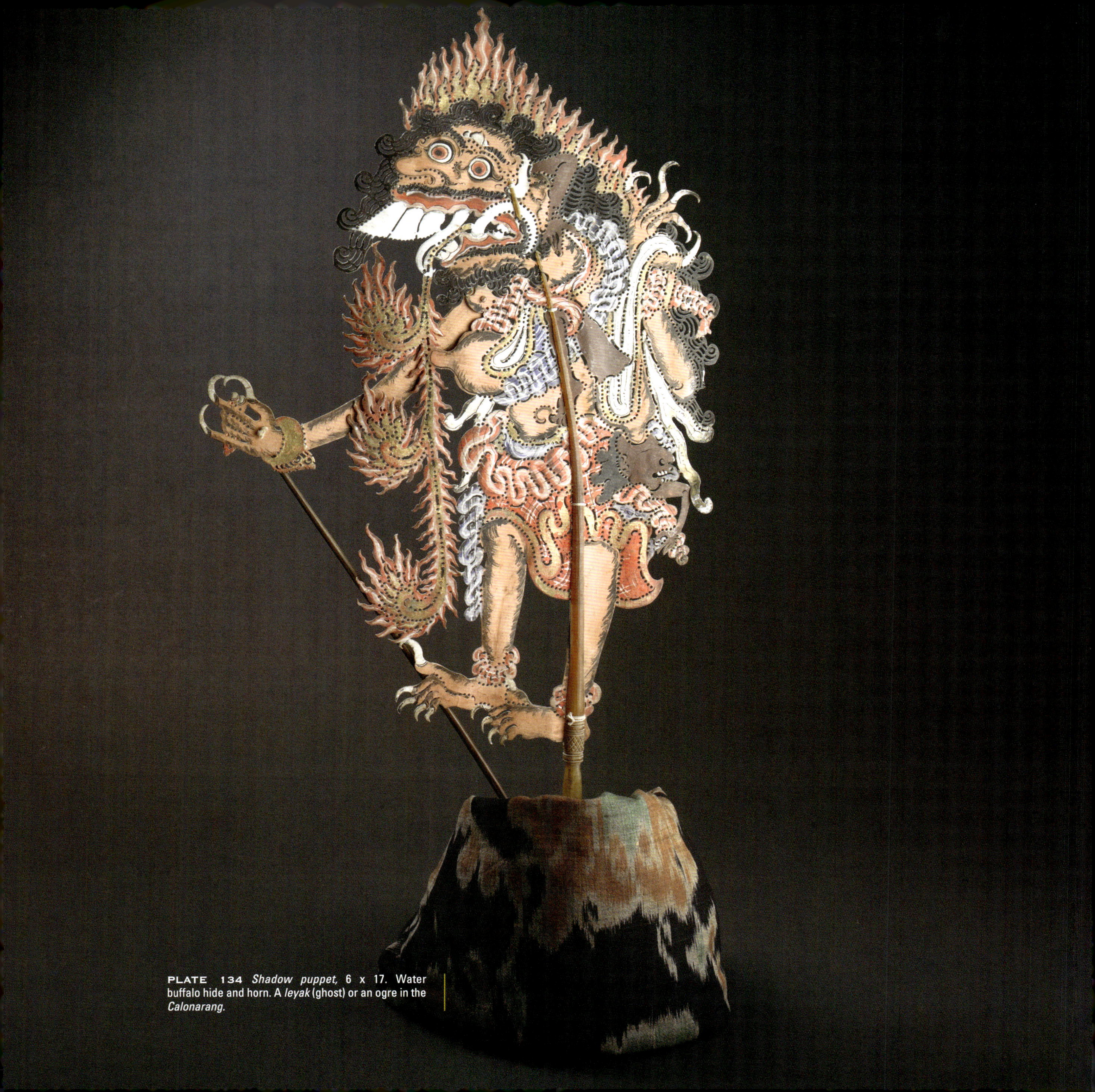

PLATE 134 *Shadow puppet,* 6 x 17. Water buffalo hide and horn. A *leyak* (ghost) or an ogre in the *Calonarang.*

CHAPTER 8

Calonarang: *Witchcraft and Magic*

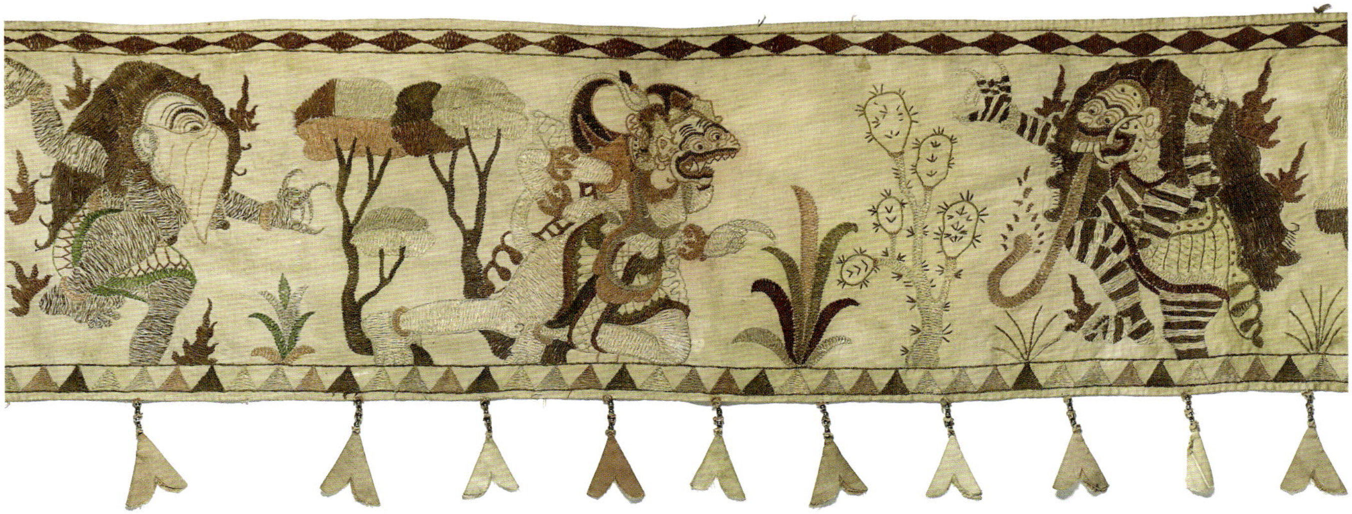

The historical background of this tale begins in Java around A.D. 1019, when a Balinese prince, Erlangga, becomes a king of Java. His mother, Mahendratta, is a Javanese princess who had ruled Bali with her Balinese husband, Dharmodayana. Mahendratta is a practitioner of black magic; she prides herself on being more powerful than anyone, including her husband. She engages in secret rituals of exorcism and uses questionable astrology in her personal life and royal duties. These things vex her husband so much that he succeeds in getting King Erlangga to sanction his divorce and eventually exile the troublesome wife. However, Dharmodayana does not enjoy his new freedom for long; he dies after a short illness. His wife, Mahendratta, becomes known as the Widow of Girah or *Calonarang* (widow). In this narrative tale, she is later referred to as Rangda, the witch, the name used here.

Because traditionally widowhood was considered an unnatural state, Rangda is determined to remarry. The problem is that her high caste requires she marry only a man of equal status—or none at all. Rangda's reputation for mischief is well known in the land and in any case no one wants a witch for a wife. She blames her inability to find a suitable husband on King Erlangga, who is determined not to help her and really wants her to leave his kingdom. This is the last straw, and in her anger and evil resolve she becomes "queen of the leyaks (ogres)... a bloodthirsty, child-eating witch widow and mistress of black magic."[1]

PLATE 135 **Negara.** *Ider-ider*, detail, 26 x 275. *Calonarang*. Rangda, a witch with a protruding tongue, confronts Hanuman, who usually does not appear in this story. A veiled *leyak* (ghost) also threatens him.

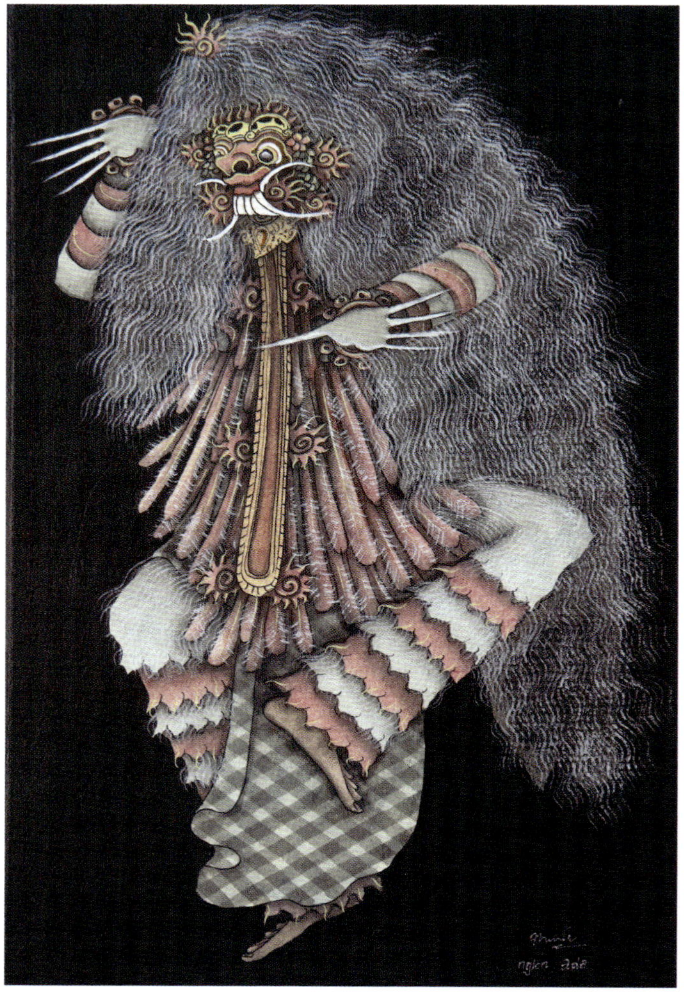

PLATE 136 *Rangda, the Witch / Widow of the Calon-arang,* 13 x 20. Acrylic on paper, artist unidentified, dated July 10, 1999.

TRANSFORMATIONS & EVIL DEEDS

One of Rangda's great powers is that she can transform herself in an instant from an ugly, long-tongued witch into a beautiful woman. However, in these Balinese embroideries she is usually portrayed in her ugly aspect, as seen in embroideries in **PLATE 135** (see page 97) and in paintings in **PLATE 136**. **PLATE 135** shows an embroidered figure that appears to be Rangda, with a veil, giant, claw-like fingers, flaming hair, and menacing eyes. It could also be a ***leyak*** (ghost) with the same scary features. Rangda is so fierce, destructive, and unrepenting that she is sometimes regarded as an incarnation of Durga, who was the wife, in her most dreadful aspect, of the god Siwa. Rangda has been described as "long fanged, long nailed, bulging eyed, hairy creature, with a long flaming tongue, with hairy pendulous breasts and her whole body sometimes crossed by horizontal black and white stripes[2]".

> *The Balinese know her well, they expect the worst of her. Whatever turn of events may take, she will be evil, she will be female... she will destroy, she will behave like fear incarnate. And you cannot kill her. It is not even any use to play out her death... [in a dance/drama] for she is always there, everlasting and indestructible, just Rangda.*[3]

It is obvious she is a formidable and fierce force, quick to act against anyone opposing her needs. She is especially angry at King Erlangga, who issues a royal mandate preventing her remarriage. She is a permanent widow; her only recourse is to find a husband for her equally bewitched daughter, Ratnamenggali (**PLATE 137**). Ratnamenggali can also transform herself from an ugly to a beautiful woman, as shown in **PLATE 141** (page 102). However, no man in Erlangga's realm wants a witch such as Rangda for a mother-in-law. Rangda's frustration explodes into a series of destructive and violent acts. She and her evil minions overturn cemetery markers, dig up graves, throw babies into the air, and generally wreak havoc throughout the kingdom. Clearly, something needs to be done to stop her onslaught.

King Erlangga secures the help of the court sage, Mpu Baradah, who sends his son to marry Ratnamenggali and at the same time learn the witchcraft secrets of her mother. The marriage is, of course, short-lived after the son fulfills his mission and gives his father the magic remedies to counter Rangda's evil actions. All the dead babies are restored to life and all the markers and graves are returned to their original state. Rangda's powers are temporarily gone and her daughter has been unceremoniously jilted. Rangda is exiled and peace is restored to Erlangga's kingdom.

RANGDA & BARONG

The *Calonarang* is reenacted in Bali in the form of a popular dance/drama called the Barong[4]—one of the most common and popular entertainments for tourists and local people. It pits the Barong—a mythical lion, boar, or bear— against Rangda, the witch. The Barong has a large articulated mask for a face and a long brightly costumed body, which is moved by two men who are hidden from view, much like the Chinese New Year dragon. A fight is staged with loud noises and frightening gestures; blows are feigned between Rangda and the Barong but neither is killed. At the end of the contest, Rangda is merely driven away and the Barong prevails. **PLATE 142** (page 103) is a contemporary painting of the Barong and Rangda with a long protruding tongue with many masked figures, ***gamelan*** (musicians), and various foods in a village performance.

The ***Calonarang*** is also performed as part of a Balinese shadow puppet play. Of the forty or so puppets in a ***Calonarang*** set, almost all are either demons, ogres, ghosts, weird spirits, or, of course, witches. One of these shadow figures is shown in **PLATE 134** (page 96).

SUPERNATURAL CREATURES

The general Balinese term for most supernatural spirits is ***leyak*** (ghost); there are many varieties. Ogres and demons are usually referred to as ***raksasas***, as described in chapter 2. Ceremonies are held and rituals performed in Bali throughout the year to placate spirits, to honor ancestors, and thus to acknowledge the power of both the ***leyaks*** and the ***raksasas***.

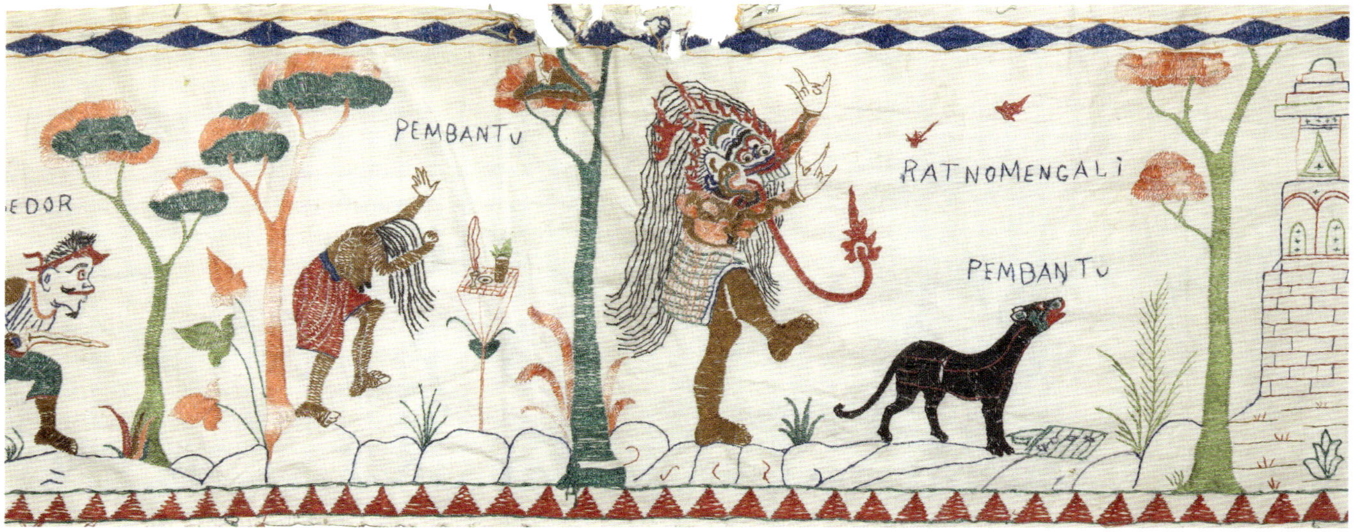

PLATE 137 caption: **Negara.** *Ider-ider,* detail, 27 x 268. *Calonarang.* Ratnomengali (Ratnamenggali), daughter of the witch Rangda, who can also transform herself from ugly to beautiful. The *pembantu,* including the dog, are her assistants in mischief.

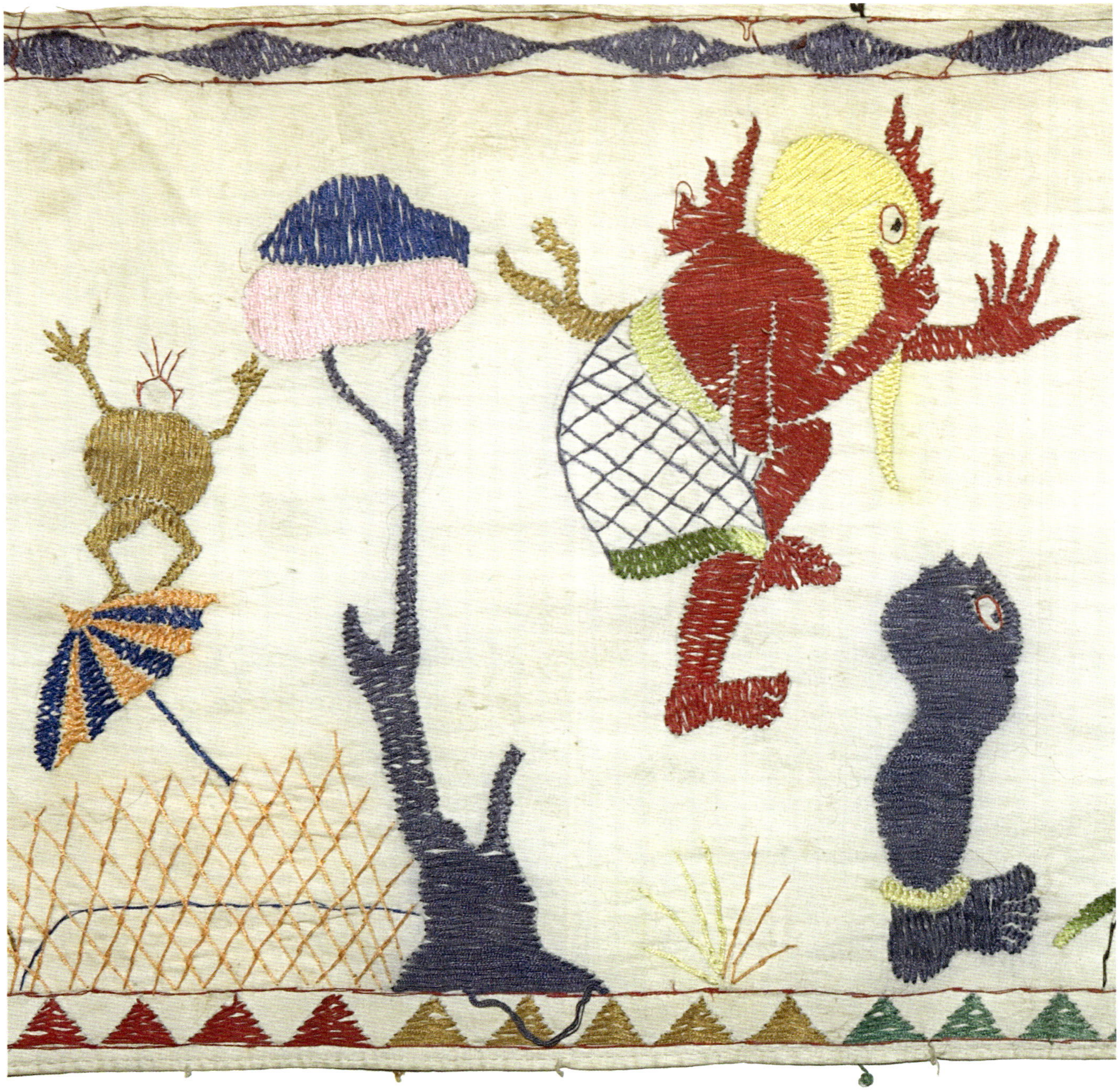

PLATE 138 **Negara.** *Ider-ider*, detail, 27 x 400. A group of weird creatures, probably from the *Calonarang*.

PLATE 139 **Negara.** *Ider-ider*, detail, 27 x 284. A temple scene showing a Balinese family, sacred structures, and banners. A ritual is performed by three men, one with a *keris* and one with an offering.

PLATE 140 **Negara.** *Ider-ider*, detail, 27 x 184. Five men ritually stab themselves *(ngurek)* with *keris* during a traditional ceremony.

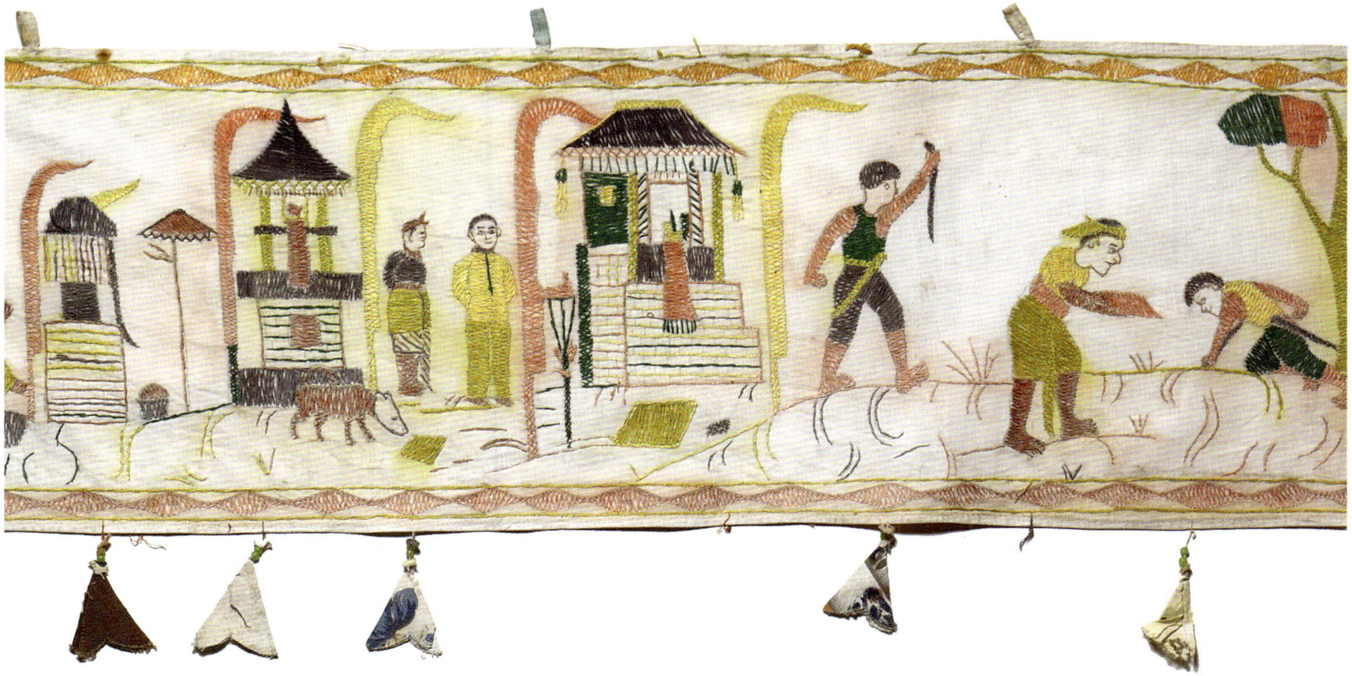

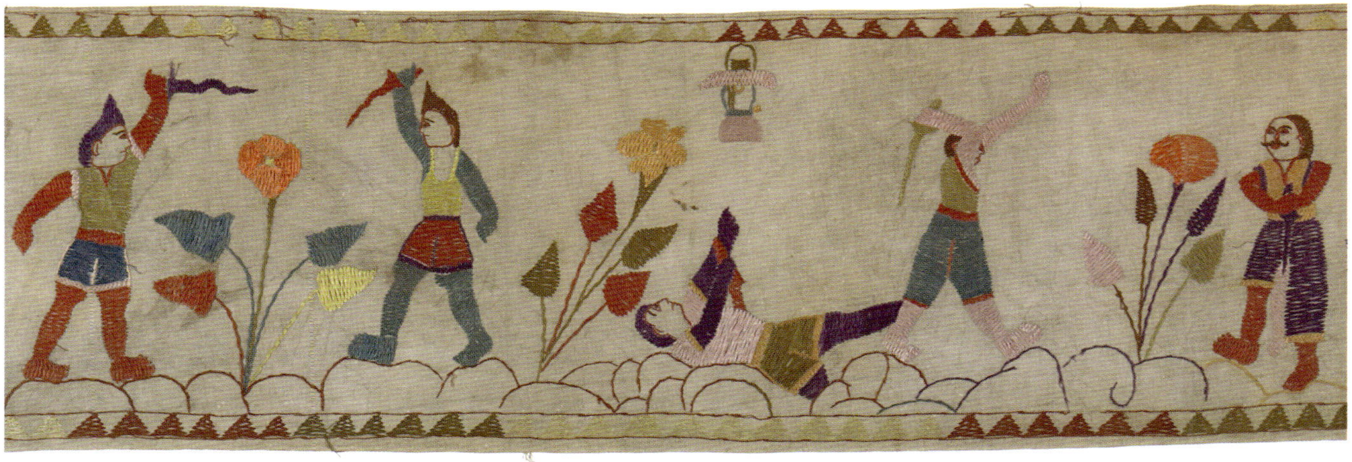

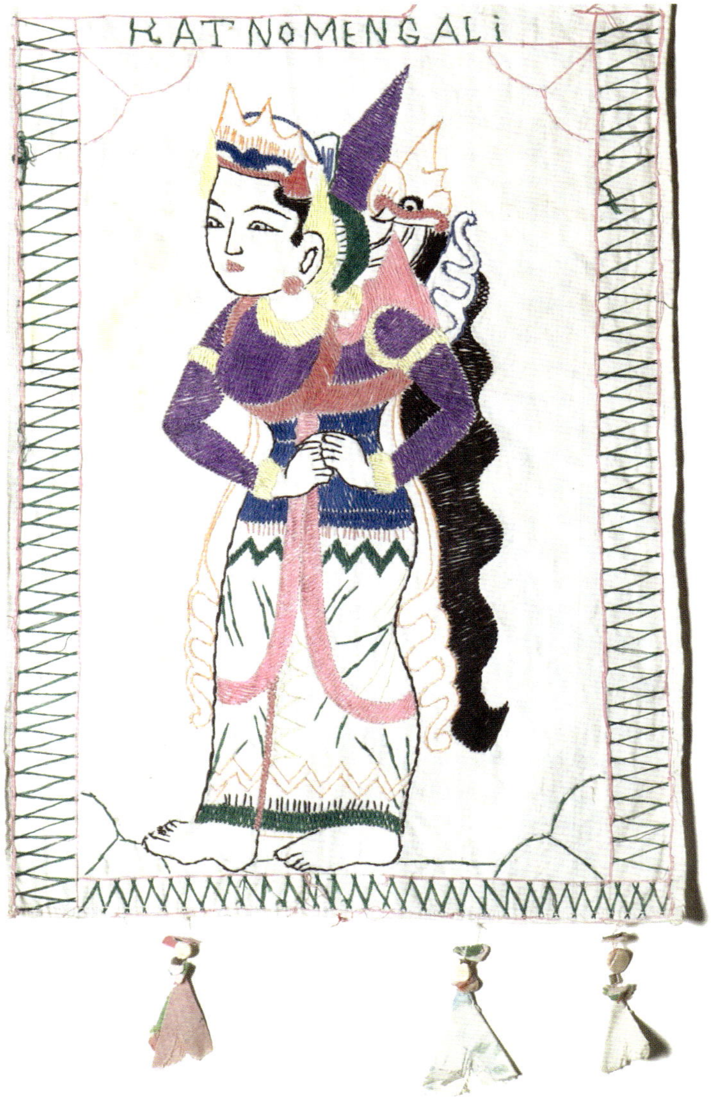

PLATE 141 Negara. *Lamak,* 11 x 18. *Calonarang.* Ratnomengali (Ratnamenggali) shown in her transformed beautiful aspect. She is the daughter of the witch Rangda.

PLATE 138 (page 100) is a good example of many weird characters found in these embroideries, including a foot with an eye, an upside-down red ***raksasa***, and an odd tiny, bloated figure standing on an umbrella. All of these figures and others like them are part of the Balinese universe, in which the dead and the living, the visible and the invisible, the natural and the supernatural are all a part of life.

ASTROLOGY & SORCERY

Astrology, talismans, and mediating offerings are common elements in Balinese culture. There are some five hundred words in the Balinese language that refer to witches, ghosts, sorcerers, astrological symbols, and magic potions.[5] Of all the world's cultures that survive from ancient times, Bali's has what is probably one of the most extensive repertoires of fearful creatures, magic objects, and protective sayings. Though fear and foreboding are common in the Balinese psyche, they are dealt with openly in their entertainments, rituals, art, and crafts; these embroideries are an excellent example. Such protective activities do not eliminate life's uncertainties, but they do render them more understandable and perhaps more controllable in a culture that strives to maintain and promote harmony among people, nature, deities, and demons.

FOOTNOTES

1. Miguel Covarrubias, ***Island of Bali***, 326. For a painting of ***Calonarang*** setting fire to a tree in front of a priest, see Höhn, ***The Art of Bali***, 94.
2. Jane Belo, editor, ***Traditional Balinese Culture***, 19. For a painting of ***Calonarang*** with her fearful and grotesque companions in a cemetery, see Höhn, ***The Art of Bali***, 80.
3. Belo, ***Traditional Balinese Culture***.
4. For a description of the Barong performance, see Jane Belo, ***Bali: Rangda and Barong***. Rangda and her evil activities are shown in two paintings reproduced in Hildred Geertz, ***Images of Power***, 76 and 78.
5. These are all enumerated and partly described throughout the volume by C. Hooykaas, ***Drawings of Balinese Sorcery***. See also Luh Ketut Suryani and Gordon D. Jensen, ***Trance and Possession in Bali***.

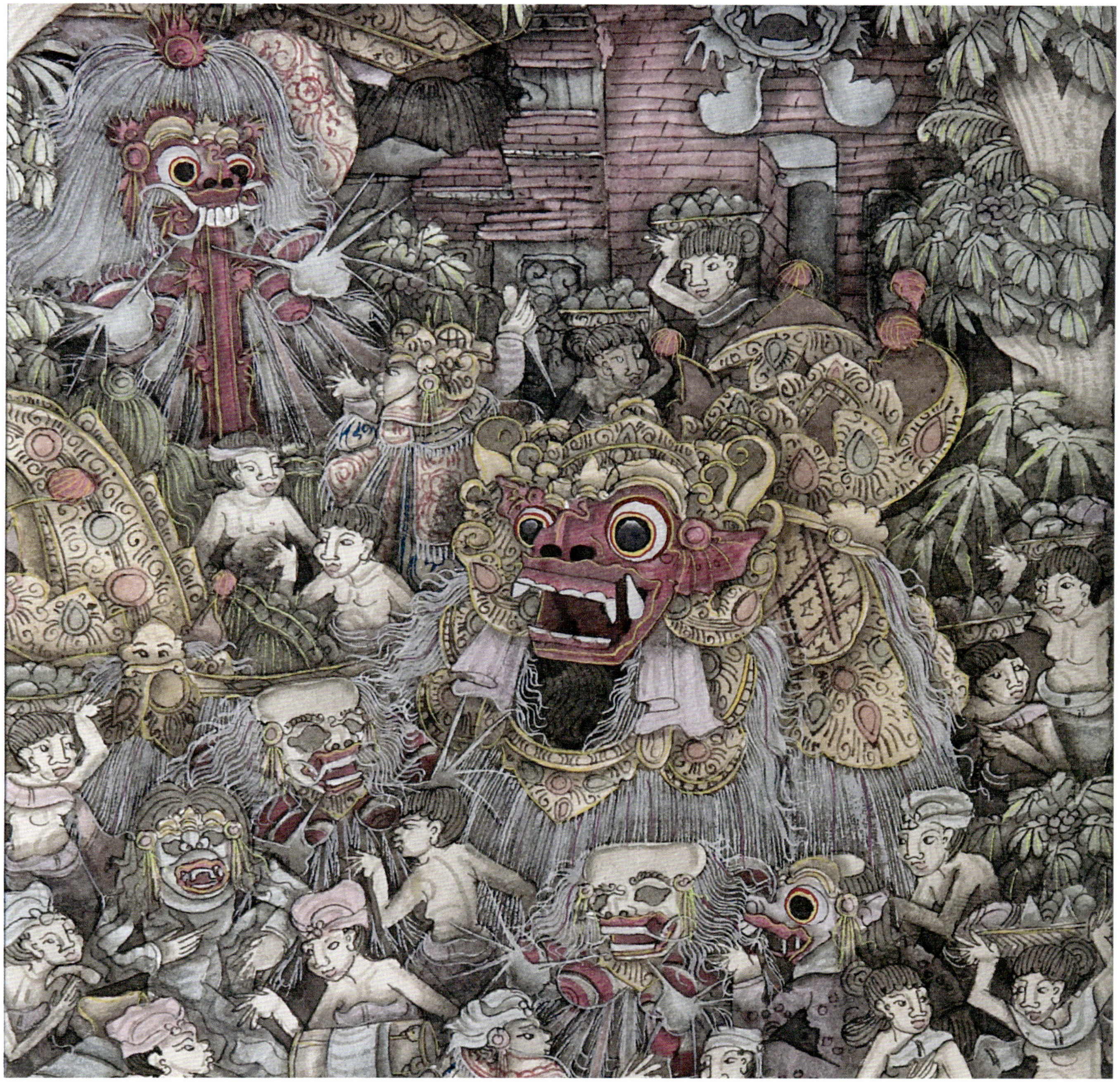

PLATE 142 **Bali**. Rangda the witch (with protruding tongue) and the Barong (with red bear-like mask) in a dance/dramatic performance in a village. Also shown are a *gamelan* orchestra, various other masked ogres, and food sellers. 14 x 23. Acrylic on paper, artist and date unknown.

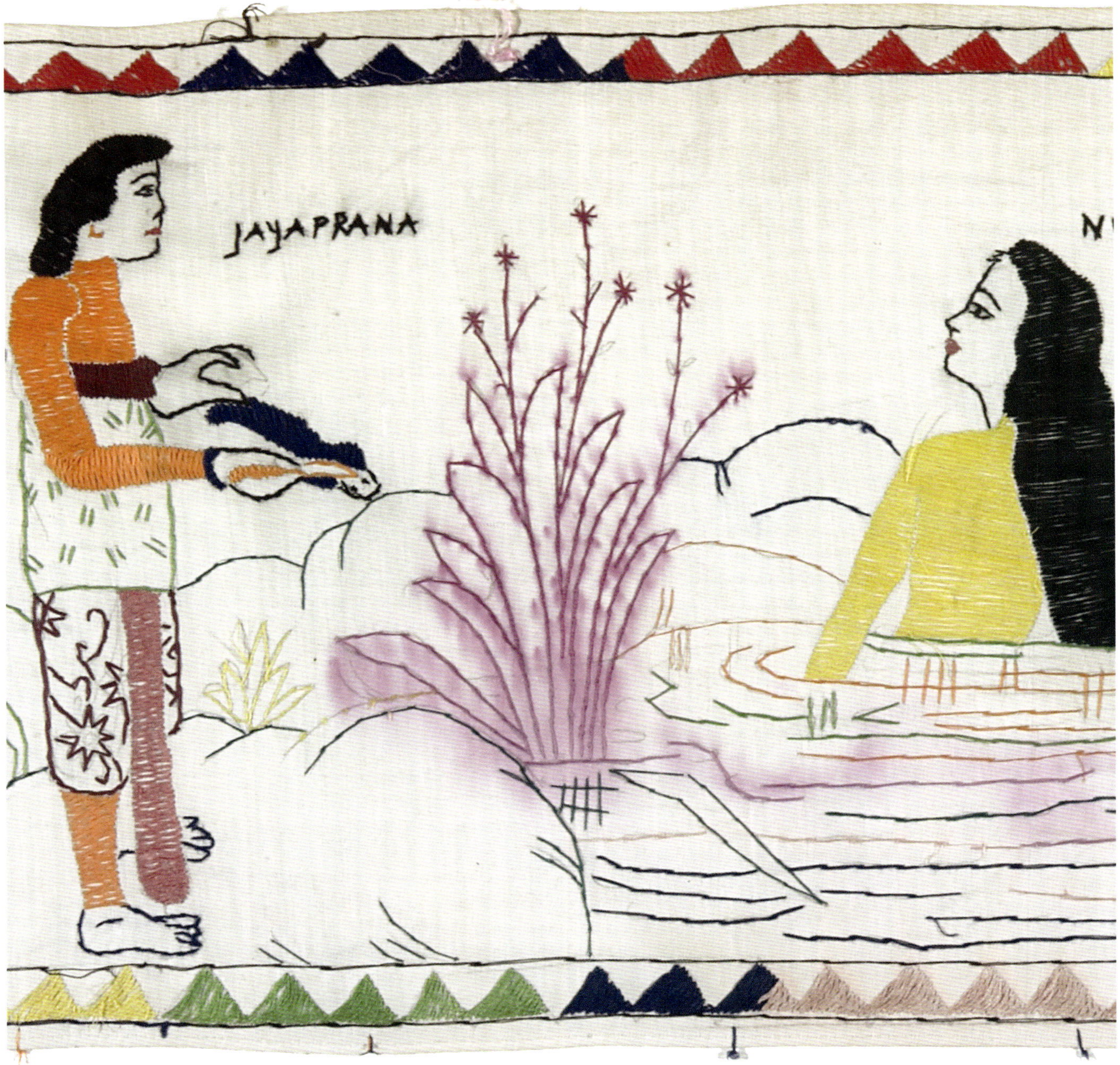

PLATE 143 Negara. *Ider-ider*, detail, 30 x 400. Jaya Prana story. Jaya Prana sees the beautiful Ni Layon Sari bathing and presents her with the gift of a tame squirrel.

Chapter 9

The Tragedy of Jaya Prana

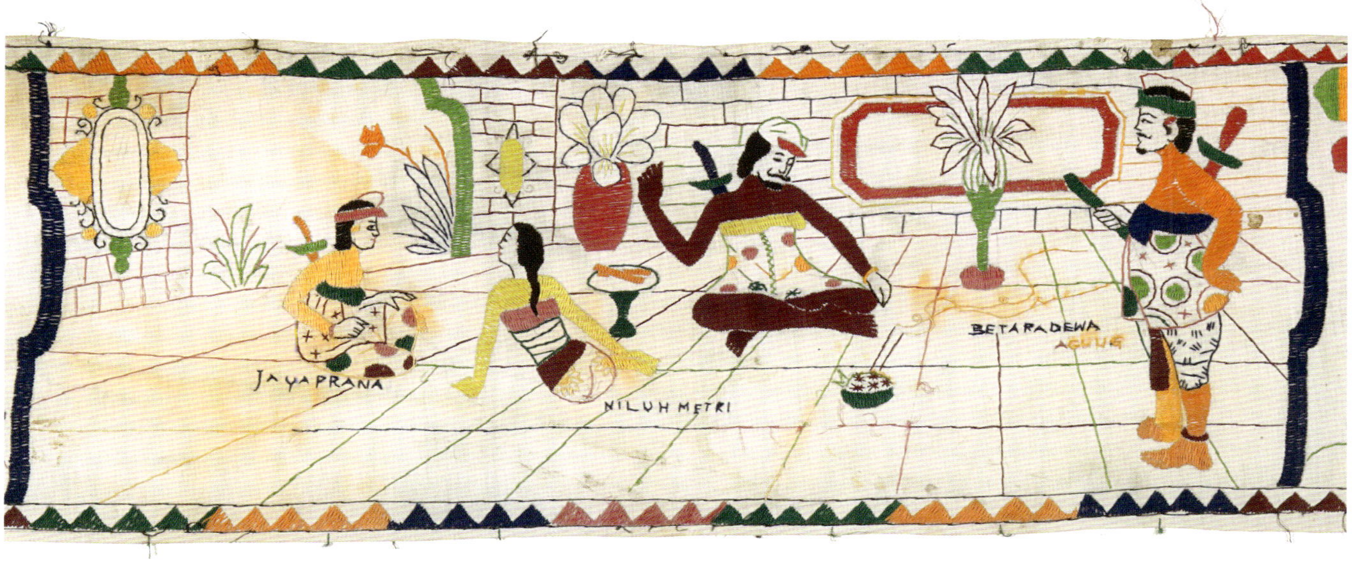

One of the most powerful indigenous Balinese tales is that of Jaya Prana, his marriage to the beautiful Ni Layon Sari, and his betrayal by King Anak Agung Gde Murka.[1] It is partly historical fact and partly legend that has been pieced together from twelve surviving manuscripts written in ***kawi***, the ancient form of Javanese language inherited by the Balinese. The story originated in Buleleng, the northernmost district of Bali, but it is well known throughout the island and has become an important part of Balinese folklore. The tale grew, over a period of many, many years, to incorporate a whole series of real events, traditional ceremonies, strange rituals, and unusual occurrences that are still well known in today's Bali. In fact, the events that occurred long after the story took place are in many ways more intriguing than the tale itself.

The story of what happened to Jaya Prana is recounted in a long poem of two hundred stanzas, which was traditionally sung rather than merely recited. It turns upon the murder of an innocent man, Jaya Prana, and the need for the murderer's family to assume some responsibility for the heinous act. Balinese traditional culture decreed that there must be some atonement by the family of the murderer so that it can be freed from future misfortunes. It is similar to the Bible tale (II, *Samuel* 11:3–27) in which David causes the death of Uriah so that he can marry his wife Bathsheba, with tragic consequences. There are similar tales in many traditional cultures around the world.

PLATE 144 **Negara.** *Ider-ider*, detail, 30 x 400. Jaya Prana story. Jaya Prana discusses arrangements for his marriage to Ni Layon Sari with King Anak Agung, her servant, Ni Luhmetri, and her uncle.

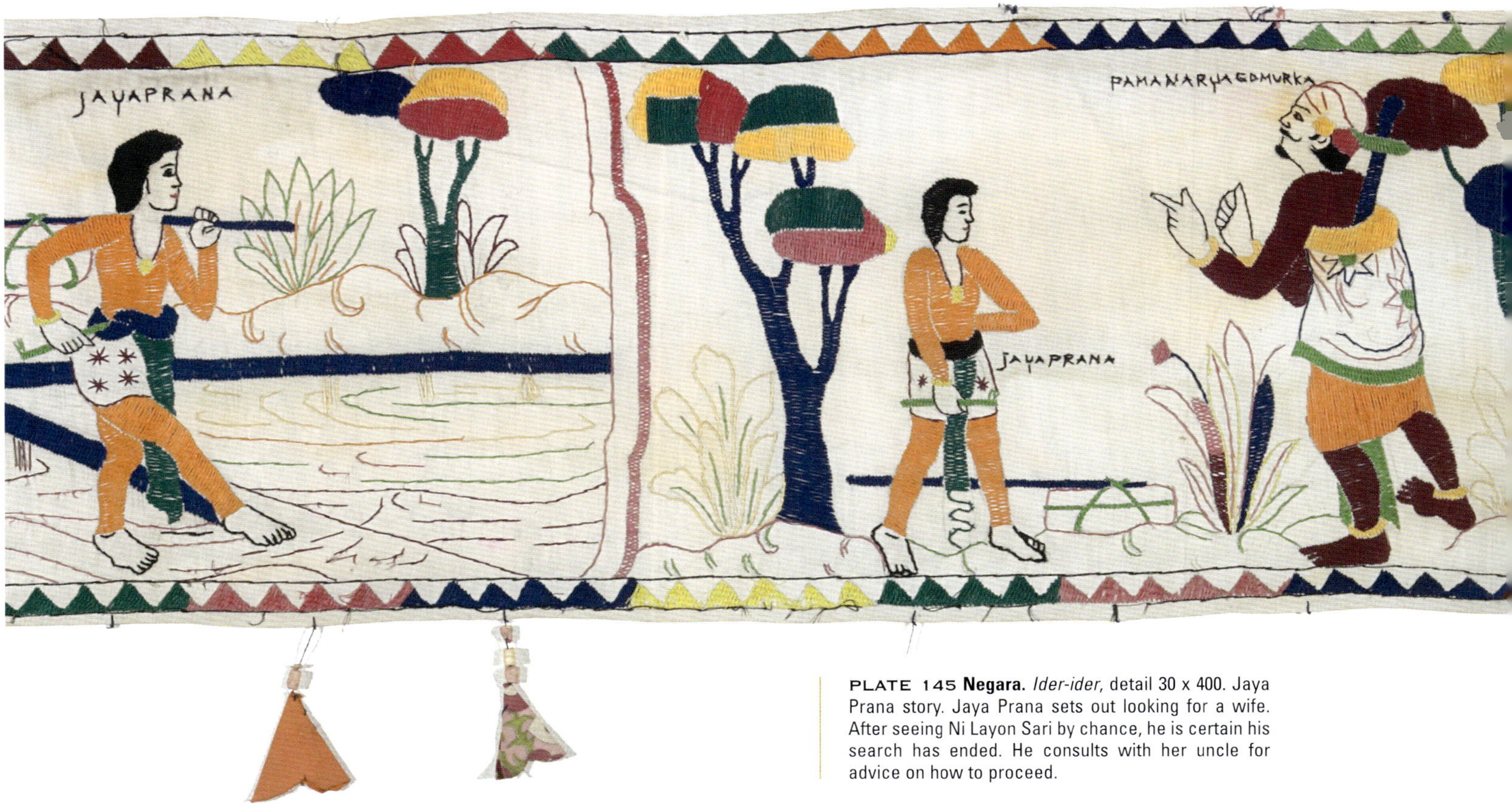

PLATE 145 Negara. *Ider-ider,* detail 30 x 400. Jaya Prana story. Jaya Prana sets out looking for a wife. After seeing Ni Layon Sari by chance, he is certain his search has ended. He consults with her uncle for advice on how to proceed.

ADOPTION OF JAYA PRANA

The poem tells of Jaya Prana, a simple village youth living with his parents. He is the eldest of four brothers; the other three have all died. One day a minister of the king, Paman Sawunggaling, passes by the village, which appears to be empty—except for Jaya Prana, who is sitting alone in a cemetery grieving for his deceased brothers. The minister returns to the palace and relates what he saw to King Anak Agung. The king, saddened by the story, summons Jaya Prana and out of sympathy for this sad youth makes him a member of his household. Jaya Prana's main duty is caring for the king's prize fighting cocks—an important task in traditional Balinese culture. The king becomes very fond of Jaya Prana and treats him like a son, and Jaya Prana comes to revere and respect his benefactor.

As time passes, the king commands Jaya Prana to look for a wife. The king's ministers help him to find a family with a suitable daughter. The embroidery in PLATE 145 shows Jaya Prana with a stick on his shoulder, setting out on his quest for a wife. By chance, he meets Ni Layon Sari. She is described in the narrative as a "peerless nymph" with long, flowing, silky black hair, a serenely beautiful face, and a stately stature. She walks on, but Jaya Prana is determined to see her again. Jaya Prana consults with her uncle, Pamanarya Edmurka (PLATE 145) for advice on how to correctly conduct himself in seeking such a bride. He is told to be patient and respectful. However, as if ordained, Jaya Prana sees Ni Layon Sari bathing in a pool near her village (PLATE 146), with the sun shining on her hair and a demure expression on her face. Jaya Prana is overwhelmed by her beauty and on the spot offers her a gift of what appears to be a tame squirrel.

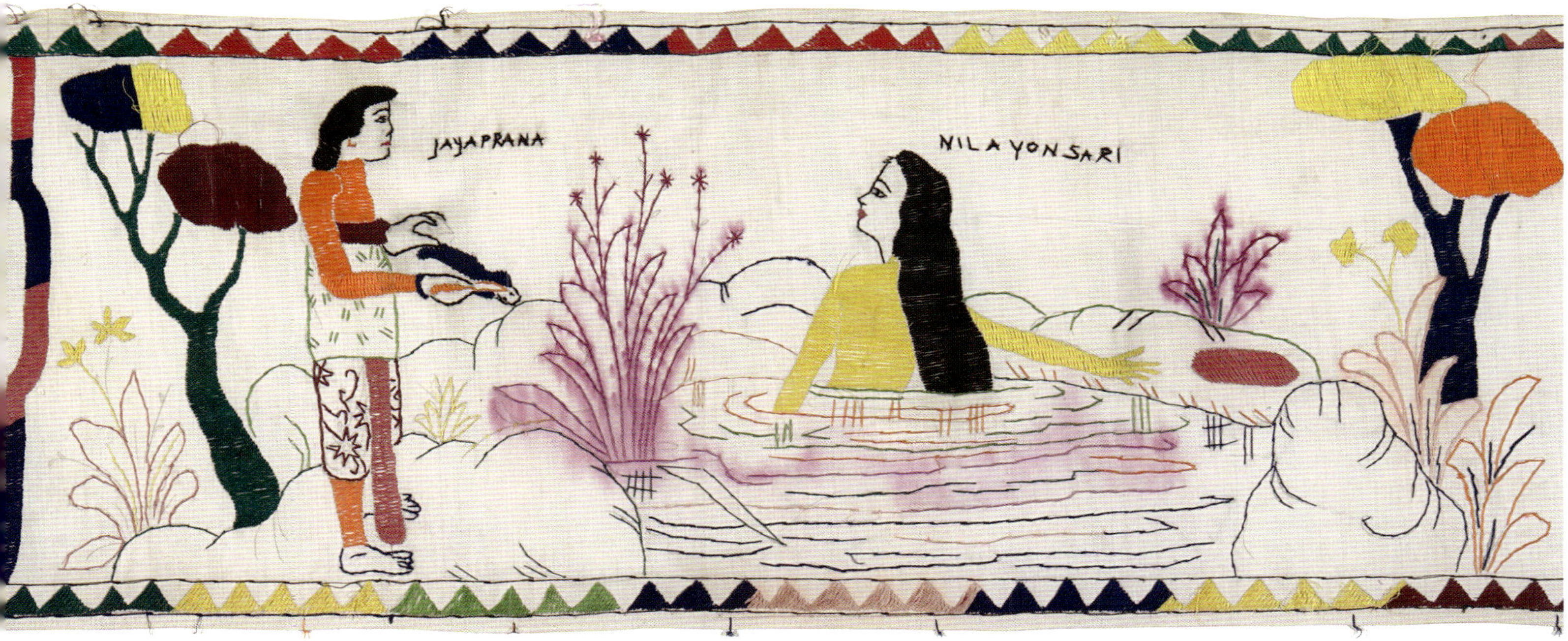

PLATE 146 **Negara.** *Ider-ider*, detail 30 x 400. Jaya Prana story. Jaya Prana sees the beautiful Ni Layon Sari bathing and presents her with the gift of a tame squirrel.

ROYAL NUPTIALS

It is obvious to all that the two appear to be deeply in love with each other. The uncle arranges an audience with King Anak Agung to discuss arrangements for the marriage of Jaya Prana and Ni Layon Sari (PLATE 144). An elaborate traditional ceremony takes place, with all the rituals, offerings, decorations, and costumes that are part of this colorful Balinese rite of passage. The bride and groom are described as the perfect couple and their respective families are elated and proud. The celebrations continue for three festive days, but something ominous is about to occur.

GREED & MURDER

King Anak Agung, seeing Ni Layon Sari dressed beautifully in a colorful silk sarong and adorned with glittering gold jewelry, becomes overwhelmed with a desire to possess her for himself. He plots with his chief minister to have Jaya Prana sent away and later killed. Jaya Prana is summoned to the court and ordered to leave immediately on a mission to investigate piracy and the supposed wreckage of a ship. Jaya Prana and his assistant Gustiarya are about to depart. They are accompanied by the king's minister, Paman Sawunggaling, who will carry out the plot. Jaya Prana is given a betel quid and "seven score" of copper coins as provisions for his journey.

Just before his departure, Ni Layon Sari tells her husband of a dream she had in which everything is swept away in a flood. At this foreboding vision, Jaya Prana somehow senses that his death may be near.

When he arrives at the seacoast destination, Paman Sawunggaling gives him a letter from the king stating that Jaya Prana must die (PLATE 148). Jaya Prana does not

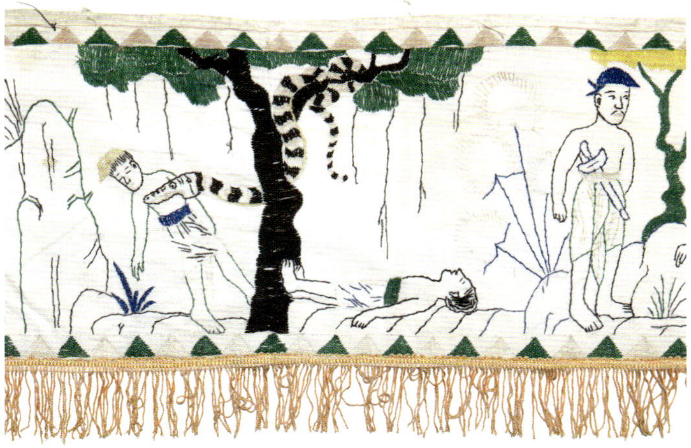

protest and accepts his unjust fate, for his allegiance to the king is so strong that he must accept any royal order. He gives up his own ***keris***[2] and the king's minister uses it to perform the dreadful deed. Jaya Prana's body is hastily buried in an unmarked grave. Immediately a strong wind comes up, creating a fearful howl. A heavy rain falls in torrents and drenches the men in Paman Sawunggaling's retinue. Suddenly, animals begin to attack the party. The scene is depicted in the embroideries in **PLATE 147** and **PLATE 149** (see page 110): a tiger is gnawing on one man, a deadly snake is biting another, while Jaya Prana lies dead on the ground. The gods in the heavens and the animals on earth have attacked, signifying that a terrible event has occurred for which many people will pay dearly. [3]

Ni Layon Sari is told that her husband died accidentally while serving the king, but she does not believe this. Her grief is so strong that she contemplates her own death and nearly succumbs. King Anak Agung summons her to his court and entreats her to live with him. He says, "Are you prepared to care for me?… So may your sorrow be consoled. I pray your favors to bestow upon me now. My jewel! Stay you always here."[4] Ni Layon Sari refuses and draws her ***keris***, threatening to stab herself. The king relents temporarily and she returns to her home. After eleven days have passed, Ni Layon Sari, still deep in sorrow, is about to commit suicide. The manuscript tells us:

How could she e'er forget her grief? Death held no terrors for her now, she had no fear and drew her *keris* ***and struck at her breast with deadly force and then she swooned and lifeless lay, so beautiful, her corpse was a goddess fair.***[5]

Her grieving family, her village, and the king's family are appalled at what has happened and fearful of the consequences. When the king is informed of the suicide, he temporarily goes into seclusion, deeply disturbed, but later he begins to act wildly insane. He runs about the palace flailing in every direction with a ***keris***, attacking servants and animals. He is finally restrained, suffers a heart attack, and dies. The tragic tale ends with these stanzas:

> ***We will not speak of those things now.***
> ***Bearers of streamers then came forth,***
> ***then sparkling gold sedans appeared,***
> ***banners were borne and big sunshades,***
> ***all was ornate in high degree***
> ***that had now come;***
> ***Both mounted then the golden chairs.***
> ***Now played one gong, now another,***
> ***played gamelan,***
> ***nymphs from heaven followed them,***
> ***the loveliest all seven were,***
> ***they went up then to heaven on high***
> ***with no time lost.***
> ***We speak not of their life therein.***[6]

Jaya Prana and Ni Layon Sari are everlastingly reunited in heaven and their formal story closes, but not its extraordinary reverberations.

A legend was born that began to be told over and over again throughout Bali. It became a symbol of loyalty and love, of greed and revenge, and of duty and morality.

PLATE 147 **Negara.** *Ider-ider*, detail, 24 x 172. Jaya Prana story. A snake attacks a member of the group that murdered Jaya Prana. The victim lies dead while the king's minister, who directed the deed, looks away.

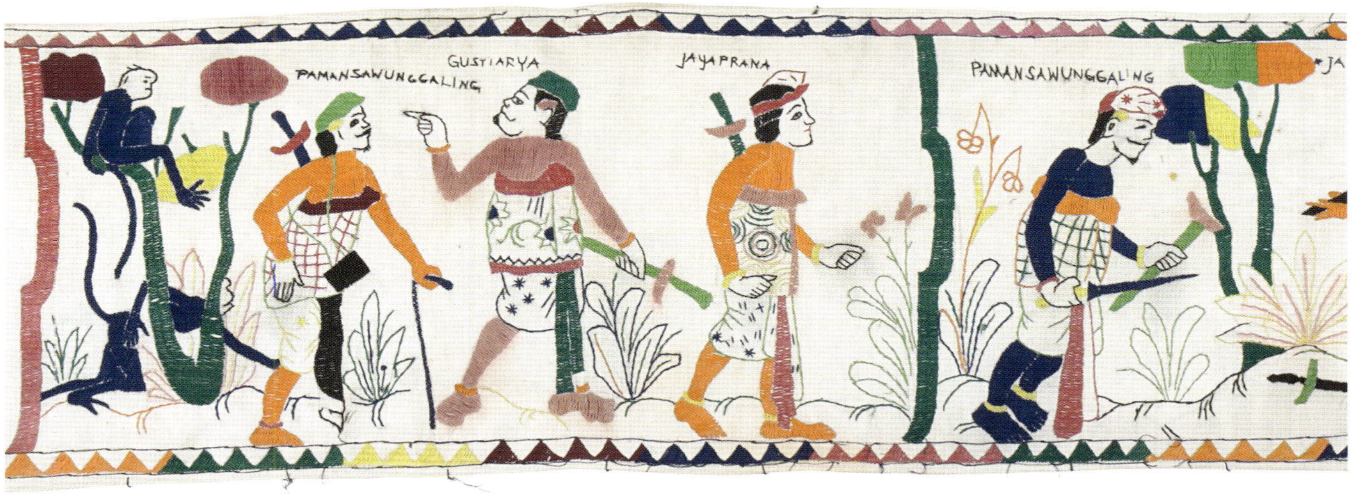

PLATE 148 Negara. *Ider-ider,* 30 x 400. Jaya Prana story. Jaya Prana is sent on a journey with agents who later give him a letter which is his death sentence.

Most importantly, the traditional system of beliefs required that the descendants of all those associated with the murderer seek atonement so that similar tragedies might not befall them. Even the families of Jaya Prana and Ni Layen Sari were obligated to also undertake actions that would bring closure to the tragedy and honor its victims. And what they all did makes for an equally remarkable story.

In Hindu Bali it is absolutely necessary to hold a traditional cremation ceremony for all who have died. In Balinese it is called a ***ngaben***. It is one of the most elaborate, costly, and highly prescribed funeral ceremonies in the world.[7] Without a proper cremation, the soul of the deceased would remain forever in torment and terrible things would befall the relatives on earth. The problem in the case of Jaya Prana was, of course, the absence of a corpse to cremate. After many years, the descendants of the villages that were originally involved finally decided to do something to correct this. But how, when, and where to do it? This would require preparations and ritual unprecedented and almost unique in Balinese cultural history.[8]

In 1934 at Gitgit, a small village some six miles from the city of Singaraja in the northern district of Buleleng, a modest memorial shrine was erected outside a temple gate. On it was a plaque inscribed in Balinese; the English translation is "to placate the spirit of an innocent man who had been murdered." The temple, called Pura Jaran Guyang, was dedicated to the memory of Jaya Prana and was being restored in the years just before 1940. The supposed site of Jaya Prana's grave had previously been established, but without the recovery of his bones, thus preventing any cremation. Once World War II began, nothing more was done until it ended.

Over many decades, tales of encounters with Jaya Prana's unquiet ghost had been widely circulated in Bali and were interpreted as the dead man's desire to return to his native village. Mishaps that had befallen the village in the past were seen to be the result of Jaya Prana's unhappiness with the lack of action on his behalf. In such a traditional society, his ghostly protestations were not to be ignored. The local people, their officials, and their priests all took this very seriously.

Reports of trance contacts between Jaya Prana and a local Hindu sage further underscored the need for a cremation. A ***balian*** (healer) was employed to contact Jaya Prana and confirm that he would be given a proper cremation. In another trance exchange, Jaya Prana gave assurances that he would provide all ceremonial expenses

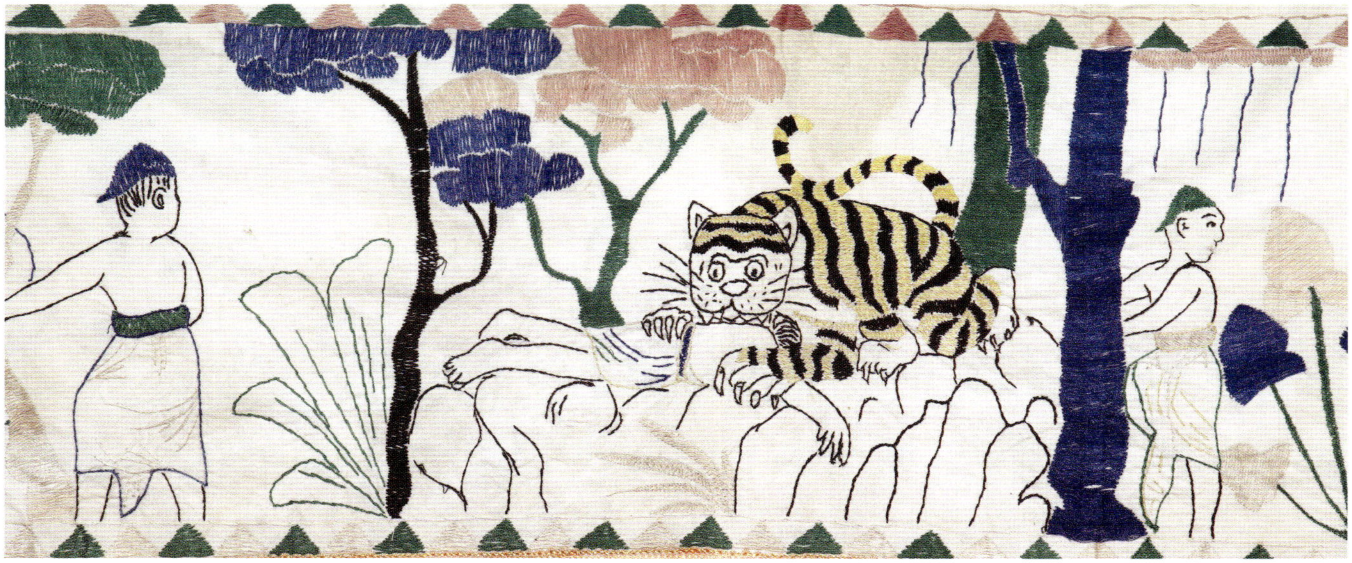

PLATE 149 Negara. *Ider-ider*, detail, 24 x 172. Jaya Prana story. A tiger attacks a member of the party that was responsible for the murder of Jaya Prana.

and guide all the preparations. The only village elder who did not believe any of this lost his child to the bite of a dog. The warning was clear to all: they must not delay.

A village deaf-mute, immune to interference, set the cremation date for August 12, 1949. All the instructions were to be received through trance messages. The major barrier was still the lack of human bones; without them, many traditional rules and caste considerations had to be reluctantly set aside.

Throughout May and July, large numbers of people arrived from all parts of Bali and even from other islands, bringing offerings. Jaya Prana's temple became a pilgrimage site where rituals and meditations were held by and for thousands of local people and visitors. They were to witness and to be a part of four traditional ceremonies that had to be undertaken before the actual cremation could take place.

The first of these, a two-day ceremony called a ***penangian***, was conducted at the supposed grave of Jaya Prana at a place called Tjeluk Trima. The ***penangian*** involved the making of an ***adegan*** (image of the deceased) along with a letter identifying the person as Jaya Prana. Now that he had been officially identified, a well-known female specialist in offerings came to take over the rituals. Contrary to Balinese custom, Jaya Prana had demanded, for some reason, that this woman not wear her gold ring. Another woman called a *makele* (mistress) had been called in as a substitute. She went to Kali Anget village to obtain holy water for use in the rituals. Unfortunately, it was the dry season and the well within the temple compound had dried up. Then a miracle of sorts occurred: the *makele* folded a leaf into a funnel and pressed it against a rock, and fifteen drops of water flowed into a holy beaker. With this requirement satisfied, made-up images of both Jaya Prana and Ni Layon Sari were placed in a special ***bale*** (traditional storage building) in Kali Anget to await cremation.

The second ceremony was the ***pembersihan***, the purification of the ***adegans***. On August 6, an unknown priest mysteriously appeared and then disappeared amid a stream of silent shuffling figures that walked under the ***bale*** containing the images. To the villagers, these priestly apparitions linked Jaya Prana with Nirartha, who first brought Hinduism to Bali. According to tradition, he had landed at a place close to where the cremation ceremonies were being conducted.

Many of the villagers appeared to be in a trancelike state and were feeling an aura of ***suchi*** (sanctity). They were exhorted to go to Kali Anget to participate. In the midst of all this, a document suddenly appeared, purported to come directly from Jaya Prana, expressing his wish for a cremation for himself and his wife. This message was accepted even though it mysteriously disappeared after being given to a village headman. Without this lost document, the foremost priest attending from the mother temple of Besakih at first refused to participate in the ceremony. He later acquiesced, due to a dream in which the gods admonished him to do so.

The third ceremony, ***pembaktian*** (devotion), took place on August 11. It consisted of a splendid long procession of hundreds of Balinese people in full traditional dress, some of them supporting a ten-foot-high figure of a black bull set on a thirty-foot-high funeral tower. These were placed in a temple courtyard awaiting the next event.

On August 12 the final ceremony, the ***pembasmian*** (the actual cremation) took place. The foremost Balinese prince, Dewa Agung of Klungkung, arrived to preside over the event, because he considered Jaya Prana part of his royal family. His participation was tantamount to regarding Jaya Prana as not just a high-caste ***ksatriya*** person but a Brahman as well. There was some criticism of this interpretation, but the majority of Balinese accepted, with some reservation, this designation of Jaya Prana and venerated him. At 2:00 A.M., a small empty coffin was placed inside the large bull figure, and bull and tower were set afire. The two ***adegan*** images of Jaya Prana and Ni Layon Sari were later placed on a seat made of lotus leaves and carried by the villagers in a long march to the seashore, where it was buried.

At long last—after many years of miracles, mysterious happenings, and tragic events—the traditional deed was completed, but an even stronger legend was born. Through its circulation in Bali it has become a well-known story. The embroideries pictured on pages 108–110 (**PLATES 147, 148,** and **149**) show only a very small part of the whole, mainly presenting some of the major characters. As far as I know, the later events of the cremation have only been the subjects of paintings.[9]

In the Balinese embroidery tradition, the story of Jaya Prana is rarely depicted. In fact, of the more than two hundred cloths that I have seen, the ones shown in this book are the only ones in my collection. The very mysterious nature of the Jaya Prana story may have had the effect of keeping artists and embroiderers away. Nevertheless, its inclusion in any embroidered cloth demonstrates again that arts and crafts use many parts of the Balinese narrative tradition. Belief and creativity are essential to this kind of folk art expression. As such, Balinese embroideries are texts, as well as religious offerings, for all to see and use, which further helps preserve ancient cultural traditions. It is indeed a rich and captivating mythology that demonstrates the vitality and attraction of ancient values.

FOOTNOTES

1. The principal source for this chapter is C. Hooykaas, editor and translator, ***The Lay of Jaya Prana***.
2. As retold in the Balinese oral tradition, Jaya Prana's ***keris*** makes him invincible until he voluntarily gives it up; the original manuscript does not relate this version. This is also the case for the attacking animals.
3. For a similar tale in which Rajah kills someone named Gusti Wayan to get his wife see Höhn, ***The Art of Bali***, **PLATES 129, 130,** and **131**.
4. Hooykaas, ***The Lay of Jaya Prana***, 99.
5. Ibid., 103.
6. Ibid., 106.
7. A reliable source for this rite of passage is Fred B. Eiseman, Jr., ***Bali: Sekala and Niskala***, vol. I, 115–126.
8. All the events and rituals connected with the actual cremation of Jaya Prana are summarized by Hooykaas, ***The Lay of Jaya Prana***, 10–15, based upon the field research of J. H. Franken, a Christian missionary who was present throughout.
9. Examples are the paintings in Hooykaas, ***The Lay of Jaya Prana***. **PLATES I, II,** and **III** portray, consecutively, *Jaya Prana's First Encounter with Layon Sari, The Animals of the Forest Wailing Beside the Corpse of Jaya Prana,* and *Ni Layon Sari Stabbing Herself* by the renowned Balinese artist, I Gusti Nyoman Lempad, who died in 1978 at the age of 116.

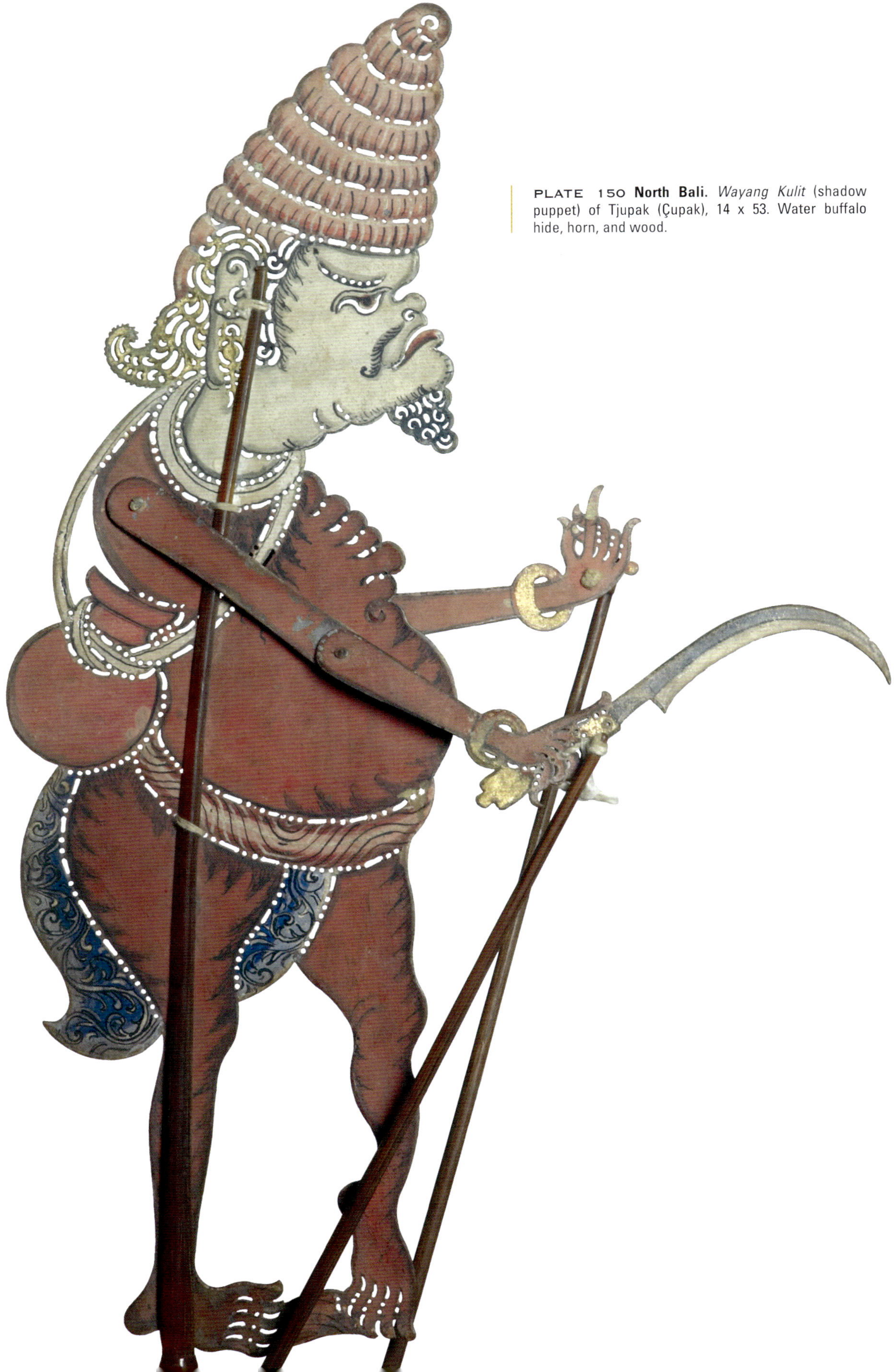

PLATE 150 **North Bali.** *Wayang Kulit* (shadow puppet) of Tjupak (Çupak), 14 x 53. Water buffalo hide, horn, and wood.

CHAPTER 10

A Tale of Two Brothers

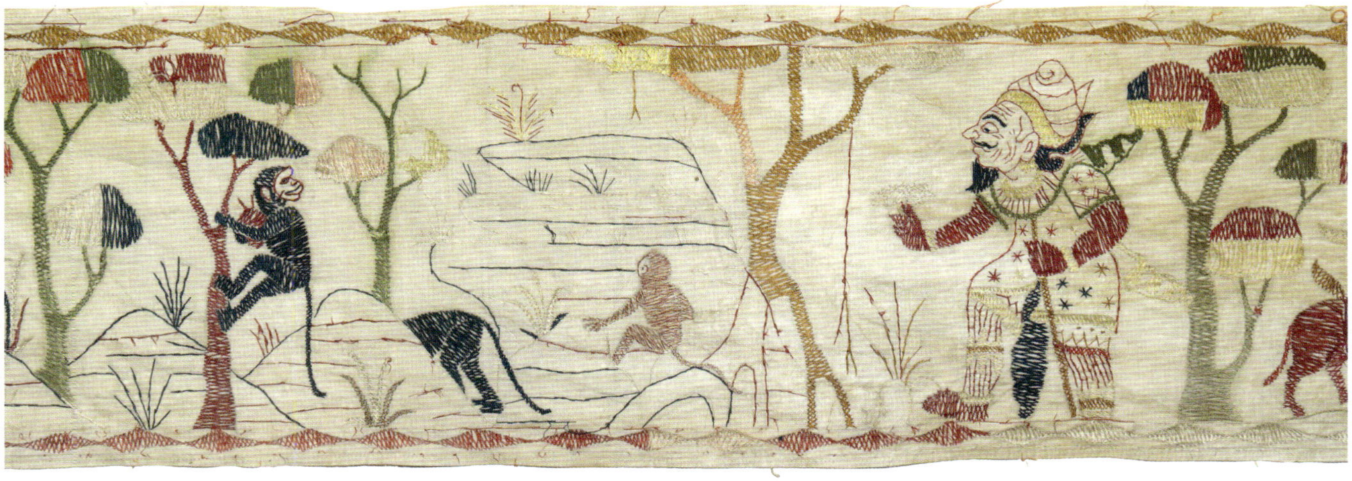

Now we come to an indigenous Balinese story of twin brothers with diametrically opposed personalities. Tjupak (Çupak) is ugly and conniving; Grantang is handsome and virtuous. This popular story is performed occasionally in a form of Balinese drama known as ***arja*** (opera).[1] A characteristic of some folktales such as this is their ambiguity in the telling and retelling, often resulting in various versions. The main one here centers on the bad brother Tjupak, who over time has become more famous than his good brother. It may be that his unrestrained cunning and greed attracts more attention, albeit negative. Such a character is perhaps easier to portray in drama and paintings. In many traditional myths, villains are often remembered and celebrated as much as heroes.

The twins are the sons of a high-caste Brahman's wife, and their origin is full of myth and mystery. One day the wife is walking in a rice field carrying food home for her husband when she is accosted by two powerful gods, Brahma and Wisnu. They have descended from the celestial heavens to inspect the earth. They are at once attracted to this beautiful but defenseless woman whom they have come upon by chance. Their power and lust cannot be contained and they rape her. The guilty gods immediately return to heaven, leaving the woman and her husband with no redress. Pregnant, the wife gives birth to twins. One baby—the firstborn, Grantang—is from the seed of Wisnu. Grantang has a beautiful face, a perfectly proportioned body, and lustrous black hair, which for the Balinese indicate his good character. The secondborn, Tjupak, from the seed of Brahma, has only one eye and one ear and a harelip; for the Balinese, all of these indicate his nasty character.

As the twins grow, they are expected to help care for the family's rice fields. Grantang does all the work while Tjupak tries to get credit for everything. While Grantang digs ditches, plants crops, and harvests them, Tjupak snares birds, chases dogs, and is given to endless idle talk.

PLATE 151 **Negara.** *Ider-ider,* detail, 28 x 540. A scene showing a holy man walking through a forest and meeting playful monkeys, one who is hiding behind a rock.

After the workday ends, Tjupak purposely covers himself with mud and returns home first to appear as if he has been working. Because Grantang always bathes before going home, his parents label him a loafer and his brother a hard worker. Grantang is punished by being forced to leave home. This is not what Tjupak had anticipated, for now he will have to really work alone in the fields. He gets permission, however, to take food to Grantang and promises to return soon—which, of course, he has no intention of doing.

After a short journey, the two brothers arrive at the royal city of Daha. There the king has called a meeting of his ministers and generals to find a way to rescue his daughter Mustikan, who has been kidnapped by an awful ogre, Detya Menarung. It is agreed that whoever accomplishes this feat will marry the daughter and inherit the throne. Tjupak, in his typical boastful manner, vows loudly that he will rescue the daughter. Grantang tries to dissuade him, but in the end the two set forth on their quest.

Tjupak unsuccessfully tries to lose Grantang or get him to go back on some foolish errand so that all the future rewards will be his alone. Tjupak eats all the food they are carrying, then says dogs have stolen it. He gives Grantang a leaky pot to fill with water and plays other tricks aimed at convincing his brother to depart, but nothing works. Finally the brothers stumble into the camp of the ogre/kidnapper.[2] Cowardly Tjupak runs away and climbs up a tamarind tree to hide.[3] The captive princess appears and promises to marry Grantang if he defeats the ogre. She says that the only way to kill him is to shoot an arrow into his mouth; Grantang promptly does this. Immediately, Tjupak jumps down from the tree, shoots another arrow into the ogre's mouth, and claims it was *his* arrow that really killed him. Kind-hearted Grantang does not argue the point. The princess is unclear about whose arrow it was and the three decide to rest for the night before returning to Daha.

While they are sleeping, the ogre's sister, Ni Butawili, steals into the camp and forces the princess down a deep well, then runs away. Of course, it falls upon Grantang to rescue her by climbing down a rope into the well. She climbs up to freedom, but Tjupak cuts the rope, stranding his brother at the bottom. The triumphant and nefarious Tjupak and the naïve princess return to Daha and report to the king. Tjupak is given a new honorary name of Mantu Anom, entitling him to many rewards. In the meantime, Grantang escapes from the well and returns to the court, much weakened and his body "as a bag of bones." Tjupak, furious that his brother is still alive, orders him to be wrapped in a mat and thrown into the sea.

The plot takes another turn when a fisherman catches the floating Grantang in his net. He takes him home and brings him back to full health. The fisherman joyfully tells his wife, "I found a son for you." The grateful Grantang gives his new mother a golden ring that the princess had given him. He begins working hard to help his adopted parents by selling flowers and vegetables in the local market. His good looks, honesty, and polite demeanor attract buyers from all over the kingdom. His fame and reputation spread even to the court. The princess, who is not yet married to Tjupak, sends for the fisherman's wife and sees on her finger the ring that she had given to Grantang. At last Grantang and Mustikan are rightfully reunited—but Tjupak stands in the way of their marriage. He fights with his brother, is defeated, and is banished from the kingdom. An elaborate royal marriage ceremony, lasting many days, unites the couple, amidst great rejoicing by the king and his people.

In the Balinese ***arja*** version, full of action, drama, and laughs, the story ends here. However, characteristic of such myths, there is another version with quite a different outcome.

This alternate version of the Tjupak tale is less known and less performed in Bali. It blames Tjupak's hideous appearance on his mother's eating of two magical mushrooms. One was torn, producing the imperfect Tjupak; the other was whole, resulting in the perfect Grantang. The tale also shifts from the popular version in Tjupak's banishment to a remote forest, where he lives in exile. A ghostly voice speaks to him in a dream and commands him to help the kingdom that had banished him. It is being destroyed by a monstrous mythical bird called Paksi Garuda, who has to eat one human a day to survive. Tjupak learns from an old woman in the marketplace that the king is in despair because the monster bird has demanded the king's daughter

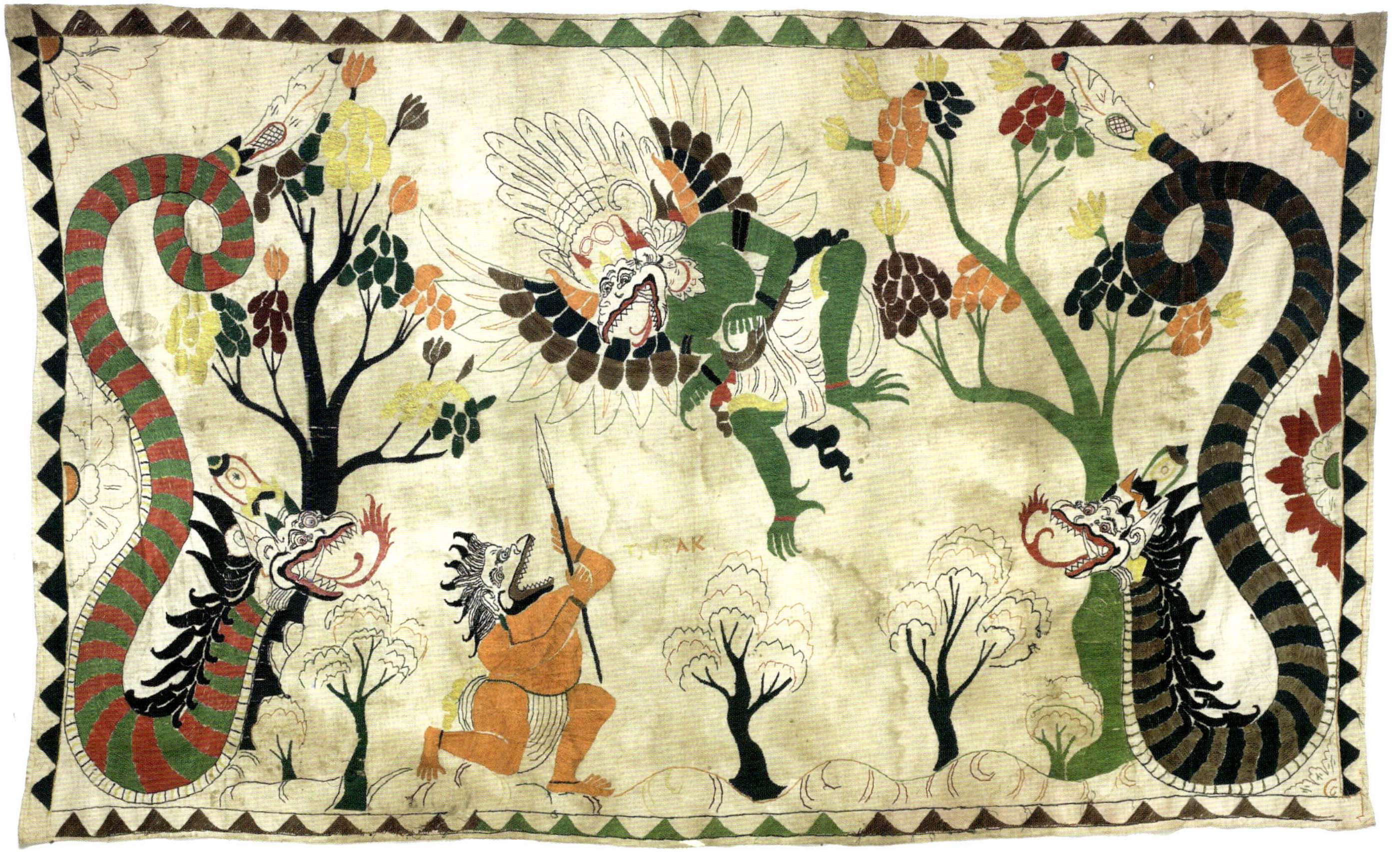

PLATE 152 Negara. *Tabing*, 85 x 135. *A Tale of Two Brothers*. The ugly Tjupak with spear, attacks and then destroys the killer bird Paksi Garuda who needs to eat one human each day to survive.

for his next meal. The embroidery in PLATE 152 shows Tjupak about to battle the giant bird Paksi Garuda, who is later slain.[4] Tjupak carries its head back to show the king and is rewarded with a stupendous wedding for himself and the princess. (A Balinese shadow puppet version of Tjupak is shown in PLATE 150, page 112.)

The married princess becomes pregnant, but she has ambivalent feelings about her new husband. She is embarrassed by Tjupak's ugliness, which is the subject of popular jokes. She is also concerned that she might give birth to an ugly child in her husband's image. The princess consults a priest and is advised to meditate and beseech the gods to make her husband handsome. The god Indra hears her prayer and is willing to grant her wishes. As a consequence, the princess gives birth to perfectly normal male twins.

Tjupak is constantly restless and unsatisfied with court life, so while his sons are still babies he sets out on a long journey of adventure that lasts many years, during which Indra had made him handsome.

His twin sons grow up and begin a search for their father Tjupak. During their journey, they stop at a palace and ask for food, but are refused any unless they are willing to marry the king's two adopted daughters, sight unseen. They refuse to do this, a fight follows, and the demanding king is slain. Before departing, Tjupak's two sons hear the king's daughters weeping uncontrollably in the palace. Much to their amazement, the two daughters are beautiful and the sons are so dazzled that they all agree to journey together. Coincidence is a common feature in folk stories and this is no exception, for by chance they meet Tjupak. He does not recognize the twins as his sons, for they have so matured, and his sons do not recognize their now-handsome father, whom they had only known as ugly. Tjupak tells his sons his name, but they do not believe him until he changes back to his original ugly self. At long last, Tjupak and his family are reunited. Father and sons are elated; they embrace each other and celebrate with food and song.

And then the story takes another surprising turn, as Tjupak begins to question the two adopted daughters about their origins. He learns that they were the twin daughters of his brother Grantang, who had been forced to give up his daughters for adoption by the king of Daha. There is more rejoicing and all journey home together. Each of Tjupak's twin sons marries one of Grantang's twin daughters and all live happily for the rest of their lives. The original tale has come full circle, with a reversed second version and, eventually, a reconnection of both.

CHARACTERISTICS OF FOLKTALES

Such a tale demonstrates many of the general characteristics of surviving mythologies and folktales across many cultures:

- Role reversal (such as the redemption of Tjupak)
- Ambiguity (such as an unclear mix of happy and unhappy events)
- Magic (such as changing Tjupak from ugly to handsome and back again)
- Coincidence (such as chance meetings, surprising discoveries)
- Supernatural elements (such as the intervention of gods and ogres)
- Stereotypes (such as one-dimensional personalities)
- Opposing versions (such as the first and second Tjupak tales)
- Omission of information (such as a reason for the adoption of Grantang's daughters)

Variations in any tale will often occur with its oral telling and retelling and its writing and rewriting over the passage of time. When myths or folk stories are performed as dance/drama or puppet plays, as they are in Bali,[5] or serve as the subject of painting and embroidery, artists will make adaptations, omissions, additions, and the like. These alterations may stem from various factors, such as the impact of historical events, the languages of performance or transmission, the kinds of religious practices, and the character of indigenous social structures. Field research might reveal how these factors affected the character and content of traditional objects and in this case, how the image of Tjupak and his brother came to be present on a Balinese embroidery.

FOOTNOTES

1. My major sources for this tale are a few Balinese informants, and Beryl De Zoete and Walter Spies, ***Dance and Drama in Bali***, 143–147 and 275–278 and Jane Belo, ***Traditional Balinese Culture,*** 183–185. For a painting of the Tjupak tale, see Hildred Geertz, ***Images of Power***, 54. For photographs of wooden masks of Tjupak and Grantang, see Margaret H. Dunningham, ***Balinese Folk Art***, nos. 41 and 42.
2. For a painting of this man-eating ogre, see Höhn, ***The Art of Bali***, 63.
3. For a painting of Grantang battling the ogre and Tjupak hiding in a tree see Geertz, ***Images of Power***, 55.
4. This is the only cloth containing any of the Tjupak myth that I have seen, and it relates only to the second version.
5. For example, see the changes noted in the Sampik/Ingtai story on page 118.

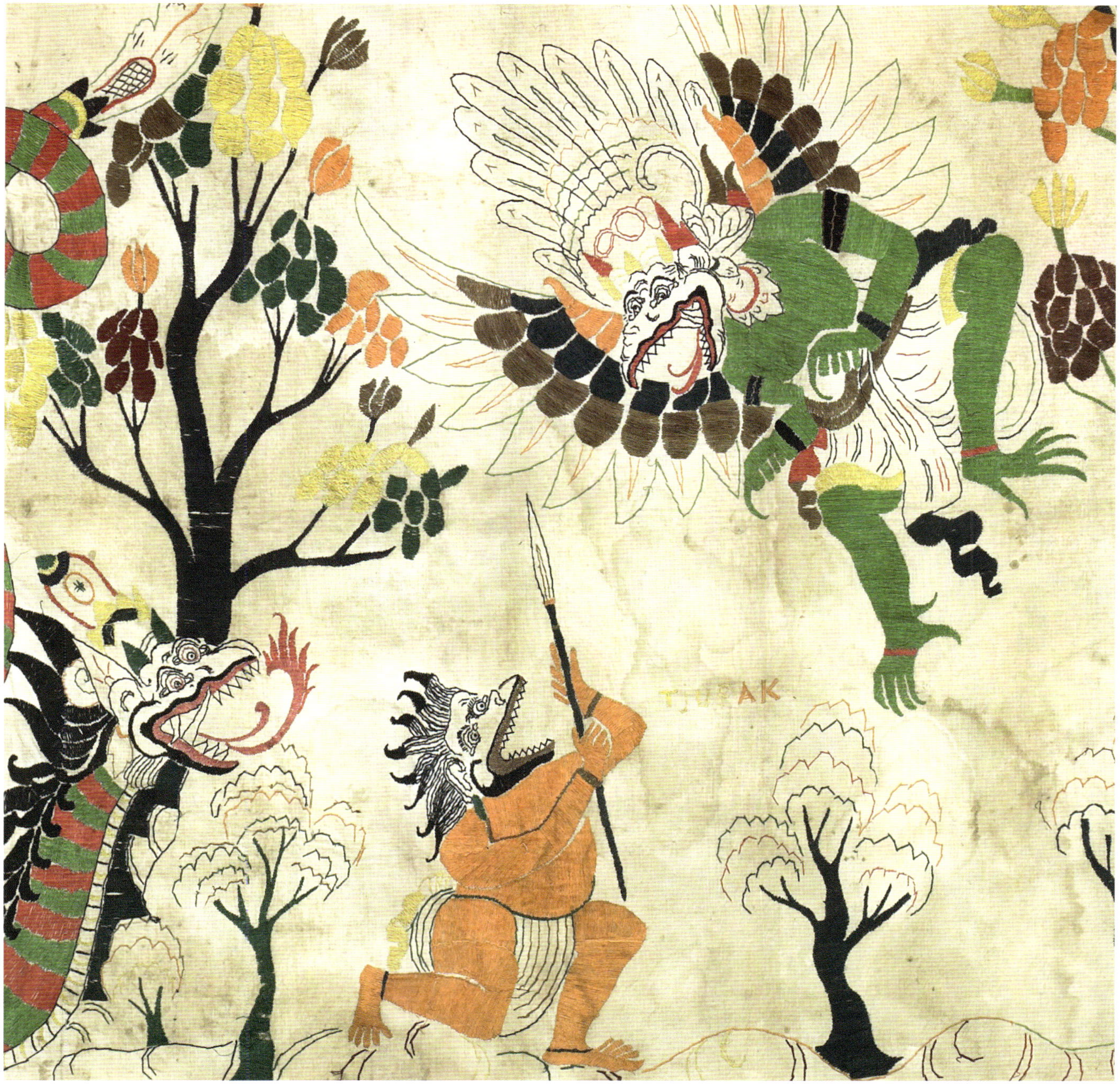

PLATE 153 **Negara.** *Tabing* detail, 85 x 135. *A Tale of Two Brothers.*

Chapter 11

The Butterfly Lovers: A Chinese Folktale in Bali

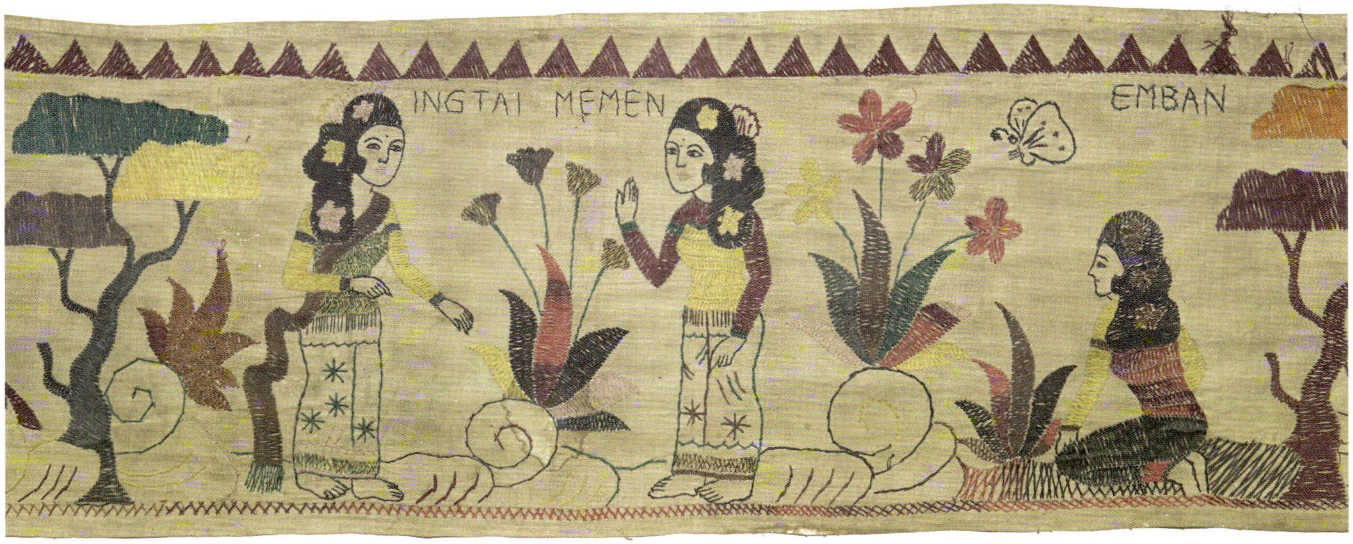

China was in contact with some of the Indonesian islands as early as the fifth century A.D.[1] Continuously afterward, small Chinese immigrant communities were established in sparse settlements in many parts of Indonesia, particularly in Java, Sulawesi, and Sumatra. These so-called Overseas Chinese brought with them skills and traditions from their homeland. These were expressed in arts and in crafts, such as Chinese designs in painting and especially in batik cloths. The artisans incorporated such Chinese motifs as the mythical phoenix bird and distinctive ways of depicting clouds, rocks, and water. In Bali, Chinese coins were used as decorations, as parts of wooden images of Dewi Sri, and in offerings to Hindu temples.

When the Dutch first arrived in Indonesia at the end of the sixteenth century, they found that many printed books in Chinese were available, especially in Java. During the nineteenth century, more and more were published or appeared in manuscript form. Some were translated into Javanese and into what was then called Malay. In 1881, a Javanese translation of a Chinese tale was made by a Chinese man living in north Bali. Other manuscripts of Chinese romances and histories existed and some have been found in Bali. The earliest dated one is from 1915.[2]

One of the most famous Chinese folktales was first serialized in a Javanese language newspaper in 1878. It was called "The Butterfly Lovers" or the tale of Liang Shambo

PLATE 154 Negara. *Ider-ider*, detail, 27 x 245. *The Butterfly Lovers* story. Ingtai, her mother (Memen), and her servant (Emban) discuss Ingtai's desire to go to school.

and Zhu Yingtai (Ingtai in Bali). This story had been a theme for drama in China since the eleventh century. The Hokkien names for them in what was then the Dutch East Indies were Sampik and Ingtai. A Balinese translation appeared around 1915, but there is some evidence it had been in circulation as a tale before 1883. The translator was Ida Bagus Ketut Sari, a thirty-six-year-old Balinese man. He is reputed to have acquired the Sampik story from an old Chinese merchant who lived in Sanur, Bali, in the late nineteenth century. This Chinese resident was regarded as a scholar and was a friend of the local king of Badung District. It is supposed that the interest of this Chinese man in the Sampik tale may have been inspired by his own secret love affair with a Balinese maiden. He was eager to see this romance published in Bali because it mirrored his own romantic difficulties over loving someone who was not Chinese. Disapproval came from his own community and the Balinese parents of the young woman.

There are some examples of the text of this story on ***lontars*** in libraries in Jakarta, Denpasar, and Singaraja. The tale of Sampik and Ingtai has been performed as a popular ***ketoprak*** (modern drama) in Java; a major performance was held in Bandung in August 2002. In Bali it is played as part of the ***arja*** (traditional opera) repertoire, usually in connection with local festivities. This tale has survived in Bali despite some prejudice against Chinese-Indonesian citizens.

There are several versions of the original Chinese story. One is a Szechuan opera called ***Love Under the Willows***;[3] another is found in a novel entitled ***Liang Shambo and Zhu Yingtai***.[4] It is still extremely popular in China in prose, performance, and song. It is clearly one of those tragic romantic tales that is attractive to all sorts of people and it is not surprising that it has found a home for more than one hundred years in Balinese popular culture. Its depiction on Balinese embroidery, its popularity as a folk-tale, and its place in Balinese opera attest to this. I found all sorts of people in Bali were quite familiar with this story of two tragic lovers. Drivers, artists, shop owners, waiters, farmers, gallery owners, teachers, grade school children, young and old, men and women–all knew the story.[5] It has features that clearly transcend geography and culture, enabling the Sampik and Ingtai folktale to persist in popularity today in both Bali and China.

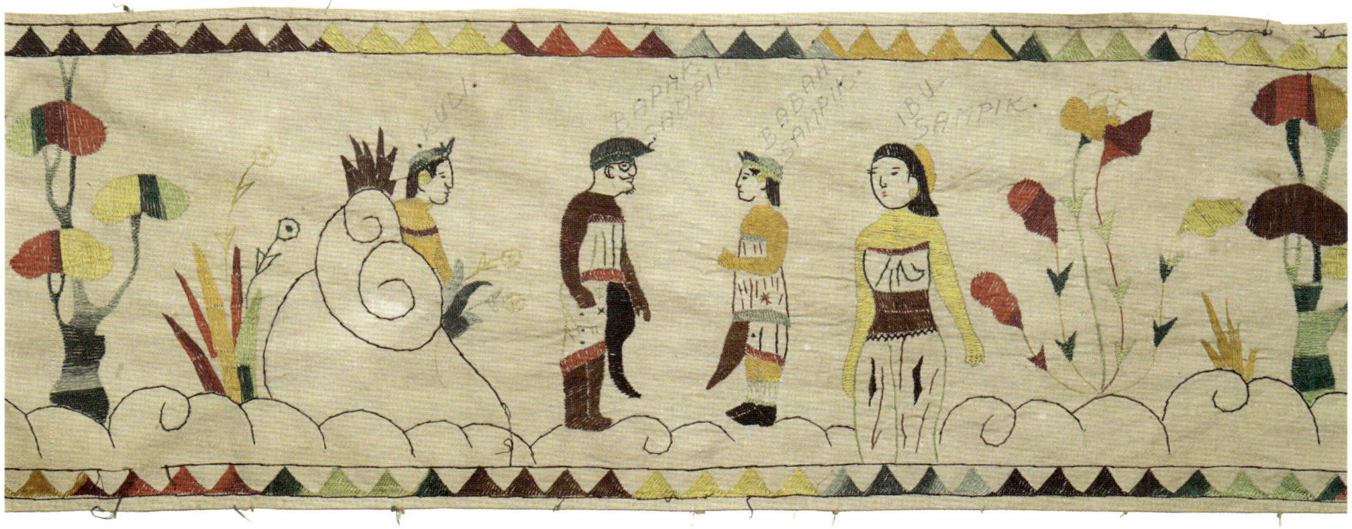

PLATE 155 **Negara.** *Ider-ider*, detail, 27 x 360. *The Butterfly Lovers* story. This is son *(babah)* Sampik's family: his mother *(ibu)*, his father *(bapak)*, and his servant *(kuli)*.

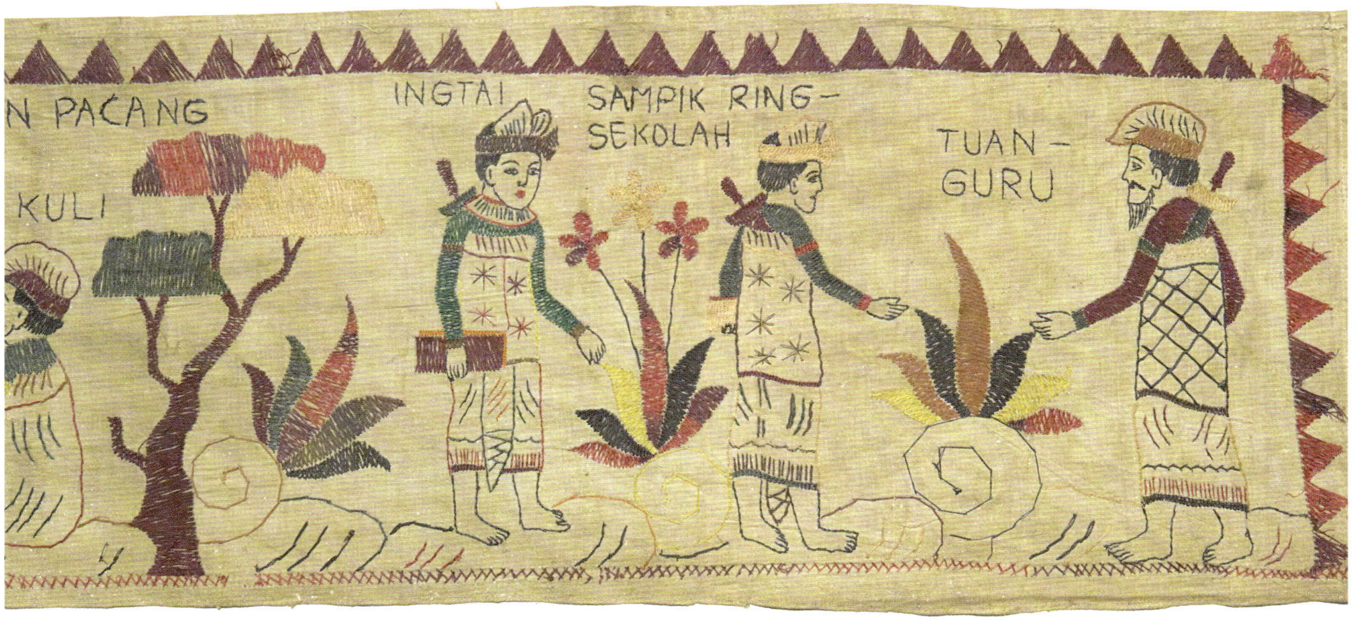

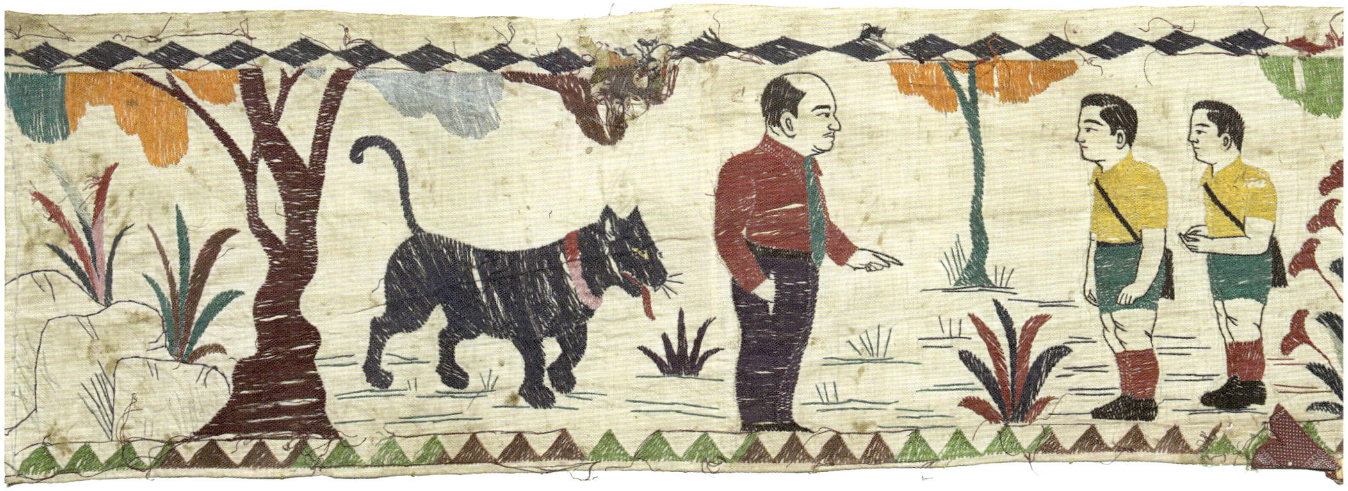

PLATE 156 **Negara.** *Ider-ider*, detail, 27 x 245. *The Butterfly Lovers* story. Here are Ingtai disguised as a man, her roommate, Sampik, and their teacher *(Tuan Guru)* at school *(sekolah)*.

PLATE 157 **Negara.** *Ider-ider*, detail, 27 x 292. *The Butterfly Lovers* story. The father of Ingtai talks to two schoolboys. All three are in modern dress.

This folktale originated in China some time between the fifth and tenth centuries. Its setting is Shangyu and Guiji counties in Zhejang Province. On the outskirts of Shangyu county in Zhuija village live a wealthy man name Zhu Gangyan and his wife. They are nearly seventy years old and have eight mature sons who have married and moved away, and they long for a daughter. As if by some miracle, a baby girl is born to them. She is named Zhu Yingtai (Ingtai); her parents dote on her and deny her nothing. By the time Ingtai reaches the age of sixteen she yearns to go to school, something that Chinese girls did not do in those times. They are expected to get married and raise a family or to stay home, and in any case, to always respect their parents' wishes. Ingtai will have none of this and constantly pleads with her parents to permit her to go to school. Her mother is generally supportive but her father is adamant in his refusal. Still, Ingtai will not give up her yearning to study.

One day, while walking near her home, she stops to talk to a group of young men on their way to study at a famous school in Hangzhou. Ingtai quickly returns home with an even stronger desire to go to school, but she knew that schools do not accept women as students. Headstrong as she is and over her parents' protests, she put on men's clothes and in this disguise she rejoins the traveling student group. Their leader is named Sampik; he is tall, slim, cheerful, and hospitable to this "male" newcomer.

The journey to Hangzhou takes many days, during which the group shares food and stories of their lives. Ingtai and Sampik become close friends, vow to be spiritual "brothers," and agree to share a room in school. Sampik notes that Ingtai's passion and eagerness for school seem excessive, even for a "man." Nevertheless, he welcomes the companionship and is pleased to have made a new friend. Schoolmates they will soon be. Ingtai's educational journey has finally and joyfully begun.

A thunderstorm suddenly arises, showering the students with raindrops the size of grapes. Strong winds bend trees, leaves are scattered, and swirls of mud are churned up. The clouds are black and ominous; they portend something uncertain and troubling for the future.

Sampik and Ingtai arrive at school and are assigned the same room. The room is sparsely furnished with two chairs, one table, two lanterns, and only one small single bed. Ingtai, still trying to protect her deception, is puzzled about the sleeping arrangements. She makes a strange request that rope be stretched lengthwise as a dividing line on the straw mattress, one side for Sampik and the other for Ingtai. She also makes Sampik agree that whoever crosses over into the other's part during the night must pay a fine. Ingtai is nervous about this sharing, but time passes without incident and they both concentrate on their studies. Day by day Ingtai grows more and more fond of Sampik. He treats her as a friend and schoolmate; she dreams of him as a lover and future husband.

The school term is about to end. The last day is extremely hot and humid. Ingtai and Sampik go off on a final walk around a very blue lake. Their faces are reflected in the calm water. Ingtai is thinking of having to go home and how much she will miss Sampik. She is overcome by thoughts of longing and love. She impulsively runs to the water's edge, removes her clothes, and wades into the lake. She stands there naked in the shining sun and the blue water. Sampik is stunned; his roommate for months, his spiritual "brother" is a woman! Ingtai smiles at him; he is elated. Their life as lovers has begun.

They talk and talk about their families, their goals, and their futures. They agree that, after returning to their respective homes, in thirty days Sampik will visit Ingtai and ask her parents for permission to marry their daughter. Such are their happy plans; they part with an embrace. Around them the long-stemmed rice plants are not yet ready to be harvested; they bow ever so slightly in the light wind. Two mandarin ducks, symbolic of a long and happy union, glide silently past them in the lake. It is a good sign for the time being.

Ingtai travels home quickly, but with apprehension about her parents' reaction to her marriage plans. She tells her father that she wants to marry Sampik. He becomes very angry. In China a daughter does not make such decisions; her father forbids any more talk about such a marriage. In one version of the tale, Sampik actually visits Ingtai's home, where he is refused entry by her father and forced to return to his home. Another, more common version

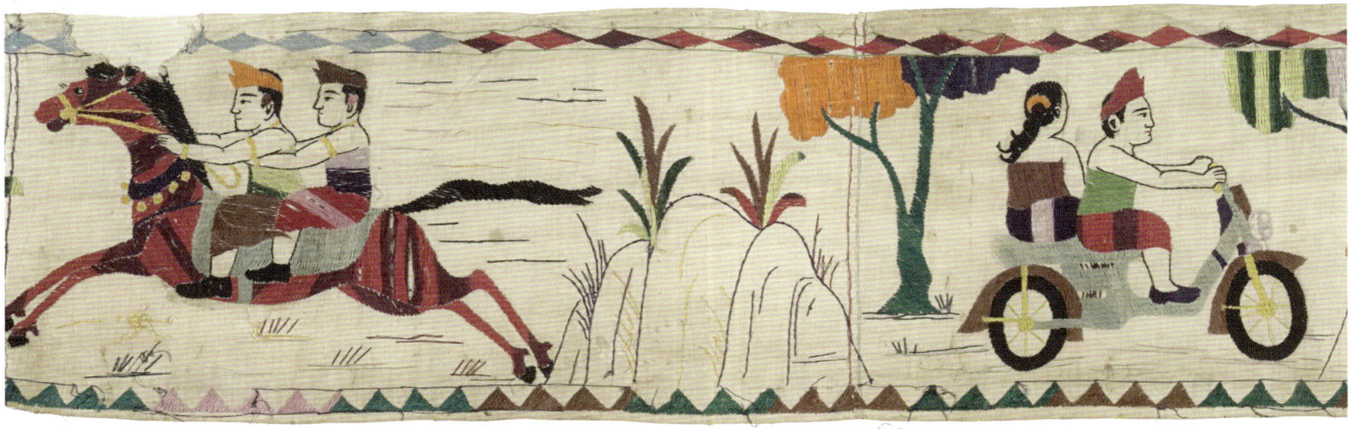

PLATE 158 **Negara.** *Ider-ider*, 27 x 292. *The Butterfly Lovers* story. Sampik and his servant Kuli ride off to school on a horse. Sampik and Ingtai ride a motorcycle while at school, obviously a modern addition.

tells of the sickness of Sampik, which prevents him from coming to Ingtai in thirty days as he had promised. In both versions, Sampik becomes gravely ill but Ingtai does not know this and she becomes concerned after several months have passed with no word from him.

Ingtai's father grows impatient with his daughter; he wants her to marry a man of his choice. In fact, he has received a formal request from the provincial governor offering his handsome but dull son for Ingtai's hand in marriage. Her father's stern demand and the power of a high official leave Ingtai with no choice. Elaborate marriage plans are agreed upon by both families and finalized. As the wedding day approaches, Ingtai becomes more and more depressed. She will not eat or leave her room. She can think only of Sampik and his absence and her misfortune in not being free. She nearly dies, but her servant and her mother nurse her daily and make her well.

The wedding takes place as planned, but Ingtai wears a white dress, which in China is a symbol of mourning, not joy. The groom is Ma Wencai, a likeable young fellow but with a puffed-up view of himself as a prize husband.

In the meantime Sampik is near death; traditional Chinese herbal medicines have no effect. His family have lost hope. Sampik dreams that Ingtai can never be his bride. He tells his parents that after his death he wishes to be buried in an unmarked grave alongside the main country road, and they agree. On the day of Ingtai's wedding, Sampik dies of his illness. Most people believed that somehow he had learned of Ingtai's wedding and died of a broken heart. His parents bury Sampik in the place and manner that they have promised, in an unmarked grave.

The sad bride and the confident groom set out on a honeymoon journey in a fine carriage drawn by two black horses. After a few days of traveling on the main highway, the carriage approaches the unmarked grave where Sampik is buried. Ingtai suddenly cries out for the horses to stop; before her husband can stop her, she leaps from the carriage. She stops at the grave and in an instant disappears. It is as if the earth has opened up and gently swallowed her. Ma Wencai rushes frantically from the carriage and runs to the spot where he last saw her. He thinks of digging into the earth, but before he can do so, from the gravesite two beautiful butterflies arise and fly away.[6] Sampik and Ingtai are united in death and transformed into another life-form. Their love for each other is so sweet, so strong, and so perfect that nothing can keep them apart.

The Sampik/Ingtai story is well known in Bali as part of the ***arja*** but it is performed only occasionally.[7] I first saw it at an evening performance held in the Art Center of Den Pasar during the annual Balinese Festival of the Arts. In general, the plot followed that found in the Szechuan opera, *Love Under the Willows,* which differs somewhat from the version in the Chinese novel. The performance was free. Vendors selling food walked through the audience; a few children were popping balloons. The opera lasted about two hours with no intermission. The actors appeared to be all Balinese but I was not sure of this because they used makeup to simulate Chinese facial features. The costumes were a mixture of Balinese and quasi-Chinese dress. The audience was a mixture of young and old, many Balinese and some Indonesian Chinese, and their sympathy seemed to be mostly with Ingtai.

This performance differed in several respects from the traditional Chinese version described previously. For example, Sampik is regarded by servants as stupid for not seeing through Ingtai's disguise and for not catching on to Ingtai's many hints about her gender. Also, Sampik and Ingtai agree to meet in ten days after school ends but for some reason he thinks it is thirty days. Both finally meet but by this time Ingtai is engaged to another man. Sampik feels betrayed, becomes very ill, and sends a letter via a bird explaining his unfortunate situation. Ingtai replies using the same bird as a messenger with a letter stating that she still loves Sampik and suggests some herbal remedies for his illness. Sampik dies and is buried in a grave marked by a blue headstone with his name clearly written on it. When Ingtai sees the grave, she declares, "You died because of me and now I come to you. The earth will open up to receive me if your love is powerful enough." Ma Wencai (Ma Tjoen in Bali), Ingtai's husband, is so bewildered and angry that he gets someone to dig into the grave, but no bodies are found. Two butterflies and two yellow bees fly away. After much digging, two blue stone coins are found. Ma Tjoen throws the coins into a river thinking he is performing some kind of ritual. The two coins land in the river, and one becomes a teak ***(jati)*** tree symbolizing Sampik, the other becomes bamboo ***(bambu)*** symbolizing Ingtai. People believed that if you put these two trees in water in the same container they would be united even though they are different species. It turns out that Sampik and Ingtai as a couple were gods before they became human. However, once on earth, they separated and could not be made to be together. When they died they became gods again united forever. And so this performed version that I witnessed ended. It is an apt example of how some folktales change when they are transferred from one culture to another.[8]

PLATE 159 Negara. *Ider-ider*, detail, dimensions unknown, July 2003. *The Butterfly Lovers* story. Ingtai sits by the bedside of the gravely ill Sampik just before he dies. This scene is neither in the original story from China or in the Balinese *arja* (opera).

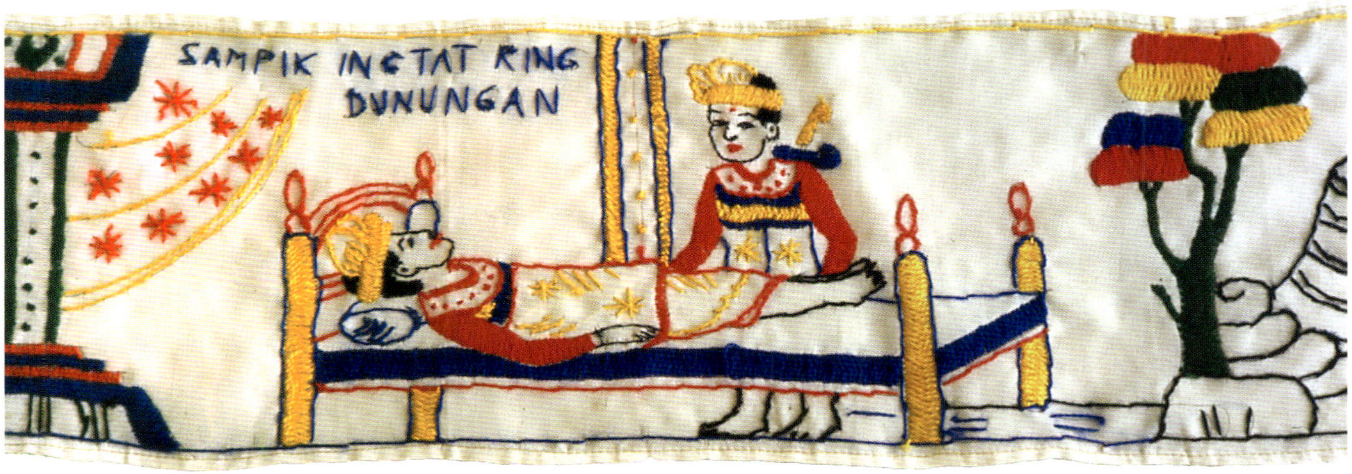

PLATE 160 **Negara.** *Ider-ider*, detail, 27 x 245. *The Butterfly Lovers* story. Ingtai is disguised as a man; Sampik is unaware of Ingtai's true gender.

As I walked home that warm evening, under a clear night sky with the Southern Cross overhead, I thought that perhaps true love could be eternal even in ancient times, when parents arranged everything and differences of status and gender kept people apart. Many years later, that thought came back to me when I unexpectedly found Balinese embroideries that depicted the Sampik and Ingtai story.

Given the size limitations of embroidered cloths, only small parts of any story can be shown. The three embroideries in my collection, however, depict all the main characters. All of these cloths are long, narrow ***ider-iders*** in which the characters are grouped into scenes that do not necessarily follow the sequence of the story, but they do give some sense of what is going on—and as an aid, all the characters have embroidered names. PLATE 154 (see page 118) shows Ingtai and her mother (Menen), perhaps discussing Ingtai's wish to go to school. A different style cloth, with penciled names, is that in PLATE 155 (page 119), which shows the Sampik family: father ***(bapak)***, son ***(babah)***, mother ***(ibu)***, and their servant ***(kuli)***. PLATE 156 (page 120) depicts Ingtai and Sampik in school with their teacher, Tuan Guru. Ingtai is disguised and carries a ***keris***, which only men do. The ***ider-ider*** in PLATE 157 (page 120) is an apt example of the use of modern elements in a traditional story. One scene depicts the father of Ingtai talking to two schoolboys, all three of whom are in western dress. A second shows Sampik and his servant Kuli on a horse, contrasted later in a third scene with Sampik and Ingtai riding a motorcycle (see PLATE 158, page 122) .

It is not clear why a folktale from China should appear on these embroidered cloths that are used mainly in Hindu temples and Balinese homes. The Sampik/Ingtai story does not have any ritual significance in Balinese belief or religious practice; it may be merely a vehicle for illustrating a popular story that is both performed and painted in Bali. It may also have been commissioned by or for a local Chinese person with nostalgia for the past or the desire to honor a friend.

FOOTNOTES

1. For an example of early contacts, see Fa-Hsien, ***The Travels of Fa-Hsien (399–414 A.D.)***.
2. Two sources for Chinese literature in Indonesia are Beryl De Zoete and Walter Spies, ***Dance and Drama in Bali***, 321–323, and Ann Kumar and John H. McGlynn, "A Legacy of Two Homelands: Chinese Manuscript Literature" in ***Illuminations: The Writing Traditions of Indonesia***, 201–212. In Java there is currently only one puppeteer who performs Chinese stories in what is called ***po-te-hie***. His name is Tantri Yuliondini (see the *Jakarta Post*, March 5, 2003).
3. Gladys Yang and Yang Hsien-Yi, translators, ***Shan-po Liang and Ying-tai Chu, Love under the Willows***.
4. Zhao Qingge, ***Liang Shanbo and Zhu Yingtai*** (in English and Chinese).
5. The only major study of the Sampik and Ingtai tale in Indonesia is I Dewa Gede Windhu Sancaya, ***Sam Pek Eng Tay (Geguritan Sampik) dalam Kesusastraam Bali***. The first translation of the tale into Indonesian was by Boen Sing Hoo, ***Boekoe Menjanjian Tjina, Sampik-Ing Taij***.
6. A slightly different ending—in which the husband starts digging into the grave but encounters two bumblebees (not butterflies) who sting him and fly away—is described by De Zoete and Spies, ***Dance and Drama in Bali***, 322–323. One embroidery ***ider-ider*** (see PLATE 159, page 123) depicts Ingtai actually sitting by the bedside of the gravely ill Sampik just before he dies. This scene does not exist in the original Chinese folktale and seldom in the Balinese ***arja*** version—another example of the vicissitudes in folk art traditions.
7. A Balinese painting of an ***arja*** performance can be seen in Hildred Geertz, ***Images of Power***, 41.
8. This version was quite similar to the one described by Dewa Gede Windhu Sancaya, ***Sam Pek Eng Tay***.

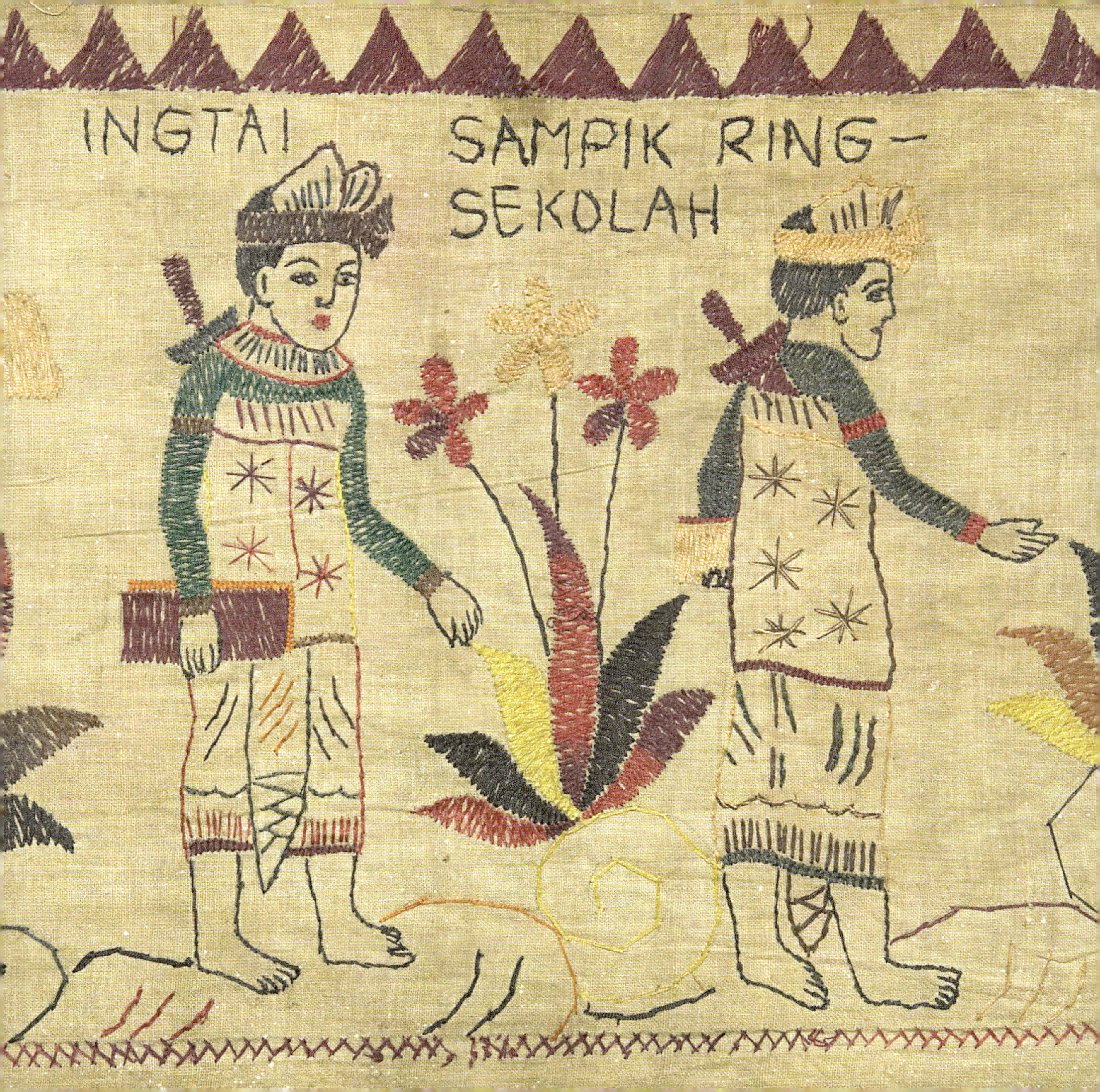
INGTAI
SAMPIK RING-
SEKOLAH

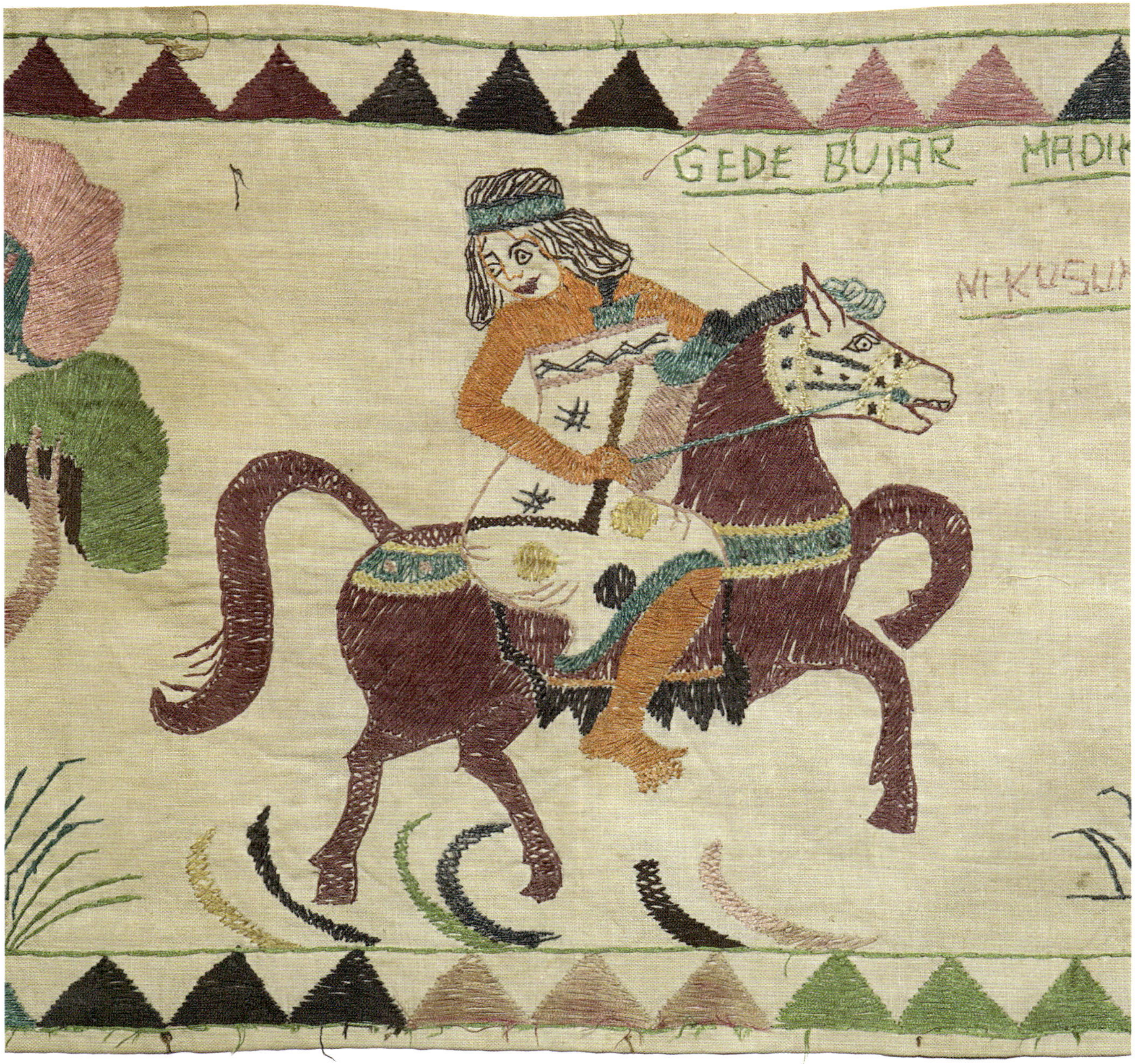

PLATE 161 **Negara**. *Ider-ider*, detail, 26 x 261. *Journey of Dukuh Siladri.* The vulgar Bujar swears as he rides away after being rejected by Kusuma Sari.

CHAPTER 12

The Journey of Dukuh Siladri

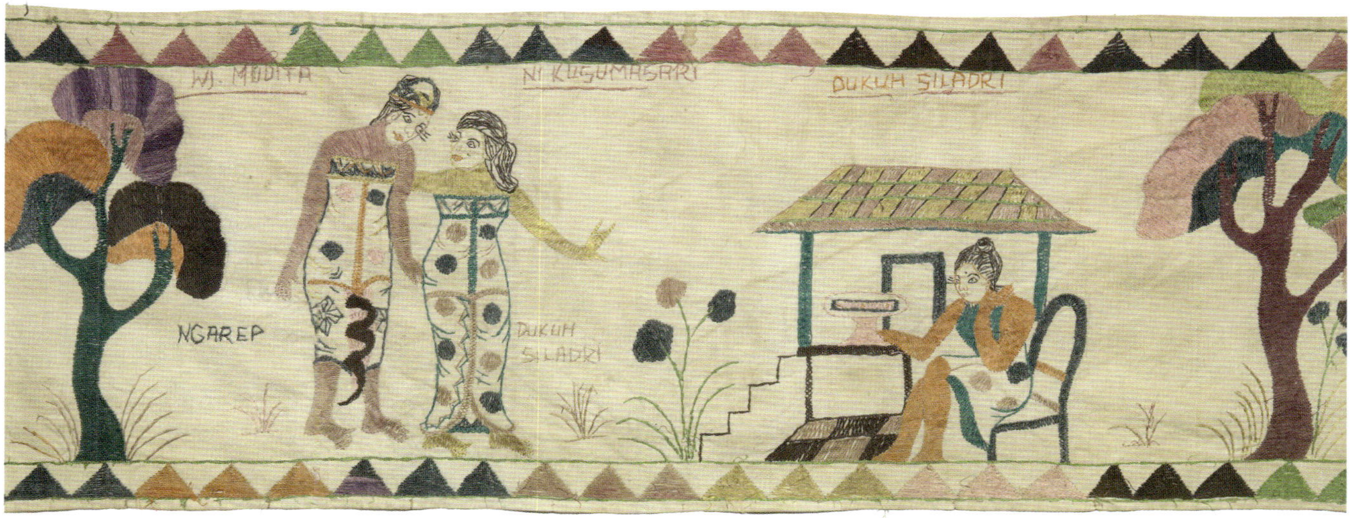

I have two ***ider-ider*** from Negara showing a small part of *The Journey of Dukuh Siladri,* a popular indigenous Balinese tale of two caring brothers, their loving children, and a rich man's malevolent son.[1] The story is complex, with many characters, surprising genealogies, villains and heroes, and a mostly happy ending. The two supposed brothers are quite different from one another. The oldest, Siladri, becomes dissatisfied with city life, its noises, its unhealthy air, and its seemingly irreligious environment. He wishes to seek solace and wisdom somewhere in the quiet countryside, preferably in a mountain retreat. His brother, Made Kerti, is very content with his life and thinks it strange that Siladri wishes to give up his comfortable existence.

They are both raised by their widowed mother, Ni Sabuk, an outspoken but caring parent who had secretly adopted Siladri as a baby. Made Kerti was her natural son, but she treated both equally with love. There comes a time when she welcomes her sons' coming of age and their intentions to marry. Siladri has chosen Kadek, a shy, beautiful daughter of a simple farmer. Made Kerti falls in love with the austere, attractive Rajin, Kadek's sister. Both appear to Ni Sabuk to be "matches made in heaven" and the brides-to-be, who had lost their mother when they were still babies, are grateful to become part of a new family.

In time a son, Mudita, is born to Siladri and Kadek, and a daughter, Kusuma Sari, to Made Kerti and Rajin. Both families appear to have a happy life, but Siladri is discontented. He still wishes to pursue the life of an ascetic, having been motivated in part by a large collection of sacred ***lontar*** that his father had left him. He learns to read these ancient texts, which were written in ***kawi,*** the old classical language of Java and Bali. Siladri reads aloud the

PLATE 162 **Negara.** *Ider-ider,* detail, 26 x 261. *Journey of Dukuh Siladri.* Mudita and Ni Kusuma Sari asking permission of Dukuh Siladri to marry.

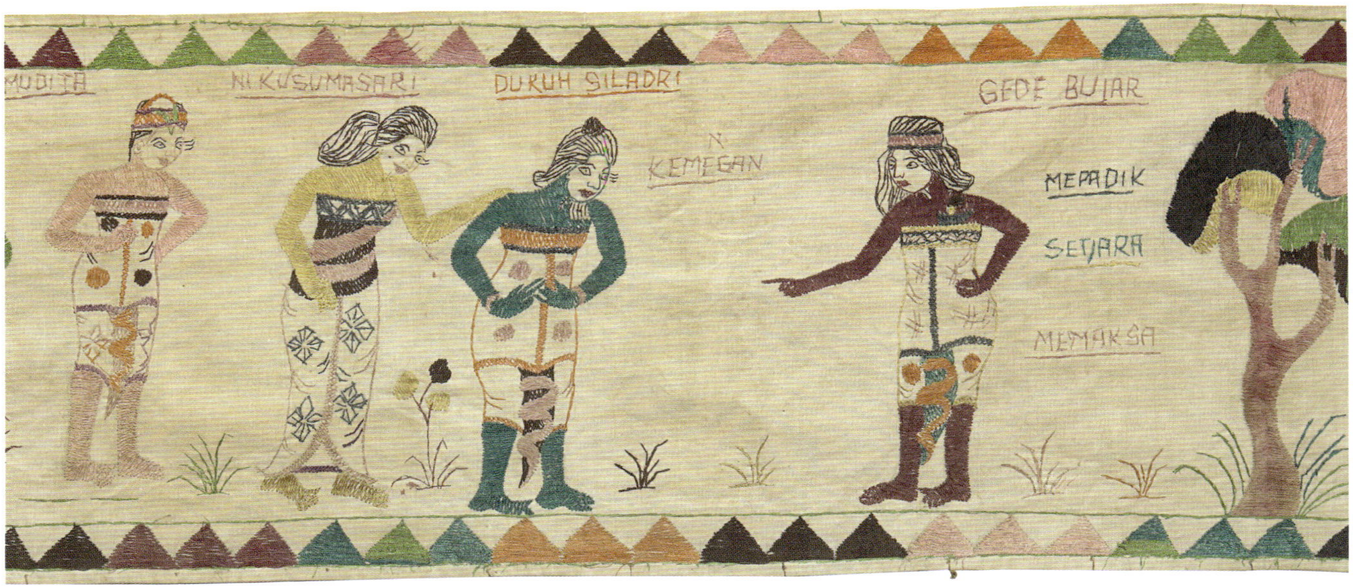

PLATE 163 **Negara.** *Ider-ider*, detail, 26 x 261. *Journey of Dukuh Siladri.* The lout and rascal Gede Bujar demands to no avail that Dukuh Siladri force one of his daughters, Ni Kusuma Sari, to marry him. Her lover, Mudita, stands ready to support her.

poems contained in them and consults with many local scholars and priests. He becomes a pupil of a master of religious practice, Mpu Dibiaja, who lives in Gunung Kawi, a very sacred place known for meditation and renewal.

In time, Siladri and Kadek decide to live in the mountains where he will, with the support of his wife, follow an ascetic life. But before doing so, they face a cultural dilemma: what to do with their only son Mudita. Balinese tradition requires that a male remain in the family home with the widowed grandmother, in this case, Ni Sabuk. Mudita is given a sacred golden ring fashioned by his father to protect him. Both parents decide not to take their son with them, although Kadek is reluctant. Siladri decides to exchange children with his brother, Made Kerti, who has the one daughter, Kusuma Sari. This is done, and the story moves into another setting.

Now Siladri and Kadek live together with their new "daughter" Kusuma Sari in the house of the holy man and teacher Mpu Dibiaja. They become part of a large family that includes many animals such as tigers and monkeys, which were reared by the holy man. Their home is surrounded by a beautiful garden busy with bees gathering nectar and flying in and out of their hives. Siladri is treated like a son by his mentor and will become his heir. Kusuma Sari matures into a beautiful young woman with a gift for healing, knowledge of the arts of magic, and a reverence for sacred texts. The faithful wife, Kadek, dies unexpectedly in a violent storm, leaving Kusuma Sari without a "mother." To assuage Siladri's grief, Mpu Dibiaja adopts him as a son and concentrates on teaching him how to become a truly religious man or a ***dukuh***. From this time on he is known as Dukuh Siladri and the Balinese myth has come to be known by this title.

Back in the city of Mameling, Mudita, the son who was left behind, matures into a handsome young man. He believes that Rajin and Made Kerti are his true parents. However, he is finally told about what happened, about the ring he wore that his real father had given him, and about Kusuma Sari.

Rajin and Made Kerti both die of a mysterious illness, leaving Mudita alone and depressed. He decides to journey to Gunung Kawi for solace and to find Siladri, his real father.

High in the mountains, by chance he meets Kusuma Sari, but they do not recognize each other because they were so young when they were parted. However, Kusuma Sari recognizes the ring that Mudita is wearing, the one given to him many years ago by his father Siladri. Kusuma Sari promises to lead him to his father. They clearly are attracted to each other, but as first cousins romance is out of the question. Their obvious instant affection for each other will have to remain suspended.

The story continues; the future will change things for them, but for now everything will stay the same. And now enters, as is customary in many myths, a most despicable villain.

His name is Wayan Bujar; his father is rich and indulgent. Bujar has no scruples, is a lazy spendthrift, and lusts after beautiful women whether they are married or not. He has a habit of marrying and then leaving each of his many wives.

His first wife, fearful of Bujar's anger and greed, fled to her parents' home, taking her dowry of jewels with her. The second wife was badly treated and ran away. The third wife became pregnant, but Bujar made her miscarry and she died. Bujar showed no remorse; carousing and drinking with seven companions were his main activities. He proposed to his fourth wife but did not attend their wedding. He refused to bring his fifth wife home with him. His sixth and seventh wives were twins who could not bear to live apart. Bujar could not cope with this triangular relationship and deserted the twins.

Bujar's father, Gde Kedampal, is exasperated with his son's irresponsible behavior but does little to restrain or reform him. No matter what, he is his only son and heir—and in Bali, such father-to-son obligations run deep.

Bujar hears about the beauty and wisdom of Kusuma Sari and is determined to pursue her. He offers Dukuh Siladri a bribe, which he refuses. Bujar is so angered by the refusal that he tries to kidnap Kusuma Sari. Dukuh transforms himself into a tiger and, with the help of other animals, forces Bujar and his drunken companions to flee. Bujar will not give up; he seeks the advice of a powerful witch named Dayu Datu. He falsely claims to be Kusuma Sari's husband and asks the witch to help get her back. His opportunity arises when Mudita and Kusuma Sari return to their city home in Mameling in order to arrange a cremation for the parents of Kusuma Sari, who had died after long illnesses.

Dukuh Siladri feels that many bad things have happened to his family, not only because of the lout Bujar, but because the cremation has been too long delayed. As is the custom in Bali, an elaborate cremation ceremony takes place. In the midst of this sacred event Bujar bursts into the scene and kidnaps Kusuma Sari. He takes her to his house, where he treats her roughly. Bujar is acting strangely: gloating over his seeming conquest, admiring his body in a mirror, and waving his arms in every direction. Even his loyal servant Pegok thinks that Bujar has gone crazy; he is obsessed with making believe that Kusuma Sari loves him and no one else.

The villagers of Mameling can no longer tolerate the terrible Bujar in their midst; they drag him out into the street. Mudita kills him with a ***keris*** and all the males in the village stab him as well. It is a communal murder, so all are responsible for the act. No one person can be held accountable for the crime. Gde Kedampal, Bujar's father, weeps and, with his spirit broken, gives away all his wealth to the villagers. He wanders about, aimless and depressed; and Kusuma Sari pities him and invites him to dwell in her house, where he lives for the rest of his life.

Kusuma Sari and Mudita are married amid festivities that lasted for three days. Their marriage is made possible because it turns out that Mudita's father, Dukuh Siladri, had originally been adopted because his natural parents were poor and could not afford to raise him. Siladri kept this secret until it became obvious that his daughter was in love. Thus Mudita and Kusuma Sari are *not* cousins and can legally marry. Their relationship is resolved, but they still have to contend with the witch Dayu Datu, who seeks revenge for what had happened to Bujar.

Dayu Datu, incarnated by the hellish Durga, gathers her destructive minions and advances on Gunung Kawi. The winds blow down trees like the great banyan. Forest animals hide in holes in the ground. All the stars are blotted out. The witch's attempted revenge ends very quickly, as Dukuh Siladri and his family of good animals destroy all her soldiers. Yet she feels her power is so great, her magic so inexorable, that she cannot be defeated. However, Dayu Datu senses something is wrong; something she did not understand is thwarting her plans. Despite his great consternation and self-doubt, Dukuh Siladri is determined to kill Dayu Datu. In doing so, he will violate all of his spiritual principles, but he will do it to save his son and daughter-in-law.

He calls out to his dead former mentor and priest to counsel him, but no answer is forthcoming. In the end, he cannot bring himself to kill Dayu Datu, so his favorite tiger and monkey volunteer to do the awful deed. Dukuh Siladri is grateful to them, but full of guilt and aggrieved over what he terms his "curse." He meditates for three days and three nights; then an apparition appears in the form of Dayu Datu. She is carrying a ***lontar*** that belonged to her father. Dukuh Siladri recognizes this ***lontar*** as one he had seen in his father's house before he had been given away by a jealous wife. Dukuh Siladri and Dayu Datu are actually brother and sister. They now reestablish a bond that had long ago been broken. Dayu Datu gives up any thought of revenge and thanks Dukuh Siladri for turning her away from evil. All is forgiven and Dayu Datu disappears into the heavens as quickly as she appeared.

Dukuh Siladri still lives in Gunung Kawi. He no longer grows old, and is invisible to all but the pure in heart, but the honey from Gunung Kawi is abundant, sweeter and more wonderful than ever, and free for anyone who can find it.[2]

On this one ***ider-ider,*** all the four main characters are represented down the length of its 261 centimeters within separate scenes. **PLATE 162** (see page 127) shows Mudita and Kusuma Sari presenting themselves to Dukuh Siladri, perhaps asking his permission for their marriage. **PLATE 163** (page 128) depicts Bujar demanding that Dukuh Siladri give up his daughter Kusuma Sari to marry him—which, of course, he refuses to do. **PLATE 161** (page 126) has Bujar riding his horse in his usual arrogant manner, vowing to make Kusuma Sari his wife no matter what. As we know, Bujar fails to accomplish this and his track record with marriage is one of utter failure.

The major emphasis of the story is on the journey of Siladri, an ordinary city dweller, to become a ***dukuh*** and lead a religious life. He is virtuous enough to be a good husband and a caring father and to become a wise man. His ascetic existence is in part enriched by his connection and friendship with animals, particularly the monkey and the tiger. They do for him what in good conscience he cannot do for himself: they slay his enemies to protect his family. Dukuh Siladri thus ostensibly escapes a moral dilemma when others carry out his intent. Yet he is full of remorse and guilt, which is only partly assuaged by being temporarily reunited with his forgiving sister and seeing Mudita and Kusuma Sari safe and happy.

In Bali, the Dukuh Siladri story is well known, but memory of it is fading away for many Balinese, particularly the children. It is going the way of tales that over time seem to have less and less relevance to contemporary life. Still, Gunung Kawi is a real place and many Balinese have journeyed to it, as did Siladri, to find serenity and peace in a spiritual life.

FOOTNOTES

1. This chapter was based in part on a novel by Diana Darling, ***The Painted Alphabet***, and on several Balinese informants including a ***dalang*** and a traditional musician.

2. Ibid., 208.

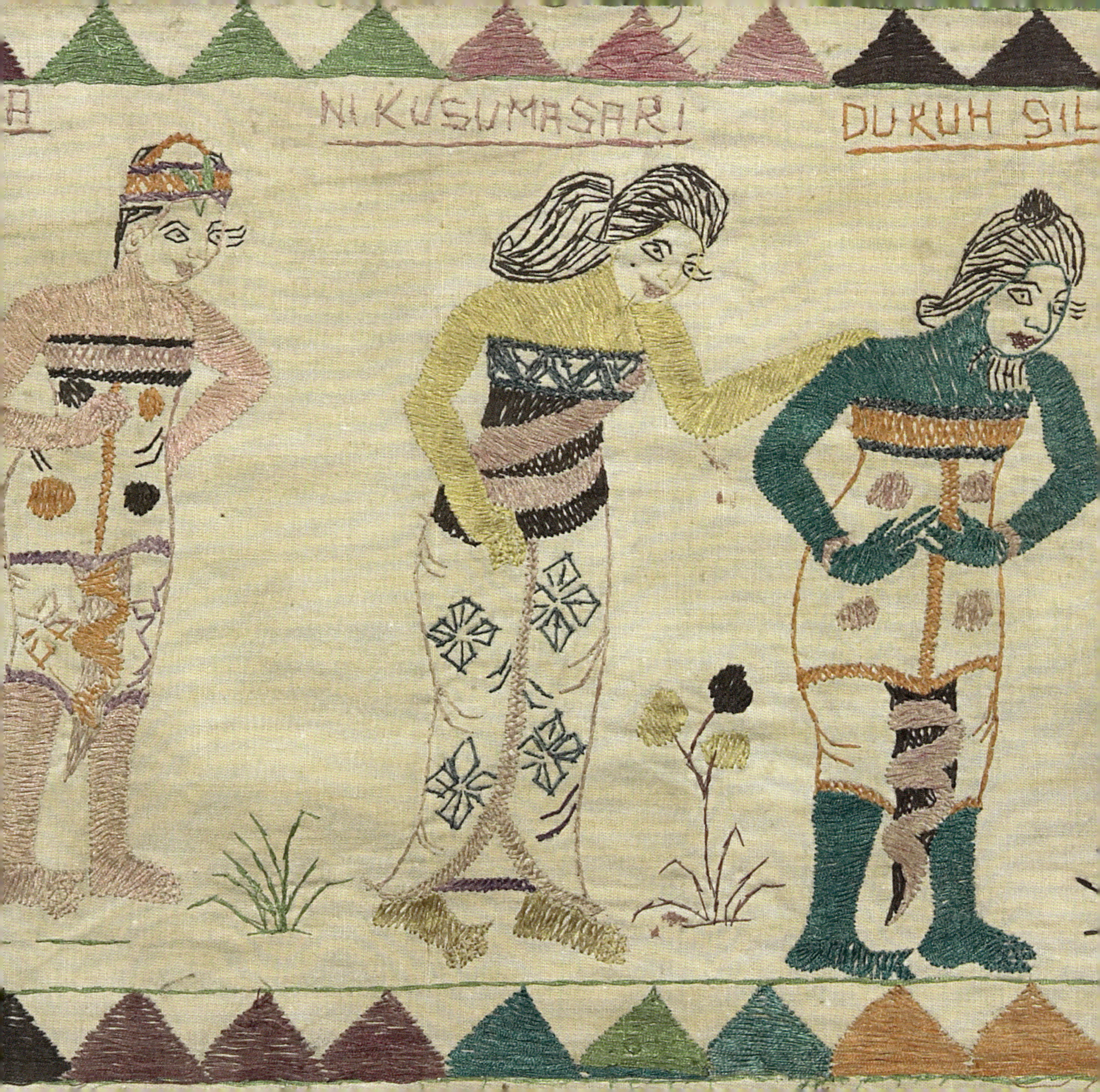

A
NI KUSUMASARI
DUKUH SIL

Epilogue

If you visit Bali today, you will still find the great epics and folk stories very much alive. They continue to be subjects of storytellers, puppeteers, painters, and woodcarvers. However, some things do not last. The embroidery tradition is dying or gone and the women who were part of it are almost forgotten. Nevertheless, the Balinese seem determined to make their mythological, religious, and craft traditions relevant to the contemporary world. In doing so, they provide something of great cultural value to their present and future generations, and to the world in general.

In Bali, Hanuman continues his antics. Rangda still fights with Barong. Rama still cries over the death of Sita. Jaya Prana is no longer a haunting ghost. Arjuna is, no doubt, meditating somewhere on a mountaintop. The endearing four clowns are still cavorting as actors on stage and chattering on the screens of the shadow puppet theater. Saraswati continues to sit majestically on her vehicle, the goose. Wisnu and his avatars are everywhere. Siwa is still in charge of the universe. My sharing of the embroideries in this book has reached its conclusion; the stories they depict will never end.

Cast of Characters and Places

Abhimanyu	Son of Arjuna
Agni	Hindu God of Fire
Ambalika	Wife of Vicitravirija
Ambika	Wife of Vicitravirija and also of Bhisma
Anak Agung	Greedy king in the Jaya Prana story
Andrada	Mother of Anjani
Anggada	Monkey solider and son of Subali
Anila	Monkey soldier who built the bridge to Langka
Anjani	Mother of Hanuman
Antaboga	King of the Undersea Snakes
Api Gana	Son of Siwa
Arimbi	***Raksasa*** wife of Bima
Arjuna	Principal hero of the ***Mahabharata*** and one of five Pandawa brothers
Ayodhya	Original home city of the Pandawas
Ayu Narawati	Goddess who inspires love of superiors
Badung	One of the Balinese districts
Bagawan Bijasa	Hindu priest
Baladewa	Elder brother of Kresna; also called *Balarama*
Barong	Mythical bear or lion and protagonist of Rangda in dance/drama
Basuki	Prominent ***naga*** who has a wife
Batara Guru	Another name for the god Siwa
Batari Serisutji	Another name for Dewi Sri, the Rice Goddess
Bayu	Hindu God of the Wind
Bedawang	Mythical turtle who carried the first mountain on his back
Besakih	Mother Temple of Balinese Hindus
Bharata	Son of Kaikeyi
Bhisma	Son of King Santanu and Ganges, the River Goddess
Bima	The strongest of the five Pandawa brothers
Bomo	The protector and offspring of Wisnu and the Earth Mother
Brahma	One of the three supreme gods of Hinduism
Brihaspati	Father of the gods
Bugis	Ethnic group in southern Sulawesi
Bujar (Wayan)	Villain in the Siladri story
Buleleng	Northernmost district of Bali
Campano	Minister of Rawana, also called Gempano
Citrangada	First son of Santanu by Satyavati
Citrasena	One of the one hundred sons of blind king Dhrtarastra
Clowns	*Bali:* Twalen, Merdah, Delem, and Sangut *Java:* Semar, Gareng, Petruk, Bagong, Çepot, and Togog
Dasartha	King of Kosala
Dayu Datu	Witch and sister of Siladri
Denpasar	Capital city of Bali
Detya Menarung	Ogre in the Twin Brothers Tale
Dewi Gadru	Wife of *Naga* Taksaka
Dewi Sri	The Rice Goddess and Goddess of Good Fortune
Dewi Sutji	One of Arjuna's wives
Dewi Winati	Wife of *Naga* Basuki
Dharmawangsa	King of East Java
Dharmodayana	Balinese prince and husband of Rangda in the ***Calonarang***
Dhimbi	***Raksasa*** wife of Bima, also called Arimbi

Dhrtarastra Blind king in the ***Mahabharata***
Drona Magician and half-brother to the Pandawas, killed by Bima
Drupada King of Pancala
Drupadi Daughter of King Drupada and wife of both Bima and Arjuna
Durasasana Nastiest of the Korawas
Durga Destructive goddess
Durokalo One of Durga's evil minions
Duryodhana Leader of the Korawas in the ***Mahabharata***
Erlangga Famous king of East Java
Gagar Mayang Heavenly Nymph
Gajah Mada Legendary Javanese prime minister and hero
Garuda Mythical bird and vehicle of Wisnu
Gatokaça Hero son of Bima and Arimbi
Gautama (Resi) Father of Subali and Sugriwa
Gde Kedampal Father of Bujar
Grantang The good brother in the Twin Brothers Tale
Gunung Kawi Ancient meditation site
Gustiarya Jaya Prana's assistant
Hanuman Great White Monkey Warrior in the ***Ramayana***
Indra Hindu god of the heavens
Indrajit Son of Rawana
Ingtai Heroine of ***The Butterfly Lovers***
Janaka King of Videha and father of Sita
Janamelyaya Later heir to Bharata Kingdom
Janantaka Demon king known as the Man-Eater
Jatayu Mythical bird and protector of Sita
Jaya Prana Hero of the Jaya Prana tragedy
Jayadrata King of Sindu, a Korawa ally, born from Bima's caul
Jembrana Westernmost district of Bali
Kadek Wife of Siladri
Kadru Enemy of Garuda
Kaikeyi Second wife of King Dasartha
Kala Muka ***Raksasa*** (demon)
Kala Rauh Monster who causes the eclipse in the ***Mahabharata***
Kalki Tenth avatar of Wisnu
Karna Older half-brother of the Pandawas
Kashyapa Father of ***raksasas*** and a sage
Kausalya First wife of King Dasartha and mother of Rama
Kenderan One of the wives of Arjuna
Kijang Mas The golden deer, a disguise of the demon Marica
Kiskindha Capital city of the monkey soldiers
Korawa One of the two principal families in the ***Mahabharata***
Kresna (Krishna) Important figure in the ***Mahabharata*** and an avatar of Wisnu
Kuli Servant in ***The Butterfly Lovers***
Kumara Son of Siwa and the guardian of children
Kumbakarna Giant brother of Rawana
Kunti Wife of King Pandu and mother of the three elder Pandawa brothers
Kusa Son of Rama and Sita
Kusuma Sari Daughter of Made Kerti and Raijin
Laksmana Brother of Rama
Laksmi Consort of Wisnu, Goddess of Good Fortune and Rice Goddess, also known as ***Dewi Sri***

Lava	Son of Rama and Sita
Lotama (Wilotama)	Heavenly nymph
Ma Wencai	Husband of Ingtai
Made Kerti	Brother of Siladri
Madri	King Pandu's junior wife and mother of Nakula and Sadewa
Mahendratta	Javenese princess who became the witch Rangda
Mameling	Home city of Siladri
Manu	Law-giver avatar of Wisnu
Marica	Chief of the demons, disguised as a golden deer in the ***Ramayana***
Maruti	Another name for Hanuman
Menen	Mother of Ingtai
Mithila	Capital city of King Janaka's kingdom
Mpu Baradah	Court sage of King Erlannga in the ***Calonarang***
Mpu Dibiaja	Holy sage in Siladri story
Mudita	Son of Siladri and Kadek
Mustikan	Daughter of the King of Daha in the Twin Brothers Tale
Nakula	Twin brother in the ***Mahabharata***
Narada	Heavenly sage born from the hand of Brahma
Negara	Capital city in the district of Jembrana
Ni Butawili	Ogre's sister in the Twin Brothers Tale
Ni Layon Sari	Wife of Jaya Prana
Ni Luhmetri	Servant of Ni Layon Sari
Ni Sabuk	Mother who adopts Siladri
Nirartha	Priest who brought Hinduism to Bali
Nitwatakawaca	Demon killed by Arjuna
Paksi Garuda	Demon foe of Tjupak
Paksi Winate	Mythical bird
Paman Sawunggaling	Chief minister of King Anak Agung in the Jaya Prana tragedy
Pamanarya Edmurka	Uncle of Ni Layon Sari
Pandawa	Victorious family in the ***Mahabharata***
Pandu	Later king in the ***Mahabharata***
Pariksit	Later heir to the Bharata Kingdom
Pegok	Servant of Bujar
Pertiwi	Earth Mother or Mother Earth; also called Prthiwi, Dewi Pertiwi in Bali, and Ibu Pertiwi
Pospowati	Another wife of Arjuna's; also called Dewi Pospowati
Pranasi (Pransil)	One of Arjuna's wives and also a heavenly nymph
Predjangga	Monkey soldier
Pulastya	Sage from whom all ***raksasas*** descended
Pura Jaran Guyang	Temple site of the cremation of Jaya Prana
Purosado	Demon king
Rajin	Wife of Made Kerti
Rama	Son of Kausalya and King Dasartha; hero of the ***Ramayana***
Rangda	Witch of the ***Calonarang*** tale
Ratih	Goddess of the moon; also called Dewi Ratih
Ratmaja	Demon king killed by Wisnu
Ratnamenggali	Daughter of Rangda
Rawana	Greedy king and kidnapper in the ***Ramayana***
Sadewa	Twin Pandawa bother

Salya	Korawa general
Samba	Son of Kresna
Sampik	Major character in ***The Butterfly Lovers***
Sanang Menaka	Heavenly nymph
Sangyang Surya	Sun God
Sangyang Ulan	Moon God
Santanu	Last king with clear succession in the ***Mahabharata***
Sanur	Balinese oceanside resort city
Saraswati	Hindu Goddess of Knowledge
Satijawati	Wife of Salya
Satrughna	Brother of Laksmana
Sempati	Eagle, brother of the mythical bird Jatayu
Singaraja	Chief city of Buleleng District in North Bali
Siladri	Main male character in Dukuh Siladri story
Sita	Wife of Rama
Sita Sundari	Daughter of Kresna and wife of Abimanyu
Siwa (Shiva)	Hindu God of Destruction and Creation
Subadra	One of Arjuna's wives, also called Sumbadra
Subali	Monkey warrior and enemy brother of Sugriwa
Sugriwa	Monkey general whose army defeats Rawana
Sukoraba	One of Arjuna's wives
Sulawesi	Northernmost major island of Indonesia
Sumitra	Mother of Laksmana and Satrughna
Supraba	One of Arjuna's wives
Supranakha	Demon sister of Rawana
Surasa	Mother of all ***nagas***
Sutasoma	Princely hero of a Buddhist animal tale
Taksaka	Prominent ***naga*** who has a wife
Tara	Wife of Sugriwa
Tjintia	Balinese God of Gods, also called Widi Wasa
Tjupak	Greedy brother of Grantang
Trimurti	The representation in one image of Siwa, Wisnu, and Brahma
Tuan Guru	Schoolteacher in the Sampik folktale
Ubud	Important city in Gianjar District
Urang-Aring	God of Healing and Plant Medicine
Valmiki	Author of the ***Ramayana***
Vivitravirya	Younger brother of Citrangada
Vyasa	Supposed author of the ***Mahabharata***
Wibisana	Brother of Rawana, opposed to war
Widi Wasa	Balinese God of Gods, also called Tjintia
Widur Budi	A demon
Wilbergaso	Minister of Rawana
Wilmano	Mythical bird vehicle of Rawana
Wise-sa	Name of a naga
Wisnu	God with ten avatars
Wiswamitra	Revered sage in the ***Ramayana***
Yama	God of Death and Retribution, Lord of the South
Yogiswara	Javanese poet and author of the ***kakawin Mahabharata***
Yogyakarta	Chief city in a special royal district in Central Java
Yudistira	One of the three main Pandawa brothers

Glossary

adegan Image made of the deceased for cremation
amerta Milk of Immortality
arja Traditional Balinese opera
avatar Other form of existence
bale Special family storage structure
balian Balinese traditional healer
banten Ritual offerings
banteng Buffalo
Baratayuda Great battle in the ***Mahabharata***
beringin Banyan tree
Bhagavadgita (also *Bhagavad Gita*) Philosophical and moral section of the ***Mahabharata***
Bhinneka Tunggal Ika Unity in Diversity; national motto of Indonesia
bidadari Angels or nymphs
bintang Star
bordir Embroidery
Brahman Highest ranking of the four Hindu varnas or social classes
cakra A magical pointed discus; weapon of Wisnu
Calonarang Widow; title of a folktale of witches and demons
cili Symbolic fertility figure
cupu Box
daitya Demon; see also ***raksasa***
dalang Puppeteer
dupa Incense
gamelan Traditional Balinese and Javanese orchestra
gerhana Eclipse
gimp Gold or silver metallic thread
griya Brahman village
ider-ider Long, narrow, horizontally displayed, embroidered or painted hangings
ikat Tie-and-dye technique for putting designs on cloth
Jataka Buddhist animal tales
kakawin Poetic form in old Balinese and Javanese narrative texts
kandas Prose forms of old Javanese literature
kawi Ancient language of Bali
ketoprak Modern Javanese folk drama
keris Traditional Indonesian weapon with snake-like blade
kijang Deer (also ***kidang***)
ksatriya Highest Balinese social caste
lalubur Ceiling canopy
lamak Small ritual offering cloth
langse Curtain or room divider
legong Traditional female Balinese dance
leyak Ghost
lingga Male fertility symbol
lontar Ancient inscribed palm-leaf book
Mahabharata Great Indian epic
Majapahit Kingdom of East Java (1294–1520)
meketu Balinese term for crown headdress
mendet Dancing

metpha	To meditate deeply
naga	Mythical serpent or dragon
ngaben	Balinese cremation ceremony
ngurek	Self-stabbing ritual
odalan	Ritual birthday ceremony for a family, business, or temple
padi	Rice plants
padma	Lotus
pamurtian	Any of the three major gods in their angry aspect
panakawan	Javanese term for a clown
panasar	Balinese term for a clown
Pancasila	Official national ideology of Indonesia
parwa	Story
pelangkiran	Stone and wood family shrine
pembasmian	One of four distinct parts of a cremation ceremony
pembaktian	One of four distinct parts of a cremation ceremony
pembersihan	One of four distinct parts of a cremation ceremony
penangian	One of four distinct parts of a cremation ceremony
penjor	Plant hangings on ceremonial bamboo poles
po-te-hie	Chinese puppet stories
pura	Temple
puri	Palace
pusaka	Heirloom
raksasa	Class of powerful beings, taking several forms: genii, giants, or demons or ogres
rantai	Chain
rebab	Two- or three-stringed violin
sedeng	To tease or entice
singa	Mythical winged lion
sulaman	Offerings
tabing	Square or rectangular embroideries or paintings
Tantri	Ancient animal folktales
tedung	Umbrella
tukang banten	Person who prepares offerings
umbul-umbul	Pennants attached to long bamboo poles, marking ceremonies
vajra	Thunderbolt symbol carried by the Hindu god Indra
wayang	Indonesian for traditional drama
wayang kulit	Nighttime shadow puppet performance in Java or Bali
wayang lemah	Daytime Balinese shadow puppet performance

Bibliography

Anak, Agung, and Thadei, Raka. "Bali," 137–166 in Fred Mayer, *Schatten Theater.* Zurich: University of Bär Verlog, Edition Georg Popp.Aryan, K. C. and Subhashini Aryan. *Hanuman in Art and Mythology.* Delhi: Rekha Prakashan, c. 1970.

Balraj, Khanna. *Kalighat.* Boston: Shambala Redstone Editions, 1993.

Barth, Fredrik. *Balinese Worlds.* Chicago: University of Chicago Press, 1993.

Beach, Milo C. *The Adventures of Rama,* Washington, D.C.: Freer Gallery of Art and Smithsonian Institution, 1985.

Belo, Jane. *Bali: Rangda and Barong.* New York: J. J. Augustin and the American Ethnological Society, 1949.

_______, ed. *Traditional Balinese Culture.* New York: Columbia University Press, 1970.

Boen Sing Hoo, trans. *Boekoe Menjanjian Tjina, Sampik-Ing Taij.* Semarang: Gravel & Company, 1885.

Bolle, Kees. *Bhagavadgita: A New Translation.* Berkeley: University of California Press, 1979.

Boon, James A. *Affinities and Extremes.* Chicago: University of Chicago Press, 1990.

_______. *The Anthropological Romance of Bali, 1597–1972.* Cambridge: Cambridge University Press. 1977.

Buck. William, *Mahabharata.* Berkeley: University of California Press, 1973.

_______. *Ramayana.* Berkeley: University of California Press, 1976.

Buurman, Peter, Wayang Golek. *The Entertaining World of Classical Javanese Puppet Theatre.* Singapore: Oxford University Press, 1988.

Cooper, Thomas. *Sacred Painting in Bali: Tradition in Transition.* Bangkok: Orchid Press, 2004.

Covarrubias, Miguel. *Island of Bali.* New York: Alfred A. Knopf, 1937.

Crill, Rosemary. *Indian Embroidery.* London: Victoria and Albert Publications, 1999.

Danielou, Alain. *The Gods of India.* New York: Inner Traditions, 1985.

Darling, Diana. *The Painted Alphabet.* Boston: Houghton Mifflin, 1992.

De Kleen, Tyra. *Mudras: The Ritual Hand-Poses of the Buddha Priests and the Shiva Priests of Bali.* London: Kegan Paul, Trench and Trubner, 1924.

Dewa Gede Windhu Sancaya. "San Pek Eng Tay (Geguritan Sampik) dalam Kesusastraan Bali." PhD diss., University of Indonesia, 1994.

De Zoete, Beryl, and Walter Spies. *Dance and Drama in Bali.* London: Faber and Faber, 1938.

Dimmitt, Cornelia, and J.A. van Buitenen. *Classical Hindu Mythology.* Philadelphia: Temple University Press, 1978.

Dowson, John. *A Classical Dictionary of Hindu Mythology.* London: Routledge and Kegan Paul, 1972.

Dunningham, Margaret H. *Balinese Folk Art.* Hamilton, New Zealand: Waikato Art Museum, 1974.

Eiseman, Fred B., Jr. *Bali: Sekala and Niskala.* 2 vols. Singapore: Periplus Editions, 1989.

Emigh, John. *Masked Performance.* Philadelphia: University of Pennsylvania Press, 1996.

Fa-Hsien. *The Travels of Fa-Hsien (399–414 A.D.) or Record of the Buddhist Kingdoms.* London: Routledge & Kegan Paul, 1956.

Fischer, Joseph. *The Folk Art of Java.* Kuala Lumpur: Oxford University Press, 1994.

_______. "Balinese Embroideries: The Birth. Life and Demise of an Extraordinary Textile Tradition." *Jurnal Seni.* July 2001, 333–348.

Fischer, Joseph, and Thomas Cooper. *The Folk Art of Bali.* Kuala Lumpur: Oxford University Press, 1998.

Foley, Kathy. "Cupu Manik Astagina," in *Voices of the Puppet Masters: The Wayang Golek Theater of Indonesia* by Mimi Herbert. Honolulu: University of Hawaii Press, 2002, 220–225.

Forge, Anthony. *Balinese Traditional Paintings.* Sydney: The Australian National Museum, 1978.

Francis, H.T., and E.J. Thomas. *Jataka Tales.* Cambridge: University Press, 1916.

Geertz, Clifford. *Negara: The Theatre State in Nineteenth-Century Bali.* Princeton: Princeton University Press, 1980.

Geertz, Hildred. *Images of Power: Paintings for Gregory Bateson and Margaret Mead.* Honolulu: University of Hawaii Press, 1994.

Goldman, Robert P., trans. *The Ramayana of Valmiki.* 5 vols. Princeton: Princeton University Press, 1984, 1990, 1992, 1994, 1996.

Goris, R. *Bali: Atlas Kebudajaan: Cults and Customs.* Jakarta: Ministry of Education and Culture of the Republic of Indonesia, c. 1960.

Hari Prasad Shastri. *The Ramayana of Valmiki.* London: 1962.

Herbst, Edward. *Voices in Bali. Energies and Perception in Vocal Music and Dance Drama.* Hanover: Wesleyan University Press, 1997.

Hirst, Jacqueline Suthren. *Sita's Story.* Calgary: Bayeux Arts, 1997.

Höhn, Klaus, D. *The Art of Bali: Reflections of Faith; The History of Painting in Batuan, 1834–1994.* The Netherlands: Picture Publishers Art Books, 1997.

Hooykaas, C. *Drawings of Balinese Sorcery.* Leiden: E. J. Brill, 1980.

_______. *Kama and Kala: Materials for the Study of Shadow Theatre in Bali*. Amsterdam: North Holland, 1973.
_______. ed. and trans. *The Lay of Jaya Prana*. London: Luzac and Company, 1958.
_______. *The Old-Javanese Ramayana with Special Reference to the Problem of Interpolation*. 'S-Gravenhage: Martinus Nijhoff, 1955.
_______. *Religion in Bali*. Leiden: E. J. Brill, 1973.
Jackson, Beverly, and David Hugus. *Ladder to the Clouds: Intrigue and Tradition in Chinese Rank*. Berkeley: Ten Speed Press, 1999.
Jendresen, Eric, and Joshua M. Greene. *Hanuman*. Berkeley: Tricycle Press, 1998.
Kam, Garrett. *Ramayana in the Arts of Asia*. Singapore: Select Books, 2000.
Katz, Ruth C. *Arjuna in the Mahabharata*. Columbia: University of South Carolina Press, 1989.
Khanna, Balraj. *Kalighat: Indian Popular Painting, 1880–1930*. Redstone Press, 1993.
Kinsley, David R. *Hindu Goddesses*. Berkeley: University of California Press, 1988.
Kumar, Ann, and John H. McGlynn. *Illuminations: The Writing Traditions of Indonesia*. Jakarta: The Lontar Foundation and Weatherhill, 1996.
Leach, Maria, ed. *Standard Dictionary of Folklore, Mythology, and Legend*. 2 vols. New York: Funk and Wagnalls, 1949.
Lugras, Leonard. *Bali: The Ultimate Island*. New York: St. Martin's Press, 1987.
Luh Ketut Suryani and Gordon Jensen. *Trance and Possession in Bali*. Kuala Lumpur: Oxford University Press, 1995.
McCrickard, Janet. *Eclipse of the Sun: An Investigation into Sun and Moon Myths*. City: Pub, date.
Morrell, Anne. *The Techniques of Indian Embroidery*. Loveland: Interweave Press, 1995.
Narasimhan, Chakravarthi V. *The Mahabharata*. New York: Columbia University Press, 1965.
O'Flaherty, Wendy Doniger. *Siva: The Erotic Ascetic*. London: Oxford University Press, 1981.
Poerbatjaraka, R. Ng. "De Calan Arang" in *Bijdragen tot de Taal-hand-en Volkenunde,* no. 82, 1926, 110–180.
Prime, Ranchor. *Ramayana: A Journey*. London: Collins and Brown, 1997.
_______. *Ramayana: A Tale of Gods and Demons*. San Rafael: Mandala Publishing, 2001.
Ramseyer, Urs. *The Art and Culture of Bali*. New York: Oxford University Press, 1977.
Rice, Stanley. *Tales from the Mahabharata*. London: Selwyn and Blount, 1924.
Richman, Paula, ed. *Many Ramayanas*. Berkeley: University of California, 1991.
_______, *Questioning Ramayanas*. Berkeley: University of California, 2001.
Ryder, Arthur W., trans. *The Panchatantra*. New York: The Limited Editions Club, 1972.
Simon, Claudine. "Cults Peculiar to the Chinese in Java," in *Chinese Beliefs and Practices in Southeast Asia*. by Chen Hock Tong. Selangkor Darul Ehsan: Pelanduk Publications, 1993.
_______, ed. *Literary Migration: Traditional Chinese Fiction in Asia*. Beijing: Culture Publication Company International, 1987.
Snead, Stella. *Animals in Four Worlds: Sculptures from India*. Chicago: University of Chicago Press, 1989.
Soewito Santoo, ed. and trans. *Ramayana Kakawin*. 3 vols. New Delhi: Sarada Rani, 1980.
Stoler Miller, Barbara. "The Universe of Rama, Valmiki's Epic Poem," in *The Legend of Rama*. Edited by Vidya Dehejia. City: pub, date.
Stutterheim, Willem. *Rama-Legenden und Rama-Reliefs in Indonesien*. München: Georg Müller Verlag, 1925.
Thomas, P. *Epics, Myths, and Legends of India*. Bombay: D. B. Tarapoevala Sons, 1961.
Tyomkin, Edward, and Margarita Vorobyova-Desyatovskaya. *The Hindu Pantheon*. Reading, England: Garnet Publishing, 1994.
Valmiki (Shri). *The Ramayana of Valmiki*. 3 vols. London: Shanti Sadan, 1970.
Van Buitenen, J. A. B., ed. and trans. *The Mahabharata*. 3 vols. Chicago: University of Chicago Press, 1973, 1975, 1978.
Vidya Dehejia, ed. *The Legend of Rama: Artistic Visions*. Bombay: Marg Publications, 1993.
Vogel, J. Ph. *Indian Serpent—Lore or the Nagas in Hindu Legend and Art*. London: Arthur Probstain, 1926.
Weitzman, David. *Rama and Sita*. Retold and illustrated by the author. Boston: David R. Godine, 2002.
Wang, Yarong. *Chinese Embroidery*. Tokyo: Kodansha International, 1987.
Wikan, Unni. <*Managing Turbulent Hearts: A Balinese Formula for Living*. Chicago: University of Chicago Press, 1990.
Wilkins, W. J. *Hindu Mythology: Vedic and Puranic*. Varanasi: Indological Book House, 1972.
Williams, Joanna. *The Two-Headed Deer: Illustrations of the* Ramayana *in Orissa*. Berkeley: University of California, 1996.
Yang, Gladys, and Yang Hsien-Yi, trans. *Shan-po Liang and Ying-tai Chu, Love Under the Willows (a Szechuan Opera)*. Peking: Foreign Languages Press, 1956.
Zhao Qingge. *Liang Shanbo and Zhu Yingtai*. Beijing: New World Press, 1998.
Zimmer, Heinrich. *The Art of Indian Asia*. 2 vols. New York: Pantheon, 1960.
Zoetmulder, P. J. *Kalangwan: A Survey of Old Javanese Literature*. The Hague: Martinus Nijhoff, 1974.

Index

ATO
BOGO